from HILLTOP *to* MOUNTAINTOP

The Life & Legacy of One Iwo Jima Flag Raiser

from HILLTOP *to* MOUNTAINTOP

The Life & Legacy of One
Iwo Jima Flag Raiser

RON ELLIOTT

forward by
Heather French Henry

Acclaim Press
MORLEY, MISSOURI

Acclaim Press
—— *Your Next Great Book* ——

P.O. Box 238
Morley, MO 63767
(573) 472-9800
www.acclaimpress.com

Book and Cover Design: M. Frene Melton

Library of Congress has catalogued the hardcover edition as follows:

Elliott, Ron, 1943-
    From Hilltop to mountaintop: the life and legacy of one Iwo Jima flag raiser / by Ron Elliott.
        p. cm.
    Includes bibliographical references.
    ISBN-13: 978-1-935001-53-9 (alk. paper)
    ISBN-10: 1-935001-53-1 (alk. paper)
    1. Sousley, Franklin R. (Franklin Runyon), 1925-1945. 2. Sousley, Franklin R. (Franklin Runyon), 1925-1945--Influence. 3. Iwo Jima, Battle of, Japan, 1945. 4. Marines--United States--Biography. 5. United States. Marine Corps--Biography. 6. Photographs--Social aspects--United States--History--20th century. 7. Sousley, Franklin R. (Franklin Runyon), 1925-1945--Family. 8. Elliott, Ron, 1943---Family. 9. Hilltop (Fleming County, Ky.)--Biography. 10. Kentucky--Biography. I. Title.
    D767.99.I9E45 2010
    940.54'2528092--dc22
    [B]
                                2010030961

First Paperback Edition, Printed 2021
ISBN: 978-1-956027-04-4 | 1-956027-04-1

Printed in the United States of America
10 9 8 7 6 5 4 3 2 1

Contents

Preface 6

Foreword 8

Dedication 9

Chapter 1 – Saturday, March 1, 1975 13

Chapter 2 – Tuesday, May 29, 1928 18

Chapter 3 – Saturday, October 6, 1934 24

Chapter 4 – Friday, June 12, 1942 31

Chapter 5 – Sunday, July 11, 1943 38

Chapter 6 – Sunday, December 26, 1943 48

Chapter 7 – Saturday, January 22, 1944 61

Chapter 8 – Wednesday, February 16, 1944 86

Chapter 9 – Friday, March 3, 1944 97

Chapter 10 – Wednesday, March 15, 1944 104

Chapter 11 – Tuesday, August 8, 1944 120

Chapter 12 – Tuesday, September 19, 1944 131

Chapter 13 – Monday, February 19, 1945 146

Chapter 14 – Friday, February 23, 1945 166

Chapter 15 – Wednesday, February 28, 1945 179

Chapter 16 – Monday, April 9, 1945 202

Chapter 17 – Sunday, May 13, 1945 208

Chapter 18 – Saturday, May 8, 1948 216

Chapter 19 – Tuesday, November 9, 1954 222

Chapter 20 – Sunday, June 3, 1984 229

Chapter 21 – Saturday, November 9, 2002 234

Epilogue – Saturday, May 1, 2010 238

Endnotes 244

Bibliography 248

About the Author 251

Index 252

Preface

Despite the fact that in the index of any comprehensive World War II history book you will find a listing for "Sousley, Franklin R.," few of his countrymen know the role that Franklin played in American history. The minister, Gilbert Fern, said it best in his eulogy, "When Franklin went into the service, he had a date with destiny." Indeed, the boy born in the tiny hamlet of Hilltop, Kentucky had an appointment to become a national icon on a mountaintop on Iwo Jima.

When I suggested this project to my publisher, he agreed that Franklin deserves more recognition that he's received, but questioned how I could write a biography of someone who only lived to age 19. In answering that question, I realized that while Franklin Sousley was, in one sense, just a country boy who died in defense of his country at age 19, in another sense, he was born the day Associated Press photographer Joe Rosenthal snapped his famous picture of Franklin and five other men raising an American flag atop Mt. Suribachi. In that sense, Franklin will live as long as the United States of America endures.

This book, then, is not biography. Nor is it a history of the war or of America during the war. It is an attempt to provide the story of Franklin's short time on earth as well as his legacy that lingers still. That Kentucky farm boy has had a lasting impact on his little community, his state and his nation. Franklin gave no more than the other thousands of men and women who fought and died to preserve democracy, but it was his fate to become a lasting and highly visible symbol for all of them. While the iconic nature of the flag raising photograph fuses the men into a single historic unit, they remain six individuals and each was an American woman's baby boy.

I promised Franklin's family (and each of the many others I spoke with) that I would get at the truth. I did that in many instances, sometimes to the chagrin of the family, but we all agreed that the facts are just the facts. So, I've presented them just as discovered, even to vexation and when in conflict with what is presented elsewhere. Sometimes the truth is elusive, so when I was forced to take my best estimate at what actually happened, I labeled it as such.

Someone once told me that footnotes are what historians use to blame their mistakes on each other. I think there's some truth in that and it's one reason I dislike using them, another being that, as a reader, I find them distracting. On the other hand, the reader does have a right to know where I got the information, so I have included some endnotes (which are hopefully less distracting) at points where I deemed the source of the information to be important.

A word about political correctness, of which I am no fan, is in order. In this, as in my previous books, I have avoided anachronisms, sometimes at the expense of political correctness. When given that choice, being true to the time, place, speech patterns, opinions and beliefs of the people in this story is, quite simply, more important.

I was amazed at how people stepped up to help me. First and foremost, Dwayne Price and Florine Moran, Franklin's closest living relatives provided information, pictures and opinions valuable beyond measure. I also owe a great debt to those relatives I didn't get to meet; Goldie Price, Ray Mitchell and Mildred May who preserved Franklin's legacy. Through his letters to his mother, Franklin himself provided much information. Dave Severance, who was Easy Company's commander on Iwo Jima, shed light on issues I would never have otherwise understood. The folks at the Fleming County Public Library were helpful as was Jerry Raisor. Edward Block, Harlon's cousin, provided valuable information on the wayside panels. James Donovan, founder of the Marine Corps War Memorial Foundation, was very helpful with the history of the Marine Corps Memorial and pictures. Speaking with Tom White about the monument on Franklin's grave was an informative pleasure. A special thanks goes to Whitney C. Mahar and the staff at the National Personnel Records Center in St. Louis, Missouri for the highest level of professionalism and service. And then there's the usual suspects: my friend and wife Carol, friends John Snell, Jim McQueen and Ron Bryant all deserve special credit for listening to me babble on with excitement, and Doug Sikes makes the effort of publishing a book a joy.

So, here's Franklin's story as complete, honest, entertaining and factual as I can tell it. Because he didn't come back to tell it himself, I've endeavored to do it for him. As another Kentucky country boy myself, I can relate to much of his story, but I cannot relate to and cannot help but wonder how he would feel about having become a national icon. As you read his story, I hope you'll be able to relate to some of his emotions and I hope you'll reflect on those things that we cannot understand. Above all, I hope you'll join me in rendering eternal gratitude to Franklin Sousley and those thousands of others who sacrificed so much to save the American way of life for us.

Foreword

There are moments in history that will live on forever. Moments that have been captured, miraculously, that will be frozen in time to remind us of our past, to encourage us in our present and, God willing, remind us in the future that we need to look to the past in order to move forward. The image of the flag raising at Iwo Jima is one of those events, one of those photographs that captured our American spirit. It reminds us of our past but yet begs of us the question whether we will be strong enough in the future to live up to the courage of thousands of heroes' lives lost in the past. Whatever transpired to cause the miracle of the flag raising at Iwo Jima, no one can dispute the power it still brings today… the image of boys like Franklin Sousley, a farm boy from small town Kentucky, who by no will of his own, helped to encourage and capture the spirit of America. Sometimes words are not enough but a solitary action, even if motivated, can express to an entire world the message of greatness but with greatness comes great sacrifice. Frankin R. Sousley's family has paid for the price of the message of greatness many times over. The story of sacrifice should always be told and so should the story of a family's sacrifice for the remembrance of a loved one who paid the ultimate price. This is for future generations so they may learn and a family's sacrifice can be remembered.

As the daughter of a veteran I feel that the stories of our American heroes should be told so they may echo throughout time and space. My hope is that every American may come to respect the price of freedom, only then by respecting the sacrifice will we ever truly know what it means to be free.

Heather French Henry, Miss America 2000
Executive Director, The Heather French Foundation for Veterans, Inc.

Dedication

To the thousands of American men and women who,
like Franklin, sacrificed their lives to preserve the
democratic life for future generations.

from HILLTOP *to* MOUNTAINTOP

The Life & Legacy of One Iwo Jima Flag Raiser

Chapter 1

Saturday, March 1, 1975
Elizaville, Kentucky

I heard it long before it came into sight. The unmistakable *whump, whump, whump* of a helicopter in flight is sure to capture the attention and imagination of any eight-year-old boy. Pulling my coat a little closer about my body against the cold north wind, I scanned the low gray overcast hoping for a glimpse of the aircraft making the noise.

Although Dad and Mom and especially Mamaw had all cautioned me to be on my good behavior, I didn't think that they'd mind if my eyes were turned to the sky as the ceremonies honoring my long-dead uncle, Franklin Sousley, had not yet begun. I certainly had been given to understand that we were gathered here at the cemetery to commemorate the thirtieth anniversary of the historic flag raising on some far-away island in the Pacific Ocean. But who cares about such ancient history anyway?

As the sound grew a little louder, I slipped around attempting to put Mamaw's body between me and the wind. She glanced at me and whispered, "Don't fidget, Dwaynie." From my new vantage point, I had a clear view of the small metal sign marking Franklin's grave. I don't know who put it up or how long it had been there, but a simple marker noting that he was "one of six Marines who raised the flag on Iwo Jima, 23 February 1945" hardly seemed worthy of all this attention. I'd been to the gravesite many times before, of course. In addition to Franklin and his father, Mamaw's other sons, Malcolm and Julian, were buried in the same plot. Mamaw's second husband, my grandfather's, grave was also nearby. Even though none of her three sons had lived to maturity, it was Franklin that she grieved for most. In my youthful, blissful ignorance, I wasted no time pondering Mamaw's heartbreak associated with any of those tragic deaths, but I had seen her in tears many times as she viewed the extraordinary photograph of her son and the others straining with that flag pole.

Suddenly, an olive drab colored aircraft swooped into sight over the bare tree limbs. Bearing a red and white star-and-bar insignia and a Kentucky Air National Guard shield on each side, the helicopter came from the east, moving slowly against the crosswind and maneuvered into an open space between the cemetery and the road. As the aircraft hovered nearly motionless about 20 feet above the ground, the pilot deftly turned the nose into the face of the north wind and sat the skids ever so lightly down on the frozen turf. My eyes riveted on the rotor as the whine of the jet engine abated and the rotor began to slow in its revolutions. In a few moments, the turning had almost completely stopped when the door on the side of the aircraft popped open. Out jumped two young Marines in dress blue uniforms, each with a red stripe running down his trouser leg and a white hat atop his head. They stood at rigid attention as an older Marine (bearing the single star of a Brigadier General on his epaulets and a chest full of ribbons), a small, white-haired man and a tall middle-aged man exited the craft. I recognized the latter man as Kentucky's governor, Julian Carroll.

The crowd's attention turned to the men as another Marine approached the general snapping off a smart salute. As all the parties shook hands, the group moved to a microphone set up near Franklin's grave. Ignoring the festivities, my eyes remained on the helicopter so I saw the pilot, dressed in a green flight suit, exit the craft and unobtrusively take a place at the back of the crowd. I wonder, I thought, if I might sneak over there and ask him if there's any chance I might get a ride in that helicopter. I decided that the chances of that happening would be slim to none, but I was – in my mind anyway – one of the guests of honor and I'd surely be the envy of all my schoolmates, so it was worth thinking about. My eyes wandered to where the Flemingsburg Boy Scout troop stood, their arrangement not nearly as precise as the green-uniformed Marine rife squad or the dress blue clad Marine band formed across the way.

One of the Marines was speaking. Mamaw smiled slightly as he introduced her as Mrs. Goldie Price. Then she swelled with pride as he announced that she was Franklin's mother. Then he presented Governor Carroll and Marine Corps historian General E. H. Simmons. The small white-haired man was Joe Rosenthal, the man who captured "the" photograph of Franklin and the others struggling with the flag pole on Iwo Jima. Then he introduced another Marine with a lot of chevrons on his arm as an Iwo Jima veteran who would lead a prayer. I kept my eye on the helicopter pilot through most of the formalities, but did pay attention when Joe Rosenthal approached the microphone. He was dressed in a dark suit under a black-and-white checked overcoat, a black beret atop his head. His appearance and manner of dress were so strange to my youthful eye that I could not help thinking that there was little chance of his being mistaken for a local.

Removing his hat, he stepped to the microphone. "I was there just carrying out an assignment," he began. "I simply hoped to send back a representation of what it was like over there. There were better photographers before me and after me, but I was lucky enough to be at the right place at the right time to get the picture that represented the story of our courageous young men. It was just a 'grab shot,' sort of like photographing at a football game. If the timing is off one second either way, you get nothing." Even though I was interested in hearing what he had to say and impressed that such a famous photographer would come to our little town, I could not help noticing that the helicopter pilot had disappeared.

"We are recognizing all the young men who gave everything for their country when we pay tribute to PFC Franklin Sousley today," Rosenthal added. "For the last 30 years, I have been explaining this picture and I can only say that I was carrying out an assignment and got a lucky shot which has lasted to be recognized by everyone. " A note of gravity entered his voice as he concluded, "Men like Franklin Sousley represented the best this country had to offer. I am at a loss to find words to describe the debt that we all owe boys like him." With that, his voice cracking, he cleared his throat and with much emotion, observed, "I was also one of the ones who was lucky enough to return."

The first Marine then returned to the microphone to introduce General Simmons. Unlike Mister Rosenthal, he did not remove his hat when he stepped forward. Perhaps afraid he'd muss all the brass on the bill, I mused. "Iwo Jima is between Guam and the Japanese home islands," he explained, "and the Japanese were mounting raids from there and intercepting our B29's...." Quickly losing interest in what I considered to be ancient history, I scanned the crowd for the helicopter pilot, the idea of approaching him having not entirely left my mind. I had not spotted him when Mamaw hissed, "Dwaynie." That was enough to bring my attention back. As the General stepped back, Governor Carroll handed Mamaw a floral wreath trimmed with red, white and blue ribbons as the two of them moved to the gravesite. Joined by the General, they solemnly placed it on the ground. As they stepped back and stood straight, the Marine sergeant barked a command. In perfect unison, the rifle squad snapped their weapons across their chests and waited. At the command "Aim," they raised their rifles to a 45-degree angle followed by only a slight hesitation before the sound of seven rifles boomed in response to "Fire!" As this procedure was repeated two more times, even I could figure that seven times three was a 21-gun salute – quite a tribute to my kinsman.

All fell quiet as the rifle squad brought their weapons to their sides. A single man stepped forward from the band bringing a bugle to his lips. As the plaintive notes of Taps sounded over the little cemetery, nearly everyone had tears streaming down their cheeks, Mamaw most of all. My mood took a turn for the serious as I began to understand the reverence that the country held for my Uncle Franklin and the hurt that his mother still held in her heart. At the time, I thought her son had been dead such a long time that perhaps some of the hurt would have healed. When a faint, haunting "Taps" echoed from somewhere in the distance, even the Marines were choking back tears. I've since come to understand how quickly the years roll by and that some injuries just never mend.

Most of the crowd of 200 or so hurried to their cars, eager to get out of the cold wind. A stack of Mister Rosenthal's famous photographs appeared as he announced he'd happily autograph one for anybody who so desired. In the years since that long-ago cold March day, as I have come to realize the patriotic significance of Franklin's participation in that historic event and the honor paid him on this day, how I have wished I'd paid a little more attention. I could have spoken to Mr. Rosenthal and witnessed his autograph. I do have the picture he signed, but only because Mom saved it away until she decided I was mature enough to appreciate it. How many times have I kicked myself for knowing that I, Dwayne Price had a golden opportunity to help honor my uncle Franklin Sousley, but as it was, I let out a long sigh of disappointment as the helicopter blades began to roar and the dignitaries boarded. Mom took my hand as we started for the car. My best chance for a ride in a military helicopter disappeared with the chopper as it sailed away over the bare treetops.

Many years would pass before I came to appreciate the significance of what my uncle Franklin Runyon Sousley had done. What Franklin and the millions of other farm boys and millworkers and ranch hands and mechanics did was no less than save our way of life. Franklin and so many others sacrificed their lives to preserve democracy for those of us standing in the cemetery that day. Because of their courage and willingness to serve, American freedom is safe for us, as it was for our parents and as it will be for our children and their children.

Little did I suspect on that long ago day that Franklin Sousley and his legacy would become major factors in my life. It's nearly 70 years now since he and the others raised the Stars and Stripes on a mountaintop on that God-forsaken island in the middle of the Pacific Ocean. Yet the interest in Franklin and his fellows is as strong as when Joe Rosenthal's classic photograph first appeared in the newspapers. The patriotism and teamwork inspired by that image has not waned. Franklin and so many others died on Iwo Jima many years ago, but in a way, he was born on February 23, 1945 when Mr. Rosenthal snapped that picture. I've been asked if my uncle was a hero. I swell with pride when I answer that question. While my uncle was one of millions who served, he's my only uncle who did. And, while he might not be known by name, he's part of an American icon that has and will continue to inspire every American who views it. To my mind, Franklin R. Sousley is a greater American hero than George Washington, Davy Crockett and Daniel Boone combined!

Chapter 2

Tuesday, May 29, 1928
Hilltop, Kentucky

Mildred May knew that the knock on her door would bring no good news. Opening the door revealed her sister, Goldie, with tears streaming down her cheeks. In the gathering dusk, she could see Goldie's husband, Duke Sousley, hurrying away toward the road. Goldie held her four-year old son, Malcolm, in her arms; two-year old Franklin stood at her side holding her hand. "How is he?" Mildred asked, stepping aside to allow the trio to enter the house.

"Not good," Goldie said through her tears. The doctor says he needs an operation right away. She gently laid Malcolm on the couch. Turning, she lifted Franklin to sit beside his brother.

"An operation?" Mildred exclaimed. "What is it?"

"Appendicitis," Goldie replied with a sigh, sinking to the couch between her sons. Malcolm moaned quietly as she patted his hand.

An observer would not have questioned the fact that the two women were sisters. Both in their mid-twenties were tall and slender. Although Goldie's hair was two shades redder than Mildred's, the family resemblance was unmistakable. "What can I do?" Mildred tried to sound reassuring.

"Well, Duke's gone to see if Mr. Neal will take us to the hospital in Lexington in his car. I'll need you to look after Franklin if he will." With that, Goldie handed over a bag of clothes. She pulled what appeared to be a stuffed sock from the bag. "He sleeps with this 'snugglie'," she announced.

"Oh, you know Everett Neal will drive you. He's a lot more to this community than just the owner of the general store. He's been as generous with the use of his car as he is everything else." Mildred lifted Franklin from his seat on the couch and held him on her lap in a chair, smoothing his rust-colored hair. "It's nearly two miles to the store, though." Indicating Malcolm lying beside his mother on the couch, she asked, "Is he in pain?"

"No, the doctor gave him something." A new burst of tears began to flow. "I just hope it'll last 'til we get to the hospital." Then Goldie mused more to herself than to her sister, "Duke's used to walkin'. He walks that far to work ever' day."

"Y'all must be hungry," Mildred said, "let me get you something to eat." Franklin, on her lap, perked up, "Cake?"

"No, honey," Mildred answered, "you need some good, nourishin' food." Rising, she deposited Franklin next to his mother then headed for the kitchen.

"Oh, don't bother," Goldie weakly protested. She suddenly realized that she had been so busy with Malcolm and the doctor that she had not eaten anything all day and was hungry. Worse, she had not fed Franklin. Although he must be ravenous, the child had not protested.

"Oh, it's no bother. I've got some cornbread and beans from supper right here," Mildred answered from the next room. "I'll just heat it up." Goldie heard her poking up the embers to refresh the fire in the stove.

Smelling food, Franklin jumped to the floor following his aunt into the kitchen. "Don't bother with nothin' for Malcolm," Goldie advised. Still patting the boy's hand, she noticed that he had drifted off to sleep, so she followed Franklin into the next room. Although the weather was warm, the heat from the stove was welcome as was the aroma of food. "Duke will be hungry, too, but I don't guess we'll have time for him to eat." Then, thinking aloud, "Wonder how long he's been gone?" A huge sigh escaped her lips as she pulled out the ladder-back chair and sat at the table.

"Oh, he's most likely at the store by now," Mildred opined, stirring the pot of beans on the stovetop. We'll fix him up with some food to take along." Ladling beans, she sat a steaming bowl in front of Franklin then another for her sister. Although he knew he should wait for his mother to say grace, the child snatched up a spoon and attacked his food.

The next few minutes passed in silence, Franklin noisily slurping his food while Goldie nibbled and Mildred held her own counsel. At length, Franklin slid his bowl toward his aunt, "More?" he requested. In response to Goldie's nod, Mildred placed the refilled bowl in front of the child. "A good appetite is a sign of a healthy boy," she said, smiling at the child.

Goldie left her place at the table several times to peek at Malcolm sleeping on the couch. "The medicine appears to be workin'," she informed, sitting again. "He's sleepin' peacefully." Before Mildred could reply, a noise out front caught everyone's attention. Franklin rushed to the door. Peering out through the screen into the gathering dusk, he exclaimed, "Daddy!" The two women moved to the door, standing behind Franklin. A car sat at the edge of the road, Everett Neal at the wheel. The passenger door was open as Duke was exiting the vehicle. "Think he'll want to eat?" Mildred asked.

As if to answer her question, Duke yelled, "Come on, Goldie, we got to go!" He slammed the car door and started toward the house at a trot. Picking up Franklin, Goldie gave him a squeeze before handing him to Mildred.

"You be a good boy and do as Aunt Mildred says," she said, turning toward Malcolm, still sleeping on the couch. He smiled wearily as she gathered him in her arms. His eyes opened slightly, briefly revealing dilated pupils before he lapsed back into drug-induced sleep.

"Let's go," Duke shouted, opening the screen door. His voice softened somewhat, but lost none of its urgency, as he entered the front room. "It's past 8 now," he observed, shooting a glance at the clock on the mantle above the fireplace, "it'll be ten by the time we get there." Mr. Neal had readily agreed to transport them to Lexington, so Duke had wasted no effort on persuasion. He was so intent on getting to the store and then back to Mildred's house he forgot that worry about his son was the object. "How's he doin?" he asked, his voice now laced with concern.

Handing Malcolm to his father, Goldie kissed the child on the top of his head and managed a weak smile for Mildred, who entered the room with a brown paper bag in her hands. "The medicine's still got him knocked out," she replied.

"Here's some food for you and Mr. Neal," Mildred said, addressing Duke.

"Thank you, Mildred. And thanks for keepin' Franklin," Duke said as Goldie accepted the bag. He shifted Malcolm in his arms to push open the screen door. Mildred stood in the door in their wake as they rushed to the car. Seeing Mr. Neal looking toward her, she managed a weak smile with her wave.

At the car, Duke handed the child to his wife before opening the rear door for her. As she slid into place, she gently pulled Malcolm to her so that his head rested on her lap. "You OK, son?" she whispered. The boy simply whimpered in response.

"He's doped up, you know that," Duke growled angrily then immediately regretting taking out his frustrations on his wife who, he knew, had enough of her own. As Everett Neal pressed the starter bringing the engine to life, Goldie looked toward the house to wave goodbye. The car spewed up dirt from its spinning wheels as it sped away. Mildred watched from the doorway until the red taillights faded into the night. After even the glow was gone, she turned to Franklin who was crawling beneath the chairs on the kitchen floor.

"How you doin', big guy?" she asked stooping to peer under the chair.

Distracted from his play, he stopped whatever he was pretending to ask, "Mommie gone?"

"Yes," she replied with a sigh, "but she and your Daddy will be back soon." Mildred wished she felt some of the assurance she was trying to provide her nephew. The hospital in Lexington, being nearly 70 miles away over a road that was curvy and treacherous enough in daylight, in addition to a critically ill child gave her plenty to keep her mind occupied. She moved to the box where she stored wooden blocks and empty thread spools for those occasions when Malcolm and Franklin visited. "Wanna play cars?"

"OK," he said, picking up the box. She hoped she saw a bit of sleepiness in his eyes as he crawled to her. They moved into the front room where Mildred lit the kerosene lantern. Sprawled on the floor, they played with the blocks until she noticed that he began to droop.

"Ready for bed?" she asked, taking him gently in her arms. Franklin simply nodded, his red hair glinting in the flickering lantern light. In the bedroom, she pulled a nightshirt from the bag Goldie had left while Franklin pulled off his clothes and dropped them on the floor. "Now, let's say your prayers," she suggested, pulling the shirt over his head.

He knelt beside the bed. "Now I lay me down to sleep…" he recited as his mother had taught. At the end, he opened his eyes and looked at his aunt. "God bless Mommie and Daddy," he said.

"Yes," Mildred agreed, "and especially Malcolm."

"And 'specially Malcy," Franklin added, crawling under the sheet.

She pulled the sheet up under his chin and handed him the "snugglie" from his bag. "Sleep tight," she whispered, kissing him lightly on the forehead.

"Bed bugs not bite," he replied with a sleepy smile. Mildred carried the lantern into the kitchen where she banked the coals in the stove. In a few minutes, she crept back into the bedroom to observe Franklin sound asleep, the snugglie clutched tightly to his breast. Walking into the living room, she extinguished the lamp and collapsed into a rocking chair with a weary sigh. Pushing gently with her foot, she set the rocker in motion attempting to relax with her eyes closed. In what seemed only a moment, she was startled by a shout from the door.

"Yoo-hoo, Mildred. You awake?" Through a sleepy haze, she recognized her brother's voice while noting that as it was now quite dark, she must have slept for some time.

"Hold it down, Ray. Franklin's asleep."

"Franklin?" Ray asked, sitting on the couch as she re-lit the lantern. "What's he doin' here?" After she filled him in on the events of the evening, he stretched himself out on the couch and announced, "Well, I'll just sit here with you 'til they get back." In a few minutes after Mildred resumed her rocking, she noticed that Ray was sawing logs, so she extinguished the lantern once again. In another few minutes, she was sleeping soundly in her chair.

Mildred awoke with sunshine streaming in through the front window. Ray was still sleeping on the couch. She sat up, stretching her arms before she remembered that Franklin was there. Rushing into the bedroom, she nearly went into a panic when she observed that the bed was empty. A noise drew her attention to the kitchen. In that room, Franklin sat on the floor, his left arm through the right leg of his pants, playing cars with the blocks. "You did a good job getting dressed," she praised, suppressing a laugh.

Franklin's impish grin crossed his freckled face. "Breakfast? Franklin hungry."

"Comin' right up," she said, lifting the lid from the stove. "I'll get the fire started, you go wake up your Uncle Ray." Franklin ran into the front room and, spotting Ray stretched out on the couch, pounced on the unsuspecting sleeper.

Ray awoke with a start, but seeing his favorite nephew, just rubbed the boy's hair. "How you doin', buddy?"

"Malcy's sick," Franklin answered in wide-eyed innocence.

"Yeah, I know." As he did not know what else to say, but smelled the aroma of frying bacon, Ray added, "Let's go see about that breakfast."

After they ate, Mildred washed while Ray and Franklin dried the dishes. When everything was cleaned up, she asked, "Well, what do you boys wanna do now?"

Ray was about to make a suggestion when Franklin chimed in, "Go to store and get pop."

"I don't think Mr. Neal is gonna be open today," Mildred said, thereby reminding herself that the store keeper had taken Goldie, Duke and Malcolm to the hospital.

Disappointment momentarily covered the child's face but he brightened with "Go see Aunt Florine? Maybe ride Old Gray?"

"That's a good idea. Let's go." Just as they reached the front door, Everett Neal's car pulled off the road in front of the house. Duke opened the passenger door. Without glancing at Mildred and Ray, he opened the rear door to help Goldie out. From the porch, Mildred and Ray could see his sunken, red eyes. The couple stood motionless, her head leaning against her husband's shoulder, as the car slowly drove away. Mildred rushed to her sister's side, trying to speak but seeing Goldie sobbing into Duke's shoulder, could find no words.

Franklin came from the house, moving slowly toward his parents. "Mommie?" he ventured, his face clouded with non-understanding.

Goldie picked him up and hugged him tightly. She turned to look at Mildred over Franklin's shoulder. "Malcolm's gone," she sobbed. "My boy's dead."

Chapter 3

Saturday, October 6, 1934
Tea Run, Kentucky

A few weeks past his ninth birthday, Franklin Runyon Sousley was pretty much on top of the world. Despite a worldwide depression, an ailing father, a baby brother and an uncle in the house, life was good for this young man. There were plenty of pretty girls to flirt with in his fourth grade class at Elizaville Elementary School, his parents ensured that he never went hungry and there was plenty of game to shoot at in the surrounding woods. About all he had to complain about was having to work so hard on the farm, even more so now that Daddy was so ill. However on this particularly glorious Saturday morning, he and his best friend, J.B. Shannon, were going squirrel hunting with Franklin's uncle, Ray Mitchell.

"Hold on, there young man." Goldie's words halted his exit out the front door of the small farmhouse. "Have you finished your chores?"

"Aw, Mom…."

"I do not want to hear it." She interrupted. "Do I need to remind you that…."

Franklin's head drooped in knowing he'd disappointed his mother, as he interrupted her. "No, Mom, I know that you've got your hands full taking care of the house and Uncle Hoover and Daddy and Julian."

Her attitude softened somewhat at this admission. Franklin was a good boy and always did his share and then some. But, with Julian just over a year old, Duke suffering from an advanced case of diabetes and the normal household chores, she had little patience these days. Additionally, her pride was somewhat injured that economics had forced the family to move into her husband's brother's home. Nonetheless, she tried not to take her frustrations out on the son who was the source of most of the joy in her life in these trying times. "And I've got you to deal with too," she added with a smile. She was about to tell him to go ahead when her brother walked up on the porch.

"Ready to go shoot a few?" he asked, entering the house.

"Uncle Ray!" Franklin exclaimed. He cast an anxious glance at his mother before answering the question. "As soon as J.B. gets here," she answered for him. Then, "Franklin, why don't you go let the cows into the pasture while we wait?"

Dashing toward the barn, he was halfway there before he realized that she'd conned him into at least one more chore. He shooed the dairy cows out of the barn and was latching the gate when J.B. appeared over the hill, a rifle tucked under his arm. "Got plenty of ammo?" Franklin greeted his friend.

"I wouldn't say 'plenty'," J.B. said. With a grin he opened his hand displaying five .22 cartridges clutched in his palm. "Only just enough to get five squirrels," he added, his grin widening.

"Didn't anybody ever tell you not to be countin' your squirrels 'fore they're shot, Hawkeye?" Franklin teased as they walked toward the house.

"Gotta make ever' shot count," J.B. said. "I worked all week in Grand-father's cornfield to get the money to buy these."

"Yeah, I heard somethin' at school about there being a depression on," Franklin said. The fact that the world's economy was in depression actually was of little more than academic interest to these country boys. Living on the farm meant that there was usually enough to eat although they had to work hard for it and while money was scarce, they had little need for it anyway. Reaching the porch, they entered the house to find Ray and Goldie drinking coffee at the kitchen table.

"Oh, he has his good days and his bad," she was saying in response to Ray's question about her husband's condition. "He complains of being light-headed most of the time, his hands and feet are always cold and he's having kidney problems. I guess the blurred vision is the worst of it though." She paused a minute, then added, "Today is one of the bad ones. He ain't been out of bed all mornin'."

Ray considered making some remark about her having a heavy burden, but was relieved that the boys entering the house eliminated the necessity. "Say, did I ever tell you boys about me and Dan'l Boone barkin' squirrels?" he asked, good-naturedly.

"Barkin'?" the boys chimed in unison, "What's that?"

"Well," Ray began leaning his chair back against the wall, "back in ole Dan'l's day if you shot a squirrel with one of those huge caliber Kentucky long rifles like we used then, you wouldn't have much squirrel left. So, we'd just shoot at the bark of the tree right under where the squirrel was sittin'.

That'd stun him so that he'd fall to the ground. Then all we had to do was run over, kill the squirrel with a knife and we'd have all the meat left for eatin'. Didn't ruin the pelt, neither." He let his chair fall forward. As the front legs hit the floor with a "whump," he looked from Franklin to J.B. and back for their reaction.

Aside from the sport, eating the meat and selling the pelts were the prime factors in squirrel hunting; the boys were impressed with that idea if somewhat skeptical. "That'd be some fine shootin'," J.B. finally observed.

"It would, but no better'n I can do," Franklin bragged, rising to get his rifle down from its pegs where it rested over the mantle. "I don't think ole Betsy here has enough power for that, though," he added, patting his trusty .22 caliber.

"Well, I reckon that's all that'll keep you from giving barkin' a try," Ray said, laughing. "Ever'body ready?"

The boys jumped up from their chairs, eager to go. "Y'all be careful now," Goldie advised as they walked through the door. "Don't shoot nothin' you wouldn't want to bring home."

"What'd she mean by that?" J.B. was puzzled.

"It's just a little joke," Franklin informed his friend.

"Ain't we always careful?" Ray said to her. Then to Franklin, "You boys loaded?"

"'Course not," Franklin answered the challenge. "We ain't ready to shoot, are we?" Ray was gratified that the young man had learned what he tried to teach about the use of guns. This Saturday was one of those glorious fall days with the leaves in full display of their red and gold colors. The trio had walked about a half mile along the road enjoying the sunshine when a car approached. "That's Uncle Hoover in his new car," Franklin shouted, waving.

"It might be Hoover and it might be his car," J.B. noticed, "but it ain't new." Indeed, the car was well worn from many miles of use.

"Well, it's new to him," Franklin said, leaping up on the running board. "Where you bound, Uncle Hoover?" he inquired.

Hoover Sousley flashed his famous grin on the hunters. A small pension from a World War injury allowed him to own the house and farm where his brother's family lived with him and now a car. Although Duke and Goldie owned a small farm in the area, there was no house on their property, so they shared his home. "Just headed for the house," he answered. "I allow we'll be havin' squirrel for supper?"

"You bet we will," Franklin enthused.

"See ya then," Hoover said, jerking the ancient vehicle into motion as Franklin jumped from the running board.

"Load up, boys but make sure you've got the safety on," Ray ordered as the car roared away in a cloud of dust. "We'll ease over into the woods right here on Pa's land." Franklin loaded one of his four shells into the single shot rifle and they moved off into his grandfather Mitchell's property which adjoined Hoover's place. "Don't make noise shufflin' your feet through these leaves, boys," Ray advised. "They's a couple of hickory trees just over the hill here and I'm bettin' the squirrels will be after the nuts today."

Franklin and J.B. followed closely behind Ray, carrying their rifles as he had taught and walking as quietly as possible. Although the sun was shining brightly, in the woods there was that little cold nip in the air that said it was unmistakably fall. Here beneath the leafy canopy, they had no time to admire the beautiful colors of the leaves. At the top of a ridge, Ray called them to a halt. "The hickory trees are right over there," he said, pointing. "They's a rail fence running along this ridge and it makes a corner over there. When a squirrel runs along the fence with a nut in his mouth, he'll hesitate just an instant at the corner. That's where you'll get a shot."

Ray held back as the boys moved as stealthily as possible to where they had a good view of the corner of the fence. "I'll take the first shot," Franklin whispered. Assuming a prone position, he pointed his rifle toward the corner, flicked the safety off and waited. In a moment, a squirrel came scampering along the top of the fence. Franklin aimed at the corner, inhaled a breath and held it. At the instant the squirrel reached the corner Franklin squeezed the trigger and the rifle boomed. The squirrel dropped to the ground, a hickory nut still clenched in his teeth. "Hot damn, you got 'im!" J.B. shouted as they both ran to retrieve the prize.

"OK, your turn," Franklin said as they returned to the shooting position. J.B. flopped to the ground trying to remember all the shooting techniques so he could do it just as his friend had. Soon another squirrel came chattering along the fence. J.B. tried to wait, but was overeager and fired before the critter got to the corner. The squirrel jumped a foot in the air and hit the ground running in the opposite direction.

And so the afternoon went, the boys alternating shots. By the time they had expended all their ammunition, the long shadows said it was time to go to the house and they had seven squirrels to show for their nine shots. Walking along in the gathering dusk, Franklin asked, as casually as he could manage, "Say, Uncle Ray, do you reckon the hoop snakes are off the nest yet?"

"Oh, hell!" Ray seemed alarmed. "I sure do hope not."

J.B., unaware that he was the object of a joke, asked, "Hoop snake?" I ain't never heard of such. What are you talkin' about?"

"Well," Ray began, "hoop snakes are the deadliest of poisonous snakes. They nest on the ridges 'til about this time of year. Then, when they get hungry, they wait for something – or somebody – to come along. Once they've spotted some food, they take their tail in their mouth, formin' themselves into a hoop and roll down the hill. When they get close to you, they let go just in time to strike."

"Deadly poison, you say?" J.B.'s eyes were wide as he warily surveyed the ridgeline above them.

"I'll say," Franklin chimed in. "One got after me one time. I was lucky enough to see him coming, so I jumped behind a tree just as he struck. I was scared so bad I run all the way home, but I come back the next mornin' and I'm damned if the tree wasn't dead!"

J.B., beginning to smell a rat, looked from Franklin to Ray trying to catch some hint of a joke.

"Why that ain't nothin'," Ray said, ignoring J.B.'s gaze. "I was pullin' a load of corn in from the field once when a hoop snake come rollin' along the row. He struck at me but caught the wagon tongue instead." He paused for dramatic effect then added, "It was a lucky thing I had an axe with me. I managed to jump down and chop off the tongue just in time to save the whole wagon from explodin' to splinters."

"Aw, you're teasing me!" J.B. observed, now sure. All three shared a hearty laugh at his having caught on.

Back at Hoover's house, Ray asked J.B. if he needed help cleaning the squirrels. "No, thanks. Ma will be 'spectin' me home. Pa'll help clean 'em." J.B. turned to walk toward home.

"Let's store these squirrels in the shed," Ray advised. "We'll clean 'em after supper." After Ray and Franklin deposited the carcasses on a bench, they headed for the house.

They knew something was wrong the instant they saw Goldie sitting at the kitchen table with her face in her hands. Franklin rushed to her and put his arms around her slim body. "What is it Mother?"

Goldie raised her head, a look of grave concern covering her face. "It's your father," she said, choking back her tears. "He's took a turn for the worse."

"What can I do?" Ray asked.

"The doctor's comin'," she said. "You take Franklin and Julian with you over to Ma's for the night. I've got the baby's stuff all ready to go."

"I want to stay here with you," Franklin protested.

"No, honey, you go along with Ray. They'll need you to help look after Julian."

Before Franklin could protest further, Ray took his hand and led him to Julian's crib. "Help me gather up his stuff," Ray said, even though Goldie already had a bag packed. Ray scooped up the sleeping baby while Franklin picked up the bag.

"Give me a hug before you go," Goldie said with a sigh, taking her son in her arms. "Don't worry. I'll see you in the morning."

"Want me to look in on Duke?" Ray asked.

"No!" The word came out a little more emphatically than intended. "You two run along now, Ma's expectin' you and she's probably got your supper ready." Then she added, wearily, "Take your coat Franklin, it's liable to get cool this evening"

"Aw, Mom, you know I don't like wearin' coats."

Franklin got the message and protested no more when Ray softly advised, "Get your coat, son." The short walk over to his Mitchell grandparents' home passed quickly enough. Franklin was worried but knew that there was nothing either he or Ray could do to help, so they walked in silence, each holding his own counsel.

The evening was, indeed, cool, so after a good meal, Grandpa Charlie Mitchell lit a blaze in the hearth. Grandma Ortha tended to Julian and entertained her grandsons by singing some church hymns. Franklin, listening to the familiar words and watching the flames dance, soon was nodding off in the warmth.

He awoke with a start, surprised to find himself in bed with weakly early morning light filtering into the room. Rubbing sleep from his eyes, he slowly became aware of a small squeak somewhere in the room. Sitting up, he saw his mother sitting in a rocking chair. Clutching Julian to her breast, she was rocking slowly, seemingly with great effort, with tears streaming down her cheeks. With each backward arc, the floor squeaked and a tiny sob escaped her lips. "Mother," Franklin exclaimed, leaping out of bed.

"Your Daddy's gone," she said, softly draping her arm around her son's shoulders. Her sobs stopped as she faced her son and her voice was steely. "By the time we get back from church, he'll be all laid out and we'll go say goodbye."

29

Although this tragic turn of events was not entirely unexpected and despite the fact that he had tried to prepare himself, Franklin could not control his tears now that his fears were realized. "It's my fault," he blurted. "I should have stayed home."

Goldie squeezed him tighter. "No, honey, it's not your fault. Or anybody's for that matter."

"But why?" he sobbed into his mother's shoulder. "Why us?"

"The Lord moves in mysterious ways," she whispered, her voice steady but laced with sorrow. Her eyes were fixed on some distant object as she rubbed his red hair lovingly. "Get dressed, son. You're the man of the house now."

Chapter 4

Friday, June 12, 1942
Hilltop, Kentucky

"All afternoon?" Franklin was amazed that he was being relieved of his afternoon farm chores. Although his mother had remarried earlier in the year and his stepfather, Hensley Price, had taken some of the work burden from the sixteen year old, he still had plenty of toil to occupy his time around their small farm. Additionally, Goldie's current pregnancy prevented her from carrying as much of the load as she had since Franklin's father died.

"Yes," she replied with a laugh. "The only drawback is that you'll have to take Jake along." The fact that Hense had relieved Franklin of much of his role as "man of the house" had allowed him to become more of the "big brother." Usually, he enjoyed the position – even nicknaming his brother "Jake" – but dragging an eight-year-old along to the neighborhood baseball game was, to his mind, above and beyond the call.

"Well, all right. But can I drop him at Mamaw's after the game?"

"It's all arranged. Hense and I are going to Maysville this evening, so you'll be on your own 'til we get back. It won't be too late, maybe about 9."

"I can deal with it." He tired to suppress the grin that the prospect of a whole afternoon and evening of freedom gave him. "Y'all have a big time," he said, sincerely knowing that both she and Hense were due – overdue – for some fun.

She crossed the room to gather her son in her arms. Franklin, now nearly fully grown was five-feet-eleven inches tall and weighed 150 pounds. Towering over her, he returned her affectionate hug. "Well, it's mostly shopping," she informed, "but we may sneak in a dinner at a restaurant."

"Come on, Jake," Franklin yelled. "If we don't get over there, they'll start without me."

"They ain't gonna start without you," Jake observed, "you got a glove." The fact that the Sousleys owned one of three gloves in the whole area was a source of wonder and pride to young Julian. The boys ran out the door headed for Papaw Mitchell's farm where the neighborhood kids had laid out a rough baseball diamond in a pasture, using stones for bases. "Besides, you're the captain."

"One glove more or less don't matter," Franklin said, grasping Jake's hand to hurry him along. As they arrived at the field, Franklin's friend, Tommy Cologan, bat in hand, waved for him to hurry. "We're burnin' daylight," Tommy shouted, eager to get the game under way. When Franklin was an arm's length from where his friend stood, Tommy tossed the bat to him. After Franklin caught the wooden stick in his right hand, Tommy moved in to place his hand atop Franklin's. The two alternated hands on the bat in the age-old ritual to determine who would choose first. At the end of the ceremony, Tommy was barely able to grasp the handle of the bat, so protocol required that he try to throw it ten feet. As he was unable to do so, Franklin earned the right to choose the first player for his team. "I'll take J.B." he announced to begin the selection process.

By the time the game was well in progress, the usual crowd of parents and on-lookers had arrived. The boys took pride in showing off their abilities as each pretended he was Lou Gehrig or Babe Ruth or Ty Cobb, depending on how he judged his own abilities. In the case of Franklin Sousley, he fancied himself as Ty Cobb as he was a swift base runner. In fact, sometimes his friends called him "Speedy." He also prided himself in being as competitive as the "Georgia Peach" but was careful to be much more considerate of his teammates and opponents than the fiery Cobb. Lost in the game, he forgot about being in charge of his brother until between innings J.B. asked, "Say, where's Jake?"

"Oh, hell," Franklin exclaimed, eyeing the sparse crowd. The moment of panic was brief as he soon spotted Jake behind the spectators. He was playing in the dirt with a couple of kids his age.

The boys played, running and laughing, until darkness called a halt to the festivities. When J.B. Shannon, playing second base, was hit by a batted ball because it was too dark for him to see it, Franklin and Tommy agreed that the game was over. "What's the score?" Tommy inquired.

"Well, let's see," Franklin mused as he pretended to review the innings in his mind. "I make it 422 for us to nothin' for you." He placed his arm around his friend's shoulders.

"You know, that's funny," Tommy grinned. "That's the exact same score I had in mind, but the other way around." All hands got a laugh.

"What are you guys doin' now?" Franklin asked of Tommy and J.B.

"I gotta go milk," Tommy said, disappointment covering his face.

"I got a pass," J.B. announced. "What's doin'?"

"I got a pass too. We'll think of something." The two waved goodbye to Tommy as he walked away. "I gotta take Jake to Papaw's house and then we'll see what we can find to get into."

After they deposited Jake with his grandparents and wolfed down a cold supper, the boys wandered outside. "Wanna go fishin'?" J.B. offered.

"Naw," Franklin said, tossing a stone into the distance. "Me and Uncle Ray was at the fishin' hole yesterday. They wasn't bitin' so we just drowned some worms."

"Let's go swimmin' then." The pair wandered aimlessly up the dirt road toward the Hilltop General Store.

"I ain't got the energy for that," Franklin said, stretching out his arms. "Besides, Hoover's took Mom and Hense to Maysville, so he can't drive us and the Blue Licks is too far to walk." As they approached Neal's Hilltop General store, he suggested, "Let's just sit here on the bench for a spell." They found a spot on what was usually referred to as the "liar's bench," for the simple reason that the structure had been witness to many a tall tale.

Darkness gathered around the two boys. At length, J.B. asked, "Say Franklin, do you reckon we'll have to go to the war?"

"Oh, I will," he answered, with a sigh of resignation. "I would have volunteered right after the Japs attacked Pearl Harbor, but Mother wouldn't hear of it. She said it was gonna be a long war and my time would come, so I'd better finish my education."

"Well, you'll be graduatin' this comin' spring."

Franklin leaned back against the bench stretching his legs out into the road. "Yep. Fleming County High School, Class of '43."

J.B., two years younger than his friend, sat in awe of the prospect. "I figured you'd marry one of those gals you're always flirtin' with, get a little place up in one of these hollers and raise a passel of kids." In the dark, Franklin could not see the smile on his friend's face.

"Oh, I guess I did too," Franklin admitted. "But my plans kinda got upset."

"Turned you down, did she?"

"Ha," Franklin scoffed. "Ain't no girl ever refused Franklin Runyon Sousley."

"Don't tell me," J.B. said, laughing. "I've seen many of 'em just turn and walk away from you."

"Only because I'd heaped so much charm on 'em they couldn't take no more." After a giggle, he turned serious, "A lot has changed in the last six months. The Japs attack and Mom marrying Hense has made a big difference to me." After a pause, he added, "I expect lots of other folks had plans upset, too."

"So you'll be joinin' up soon as you finish school?"

"I reckon so," Franklin mused. "I'd say Mom's right on with her advice about finishing my education. This war ain't gonna last forever and a fellow'll need an education for after. I'm no longer in any hurry, though; there'll still be Japs and Germans to shoot at next summer."

"You wanna be in the Army or the Navy?" J.B.'s voice was filled with wonder.

"Oh, I don't know. Might be fun to fly in a plane and bein' on a ship wouldn't be bad, neither. I just want to get over there and make a difference. Uncle Ray says the Marines is where a man ought to be."

"Bill Pendleton's in the Navy," J.B. commented with a smile. "He was tellin' me about tryin' to sneak a bottle of whiskey on his ship. Said he dropped it on the concrete dock."

"Yeah?"

"Yeah. He said his tongue was raw for three weeks after he lapped that whiskey up off that rough surface." Both boys got a huge laugh out of that.

"Say, Jim Nash is in the Marines," Franklin recalled. "I remember when he was home back a few months ago. Looked mighty sharp in that blue uniform, I'll tell ya. The girls liked it, too." Franklin drew his legs up under the bench as he leaned forward.

"Yes, sir," J.B. chimed in, "I've heard your Uncle Ray say that goin' to the Pacific, to help the Marines pay those sneaky little yellow bastards back for what they did, is the thing to do." He thought for a minute then added, "I reckon the uniform wouldn't hurt anything, either."

"Jim told me that he wouldn't take a million dollars for the experience of goin' through that Marine boot camp." Franklin paused for effect then finished, "Then he said he wouldn't do it again for a million either."

"You do remember that Jim got killed over there someplace, though."

Franklin sat silently for a few moments, remembering. "Well, folks do get killed in wars, I reckon. Seems like there's a name in the paper ever' week. Strange, though, when it's somebody you know."

The thought sobered both boys into silence. Finally, J.B. broke the spell. "Know what? Old man Brock's got dairy cows in that lot right over here behind us." He jerked his thumb over his shoulder to indicate.

"So?"

"So, they's a roll of fencing 'round behind the store. How 'bout we coop a couple of those cows up on the porch overnight."

Franklin jumped up rubbing his hands in glee. "Great idea!" he exclaimed. "Mr. Neal keeps a can of Epsom salts in the outhouse. We'll give 'em a dose just for good measure."

The two busied themselves stringing fence between the porch supports and herding a pair of cows toward the building. Some difficulty was encountered in forcing the clumsy animals up the low step at the end of the porch, but at length, the chore was accomplished. Exhausted and giggling, the boys decided to call it a night.

"Franklin Runyon Sousley! Get yourself out of that bed this instant." The tone in his mother's voice told him all he needed to know. Franklin opened his eyes to find both Goldie and Hense glaring down at him. "Are you responsible for what happened over at Mr. Neal's store last night?" Goldie demanded.

Franklin slowly raised himself on his elbows, thinking frantically. Although sleep clouded his head, he realized that denial was pointless. But, still maybe it was worth a try. "What happened at the store?" He tried to sound innocent.

"You know damned well what happened!" Hense Price's voice was even gruffer than usual.

"J.B. Shannon's in trouble, too," Goldie added.

Franklin pulled the blanket under his chin in a gesture of resignation. "Yeah, we did it," he confessed.

"Why?" Goldie's voice was less harsh. "Why would you do such a foolish thing?"

He considered saying that it seemed like a good idea at the time, but decided that now was not a good time for levity. Having no answer, he simply shrugged his shoulders.

"Did you give a thought to all Mr. Neal's done for us? Do you remember…?" Her voice trailed off as she decided not to bring up the death of her oldest son. Again, Franklin simply shrugged, but his chin dropped to his chest in humiliation and shame.

"Well, get your ass out of that bed," Hense advised. "I expect J.B. will be over at Neal's by the time you get there." He turned to walk away, and then turned back. "Your mother is mightily disappointed in you." That remark was a stinging blow to the young man.

After he was dressed, he walked into the kitchen not knowing whether to expect breakfast. The aroma of bacon and eggs hanging in the air enhanced his hunger. Surely no breakfast would be a part of his punishment, but maybe his mother would show a little pity. The look on her face showed no such emotion. Instead, she handed him a mop and a pail. "You'd best get along," was her only comment.

The short walk to the store seemed endless. Although it was thirteen years ago and he was only three-years old at the time, Franklin vividly remembered Malcolm's death. Although it was not something he and his mother ever discussed, he knew somehow that Everett Neal had shown great kindness to his family at that time and in many ways since as well. In addition to all else, the prospect of facing Mr. Neal piled more weight on his mind. J.B. was at the pump filling a pail with water as Franklin approached the store. The cows were gone, but the fencing remained in place and the porch floor was covered with slimy cow piles. "Whose idea was this?" he asked, unable to suppress a grin.

"Pretty stupid, ain't we?" J.B. answered, lifting the bucket from the pump.

"Yep. Have you talked to Everett?"

"Yes. He took it kindly enough, I guess, but didn't see any humor in the situation." They walked toward the porch. "He said we should clear a path from the door first. He don't want to be closed any longer than necessary. It is Saturday and folks will be wantin' to shop."

"Well," Franklin drew the word out, "soon's word gets around, ever'body will want to get a look at our handiwork, too. The sooner we get it cleaned up, the better." Grasping a corner of the fencing, he continued, "I'll get the fence rolled up and put away while you flush and mop, then I'll help you with that."

The morning passed quickly as they toiled at their disgusting chore. They alternated pumping water into the pails and flinging the contents onto the floor. The buckets of water got heavier as the day wore slowly on. By noon, they were covered not only with sweat on the hot, humid summer day, but with excrement, too. Each had slipped and fallen so many times that they had ceased laughing at each other and even their hair was coated. Franklin had predicted correctly; everybody in the area had stopped by to see the show. In addition to the humiliation, the boys had endured no shortage of razzing. Both boys were flabbergasted when Everett Neal appeared at the screen door with a sandwich in each hand. "Take a break, boys" he said, "here's you some dinner."

Franklin stared in amazement. "We got no money," he managed to stammer.

"Don't matter," the store owner said. "Get you a bottle of pop and rest in the shade for a spell." He handed each of the boys a sandwich.

As neither could summons the energy to pump another pail of water to wash, they simply plopped in the grass under a nearby tree. Sitting in the cool shade, J.B. said, "I wish Mr. Neal hadn't give us this bologna and cheese. Makes me feel even worse than I did."

"Yeah," Franklin said with a deep sigh. "Makes me feel like what we've been standin' in all mornin'."[1]

Chapter 5

Sunday, July 11, 1943
Elizaville, Kentucky

F ranklin was filling a hot, lazy Sunday afternoon sitting alone on the liar's bench outside Neal's Hilltop General Store idly pitching pebbles into the road. The State highway department had recently repaved the country lane leaving plenty of pebbles to pitch and fresh tar for them to sink into.

Deeply immersed in thoughts of his present and future, two topics headed the list: the draft and girls. At this particular moment, last night's date with Marian Harding, one of his best girls, occupied his mind. A smile crept over his face as he thought of Marian. All the work there was to be done on the area farms occupied his mind as well. At the very top of the list, however, was how soon he'd be receiving that infamous "Greetings" letter from Uncle Sam ordering him to report for military service. The war was as finally beginning to turn in the Allies favor, but the cost in manpower was horrific and every able-bodied young man would be called, in most cases sooner rather than later. He'd wanted to volunteer right after his high school graduation six weeks earlier, but Goldie had convinced him that he should wait; help her and Hense out with the tobacco crop and earn some money to help out with the bills. Oh, the letter was on the way, he mused, the only question was "when?" The sound of an approaching car interrupted his reverie.

He recognized his old friend Cecil McIntire at the wheel as the car skidded to a halt in front of him. The windows were down; Cecil was covered with sweat and he, as well as the car's interior, were coated with dust. "What's doin, Red?" Cecil asked as he leapt from the car and took a seat next to Franklin.

"Oh, just contemplatin' the wonders of nature," Franklin replied, shaking hands. "I ain't seen you since old Hector was a pup. What's goin' on with you these days?"

"I'm workin' at a factory in Dayton." Cecil, dressed in a linen suit, pulled off his jacket, loosened his tie and stood to dust himself off. Franklin knew that after Cecil had been classified 4F – unfit for military service – because of a heart defect, he, like many other Kentucky boys, had gone north of the river seeking employment in Ohio. With American war production in full swing and so few able-bodied men available, there were plenty of jobs to be had. "It's a good life up there, I'll tell ya." Cecil leaned back against the bench, a satisfied grin on his face.

"Yeah? Do tell me all about it."

"Well," he began, wiping his face with a dirty handkerchief, "I'm working for General Motors at the Frigidaire Division...."

"Frigidaire? Makin' ice boxes?" Franklin was incredulous.

"Naw!" Cecil spat. "Ever'thing is war production nowadays. You know that. We're makin' propellers."

"For airplanes?"

"That's right." Cecil leaned away to stuff the handkerchief back in his hip pocket. "It's hard work, but the pay's great." After pausing for effect, he added, "And, they's plenty of women on the loose up there, too."

Franklin tried to give the impression that neither of those tidbits of information interested him. "Well, the pay workin' on farms around here ain't too good, but there is plenty enough girls to go around." Here Franklin paused for effect himself before nonchalantly adding, "I've certainly got my share. And then some."

Cecil stared off into the distance to let the moment pass. He spoke thoughtfully, "The 'baccer's planted and hoed, the hay's in the barn. Ain't you ready to blow out of this place, go somewhere, see somethin' and earn some real money?"

Try as he might, Franklin could no longer hide his interest. "Well, yeah, I am," he said with a sigh, "but the money I earn helps out Mom and Hense."

"Why, hell," Cecil leaned forward to spit in the dust at their feet. "I'll bet I can get you a job workin' at GM with me. You'd earn more in a week up in Dayton than you'll earn all summer around here. You could send home more than you're even earnin' now and still have plenty left to chase the girls with."

"Probably," Franklin said with an air of resignation, "but by the time I paid rent and all, there wouldn't be nothin' left." The farm boy didn't know much about the ways of the world, but he did know that one did not live in a big city for free.

Cecil leaned back, crossing his feet before him. "I've got a little apartment – it's just one bedroom, but it does have twin beds – you can stay with me, we'll split the rent. That'll help us both."

Franklin was interested now. "We'll have to eat out ever'meal?"

"No more'n we want to. I've also got a kitchen and a living room, too. For entertainin', you know." He gave Franklin a knowing look as he gently elbowed the farm boy's ribs.

"You really think you can get me on at the factory?"

"Almost certainly. What with most ever'body already gone to the service and somebody at the plant gets drafted ever' week, they're always short-handed."

That comment abruptly halted the grandiose dreams filling Franklin's thoughts. "Well, Uncle Sam'll soon want me too, you know."

"I reckon he will, but it don't matter. Like I said, they're used to it. You might as well make a little money and have a little fun before you do go."

Franklin slapped his knee. "By golly, I'll do it. When do we go?"

"Hold on here. Let me make sure I can get you on." Cecil thought for a moment then went on, "Tell you what, I'm goin' back this evenin', but I have to come back here next weekend anyway. I'll have ever'thing set up and you can ride up with me next Sunday evenin'." He slapped his old friend on the back, "Buddy, we'll have us some fun!" Cecil stood, shook Franklin's hand and walked to the car. "I'll see you next Sunday," he shouted as he opened the car door.

Franklin sat on the bench watching the dust cloud as the car faded away over the hill. Dayton! Working inside a factory where the weather doesn't matter! Big pay check! Girls! He was halfway home with the sugar plum dreams again dancing in his head before his mother crossed his mind. What would she say?

"Dayton! Ohio! Have you lost your mind?" Goldie wasn't exactly screaming, but the volume of her voice wasn't far below that level, either.

"Now calm down, Mother. It's not so far and besides Cecil comes back home pretty often."

"But you don't have a clue about the evils of a big city, son. There's things and people and meanness in a place like that you ain't ever even dreamed about." Wringing her hands in distress, she added, "Besides, you're needed here."

"Well, see, that's the beauty of it." Despite her distress, he could see that he was winning the discussion. "I can send you more money than I'm even earnin' now and still be here to lend a hand most weekends. Why, you wouldn't have to feed me through the week." He crossed the room to place his arms around her shoulders. "You don't think I'd abandon my best girl do you?"

Goldie dissolved into tears. "Maybe Hense will have a man-to-man talk with you," she blubbered, resigned to the fact that he'd be leaving home.

What does Hensley Price know about it? Franklin thought. He respected his stepfather for his care of Goldie, but the two of them were not close in any way and Hense had never been out of Fleming County for more than a day, anyway. But he did not give voice to those opinions, merely nodding instead.

At that point, Franklin's younger brother, Jake, entered the room. "What's goin' on?" he asked, seeing his mother in tears.

"Franklin's goin' away," she said, suppressing a sob.

"Yeah?" Jake was immediately envious. "Where you goin'?"

"Cecil's gonna get me a job at a factory in Dayton," Franklin announced, pride in his voice.

"I wish you'd reconsider, son," Goldie pleaded. "You know my two boys are my heart. I can hardly bear the thought of you being so far away."

"Why, heck, Mother," Julian said. "The draft is gonna get him any day now anyhow." He crossed the room, put one arm around his mother and shook his brother's hand. "You'll tell me all about it when you get up there, won't you?" he asked with a wink.

Franklin frowned at the ten-year-old. He had not intended to bring the draft situation to his mother's mind even though he was sure it occupied her thoughts as often as it did his own. "We'll see," he said.

The week passed quickly. Franklin had a few unfinished chores to clean up and many goodbyes to say: his friends and classmates, girl friends Marian Harding and Francis Jolly, the men he worked with on the various farms and the church folk. And so many relatives; Grandparents, Uncle Ray and Aunts Mildred and Florine. Many of those partings were tearful but by the time Cecil's car slid to a stop in front of the Prices' house on Sunday afternoon, Franklin was eager to get started. He sat in a rocking chair on the porch, a cardboard suitcase holding his meager clothing at his side. "Ready to go, I see," Cecil greeted him. "Hello, Jake," he said noticing the boy hiding around the corner, a sullen look on his face. When Jake merely glowered, Cecil asked, "What's the matter with him?"

"Oh partly sadness to see me go, partly jealousy and partly being miffed because Mother said he couldn't go, too."

Cecil grinned. "Oh, to be a youngster again. Said your goodbyes?"

"No, come on in with me, Mother will want to talk to you anyway."

Inside the house, Goldie sat rocking her new baby, James Hensley, while Hense busied himself in the back. Hearing the boys enter, Hense came into the front room and shook hands with Cecil, then Franklin. "I reckon you boys will behave yourselves?" It was more of a question than a statement.

Franklin moved to his mother's side and knelt beside her chair. Placing his arm around her, he said, "Now don't you worry, I'll be home plenty and Cecil will see to it that ever'thing goes OK." Kissing her cheek, he noted it was salty from her tears. Straightening to stand beside her, a strange new emotion filled his being. He'd seen his mother cry before but those had been tears of grief. The ones staining her cheeks now were something different and much more discomforting.

"See to it that you do," she admonished Cecil.

"Yes, ma'am." Franklin noticed that Cecil turned away, trying not to smile as he answered.

Everyone walked onto the porch. "Well, this is it, I guess," Franklin said, suppressing both smiles and tears. He shook hands with Hense and Julian then kissed his mother again. Cecil settled into the driver's seat and started the engine. "Let's go," he urged.

Franklin waved weakly to those on the porch and opened the passenger door. With a sigh, he sat. As soon as he closed the door they were off. He sat with his chin on his chest as they roared away to the north. "Ready for some adventure?" Cecil asked, pretending to ignore his companion's demeanor.

"Yeah, I guess," Franklin managed to mutter.

"Aw, come on," Cecil encouraged. "You got to get away from home sometime and it ain't like you're going very far. I promised your mother that I'd bring you back next weekend. Besides, think about all that money you're gonna make and all the pretty girls you're gonna meet."

Franklin brightened at that prospect, but still could not completely put his mother's tears from his mind. "Do I start work tomorrow?"

"Well," Cecil drew the word out, "I wasn't gonna tell you 'til later, but there's a slight problem."

"Oh?" Franklin sat up in his seat.

"No big thing, it's just that they will not allow you in the factory until they've done a background check. National security, you know."

"Why, I ain't a German saboteur if that's what they're worried about."

"I doubt they suspect that you are," Cecil said with a laugh. "It's just routine. Ever'body has to go through it. You'll go to the personnel office in the morning to fill out some forms, they'll check out all the information you provide to determine you're who you say you are and then you'll be all set."

"How long's that gonna take?" Franklin's anxiety level, already high, went up a few extra notches.

"Oh," Cecil tried to sound casual, "a month or so."

"A month?" Franklin shouted. "What the hell am I supposed to do in the meantime?"

"Calm down." The driver nearly swerved off the road as he turned to look at his alarmed passenger. "They's plenty of jobs," he observed, steering back onto the pavement, "we'll just find you something to fill in the time until you're cleared."

Closing his eyes, Franklin settled back in his seat to digest this turn of events. Cecil was probably right about him easily finding a job. Or else he would have not brought him along, right? As he became more comfortable, the gentle rhythm of the wheels on the road made him drowsy. Marian's face flashed through his mind, then the haunting memory of his mother's tears. Slowly, he became aware that he was operating some kind of huge, complicated machinery. Someone was yelling his name over the noise of the machine. He opened his eyes to find Cecil smiling at him across the front seat of the car. "Franklin! Wake up, Franklin, we're home."

Rubbing sleep from his eyes, Franklin saw that they were parked in front of a small house on an elm-lined street. Following Cecil's lead, he stepped out of the car onto the concrete sidewalk. "This is it, come on in," Cecil advised. Franklin pulled his suitcase from the back seat and followed his friend up the walk. Inside the apartment he saw that all the rooms were small; living room, kitchen and dining area, bathroom and a bedroom with twin beds. "That's yours over there," Cecil indicated.

After Franklin had stashed his clothes in the closet, Cecil suggested that they eat out, a prospect which excited a young man who had eaten in a restaurant only a few times in his life. "There's a little diner just down the street," he said, "close enough to walk." The men walked down Park Drive to the corner of Brown Street where a gleaming chrome and glass diner sat opposite the Miami Valley Hospital.

"Well, hello!" Franklin cooed as the pretty waitress approached their booth, menus in one hand, glasses of ice water in the other.

"Hi handsome," she replied, flashing a smile. She handed each a menu as she sat the glasses in front of them, "Hello, Cecil." Franklin noted her voice was different from when she addressed him.

"Hi, Gloria. I'd like you to meet my friend Franklin Sousley."

The girl shifted her weight to one foot and leaned a hip against the edge of the booth next to Franklin. "You from Kentucky, too?" He was sure her smile would melt the ice in his glass.

"Yes, and proud of it, too," he replied trying to appear as cool as Clark Gable was in the movie he'd seen last week. The fact that he'd been trying to snuggle up to Francis during the movie did not cross his mind at this moment.

"Well, welcome to the big city." She smacked her chewing gum distractedly. "What can I get you to drink?"

"I'll have a Coke," Cecil said.

"Me, too." Franklin had not taken his eyes off her.

"Back in a minute," she turned to walk away. Franklin twisted in the booth so he could watch her walk toward the fountain. "Wow," he exclaimed turning back to his companion. "You know her?"

"Just to say hello to," he replied. "I eat supper in here about once a week and she's generally around." Franklin extracted a package of Lucky Strike cigarettes from his shirt pocket. Placing one in his mouth, he offered the pack to Cecil. "I didn't know you smoked," Cecil said accepting a cigarette.

"Hell, ever'body in Kentucky smokes, you know that." Franklin struck a match, lit both their smokes and blew out the flame with a puff of smoke. "I'd like to get to know that gal," he announced, smiling. "I think she likes me."

Cecil inhaled from his cigarette as he leaned back into the cushion. He stared at his friend for a long moment before he spoke. "Listen here, now," he began but stopped when the waitress approached with their drinks.

After she took their order, Franklin again turned to watch her walk away. "You were sayin'?"

"I was about to say," Cecil began, "that one thing she knows is how to get a tip from a guy. Anyhow, I promised your mother that I'd keep you out of trouble. Now I don't intend to get in your way, but I do want to give you some friendly advice."

"Fire away," Franklin said, flicking the end of his cigarette on the ashtray.

"I know you well enough to know that you have quite a way with the girls, but I want you to keep in mind that healthy men are in short supply around here. There's a war on, you know."

"Yeah, I remember reading something in the paper about that. Men bein' in short supply sounds like paradise to me. What's your point?"

"Just this," Cecil said, crushing out his cigarette. "Be careful what you ask for – you might just get it." After a momentary pause, he added, "And you might just get something you didn't ask for."

Franklin stared across the booth into his friend's eyes. He started to make some wise comment but the look on Cecil's face told him that now was not the time. He settled for, "I think I understand."

The morning dawned bright, humid and clear, promising a hot day. Cecil was taking a tray of biscuits from the oven when Franklin awoke, the aroma of frying bacon wafting across the apartment. "Get up, we're burning daylight," Cecil admonished.

"What's the plan?" Franklin asked when he'd settled into a chair at the table.

"Well, soon's we eat, we'll go over to the plant and get your paperwork underway," Cecil replied, sliding a plate of steaming bacon and eggs across the table. "By the time that's done, it'll probably be time for my shift, so you can take the car and go find you a job."

"You know, I was thinkin' about that last night. I ain't fit to do nothin' but cut tobacco and chase girls. What kind of a job can I get?"

Cecil laughed. "Well, that's a fine resume for any young man these days. I keep remindin' you there's a war on. There are a lot more jobs than there are men to fill 'em. Many don't require any great skill, so you'll be fine."

"I ain't so sure about that...."

"Tell you what," Cecil interrupted, "I'll bet you that $5 bill I loaned you last night that you'll have a job someplace before this day is over."

Franklin was awed by the sights he took in on the way to the General Motors plant. They drove by many tall buildings, any one of which was the largest he'd ever seen until they reached the factory on North Taylor

Street. His mouth was still agape when they found a spot in the parking lot outside the personnel office. "What do ya think?" Cecil asked.

Stepping out of the car, Franklin surveyed his surroundings and announced, "This lot is bigger'n Grandpa Mitchell's farm."

"Wouldn't doubt it," Cecil said with a laugh, "and a man could hang a lot of tobacco in that building, couldn't he?" making an analogy both country boys understood. As they walked to the fence, he advised, "Now you go in that door over there and tell the girl at the desk your name and that you're here to apply for a job in assembly. She'll have all the paperwork ready for you to fill out. Just answer ever' question and don't put no lies on the paper. I'll be around here someplace when you get out." As Franklin took a few hesitant steps toward the door, Cecil added, "and don't take no wooden nickels, either."

Inside the personnel office, Franklin approached the pretty girl sitting behind a desk. Bearing in mind his friend's advice from the previous evening, he resisted his natural impulse to flirt with her, instead simply stating his business. He took the thick sheaf of papers she handed him to the counter she indicated and was embarrassed to find that he had nothing with which to write. "Excuse me, miss," he said to the girl, "could I borrow a pencil?" Without looking up, she tapped a can full of pencils sitting on the counter at her side. He took one and returned to the counter to attack the forms which proved to be the toughest test he'd ever taken. The questions covered every aspect of his young life, up to and including asking for detailed directions to the Hilltop home where he grew up. "You'll be hearin' from us," she said, making a quick check of the papers he returned.

He saw Cecil leaning against the fender of his car talking to three other men. Franklin was surprised to learn, upon introduction, that all three were Kentuckians with more or less the same background that had brought him to Dayton. As he and Cecil got in the car, it occurred to him that the big city might not be as foreign as he had first expected. Cecil pulled to a halt in front of the train depot. "Run in there and buy a paper from a newsboy," he advised.

When he returned to the car with the paper, Cecil said, "By the time we get some lunch, it'll be time for me to go to work. We'll search the classified ads while we eat, then you'll be on your own." In a downtown lunchroom, the two pored over the paper while they ate. When they arrived back at the Frigidaire parking lot, Franklin had three prospects circled in the paper. "Go find you a job then go to the apartment and get some sleep," Cecil advised. "Set the alarm so you'll be back here to pick me up at midnight. OK?" He handed over the ignition key.

"OK," Franklin said, noticing that the level of comfort he'd felt earlier was gone now. As Cecil walked away, he started the car, checking the city map spread out on his lap. His first stop was a Shell service station a few blocks from the plant. Parking the car behind the building he walked around to find a fat man sitting with his feet propped up on the desk. The man's upper body was covered only by a sweat-soaked sleeveless undershirt. He was fanning himself with a funeral home fan.

"Can I help you?" He really didn't seem interested in helping.

Reciting the lines he and Cecil had practiced, he began timidly, "My name's Franklin Sousley, sir. I'm here about the grease monkey job you advertised." He pointed to the newspaper in his hand.

Laying his fan aside, the fat man looked the country boy up and down. "Can you pump gas?" His gruff voice intimidated Franklin.

"I reckon so," he replied, summonsing his courage. He'd pumped gas into Uncle Hoover's car many times at Mr. Neal's store.

"Do you know how to change the oil in a car?" The voice was slightly less gruff now.

"No," Franklin admitted, "but I'm a quick learner."

"Where do you stand with the draft?"

Remembering Cecil's advice about lies, he replied, "They'll be after me soon enough, I guess, but the fact is that I just wanna work here until I'm cleared to work at the plant." He held his breath for the reaction.

The fat man studied Franklin for a moment. "I'm Matty," he said extending his hand. "I admire a man who'll tell me the truth. I can pay fifty cents an hour. When can you start?" Now the voice was warm.

"Well, I'm free 'til midnight."

"They's some coveralls in the back room there," he jerked a thumb over his shoulder. "Go find a pair that fits you and I'll show you how to change the oil in a car."

Chapter 6

Sunday, December 26, 1943
Flemingsburg, Kentucky

A cold wind whipped the snowflakes past the window of the Greyhound bus station. Franklin stared out into the gathering darkness, feeling nearly as gloomy as the weather. Christmas had been great; good food and wonderful times with the family. The times with his girls were not so good though and, to top it off, neither Marian nor Francis was willing to wait with him for the bus. All things considered, the long, cold, lonely bus ride back to Dayton was a most unattractive prospect. While he was enjoying his job assembling propellers and really did feel as if he was aiding the war effort, waiting for the draft notice was becoming a heavy burden. As Cecil had promised, the money was pretty good and he had been able to help out the family, but working in the swing shift from 2:40 PM until 4 AM left little time for the girl chasing he'd envisioned. In fact, at dinner at his Aunt Florine's last night, he'd told her that at the rate things were going he'd be an old man before he knew it. Many of his high school friends had been home showing off their uniforms and telling of far off lands; Franklin Sousley was eager to join the ranks of those actively serving their country.

At last the bus pulled up out front. He tightened his coat around him and stepped out onto the sidewalk where the frigid wind hit him like a slap to the face. Handing the driver his ticket, he climbed the steps gratified to see that the bus was only about half full. I'll have room to stretch out and sleep, he thought selecting the back row which featured a triple-width seat. He settled back into the cushions to watch the snow covered fields slide by while hoping that the trip would prove uneventful. About all that was dependable about wartime transportation was that it was undependable – there would always be some kind of delay. A full moon illuminated the landscape of tobacco and corn stubble fields so monotonous that he was soon asleep as the bus plowed northward through the cold night.

Snow was coming down even harder upon arrival in Dayton. Cecil had gone to visit some friends in Cincinnati, so Franklin faced the prospect of a cold walk to Park Drive. Wrapping up in his coat, he trudged along making footprints in the snow on the sidewalk until he reached the apartment. Weary from the bus ride but not yet sleepy he heated coffee on the stove and settled down with a cigarette to read the paper. The war news was encouraging, but all the correspondents made it clear that there was plenty of war left. While the Marines were mopping up on one of those Pacific islands nobody had ever heard of, the talk from Europe was all of the pending invasion of the continent. When and where would the Americans and the British strike Hitler's Atlantic Wall? Stubbing out his cigarette in the ashtray, he peered out the window at the swirling snow for a few minutes and then got ready for bed.

"Wake up! Wake up! Here it is!"

Franklin sat bolt upright in the bed to see what Cecil was yelling about. "Here what is?" he asked, rubbing his eyes.

"Your greetings from Uncle Sam," Cecil shouted, throwing the envelope toward the bed.

Franklin stabbed at the missile in the air but missed so he had to lean far over to retrieve the small brown envelope from beneath the mattress. As he eyed the envelope curiously turning it over in his hands, Cecil shouted impatiently, "Well, open the damn thing up!"

Fumbling with the envelope while still groggy from sleep and excited, he handed it to his friend, "Here, you open it."

Cecil ripped the seal and extracted the single sheet contents. "From the President of the United States of America, Greetings…."

"Yeah, yeah," Franklin interrupted, impatiently. "What does it say?"

Cecil scanned down the sheet. "It says you will report at Cincinnati for induction into the armed forces at 6:30 AM, on Tuesday, January 4, 1944." He handed over the letter.

Wide awake now, Franklin mused, "January 4, that's just a week from tomorrow. They don't give a fellow much time to get his affairs in order, do they?"

Placing two mugs on the table, Cecil poured coffee. "Well, this is it. What are you gonna do?"

Franklin sat. Stirring a spoonful of sugar slowly into his cup, he spoke thoughtfully. "Well, I guess I'll notify my supervisor at the plant today. Then…." His voice trailed off.

"What can I do?" Cecil inquired?

"I think I need to go home and talk to Ray and Grandpa Mitchell," he was still stirring and peering into the cup. "I don't think I want to just let 'em draft me. They'll stick me in the Army and then who knows?" Realizing that Cecil had asked a question, he responded, "Wanna go to Fleming County this weekend?"

"I guess I could drive you down if that's what you want."

"Yeah, thanks." Then as much to himself as his companion, he said, "The home folks will know what's best. I'll write Mother and tell her the news and that I'll be there Saturday. That's New Years day. That'll make three straight weekends I've been home."[2]

"Well, that is a streak that's about to end," Cecil observed.

The days flew by in a flurry. On Friday night, his co-workers gave him the standard big send-off that everyone who was drafted received. By the time they'd finished pounding on his back and wishing him good luck, Franklin was more than ready to go to Kentucky. He and Cecil passed the drive in idle conversation, neither willing to discuss the decision facing young Franklin. He was grateful when they stopped in front of the Price house. "Well," Franklin took his friend's hand, "how do I say 'thank you' for all you've done for me?"

With his inability to go into the service himself in mind, Cecil smiled a bittersweet smile. "I guess you can do something that'll make us all proud when you come back." He placed a hand on Franklin's shoulder. "If you do that, it'll be thanks enough." He squeezed the shoulder as Franklin got out of the car.

"Be seein' ya," was his farewell. He walked into the house to find, as expected his Uncle Ray and Grandfather waiting.

"Well, there he is," Ray greeted. Franklin hugged his mother then shook hands with his uncle, Grandfather, stepfather and younger brother before moving to the fire to warm himself. "What is the word, Franklin?" Ray asked.

Extracting the draft notice from his pocket, Franklin handed it to Ray who examined the paper. He let out a long, low whistle. "Didn't leave you much time, did they?" Ray handed the paper to his father.

Goldie rose from her chair. "Come on, Julian they's men talk to be done here." She motioned toward the kitchen.

"Oh, Ma…."

"Come along," she scolded. Julian reluctantly followed her into the other room.

"I think I'll go check on the cows," Hense announced as he exited the house, leaving the three men alone.

"Well, what do you think, Ray?" Franklin asked.

"Ain't a doubt in my mind," he answered. "If it was me, I'd join the Marine Corps tomorrow."

"Me too," Charlie Mitchell chimed in. "If you got to go, you might as well be a part of the best."

"That's what I've wanted to do all along," Franklin said with a sigh. "But now that I'm starin' right down the barrel, so to speak, I ain't so sure anymore."

Ray crossed the room to throw another log on the fire. "Look at it this way. If you let 'em draft you, you've got no say whatsoever in what they assign you to. They'll most likely send you to Europe and that ain't where you want to be."

"I agree with that," Franklin said, "I want to go to the Pacific to fight the Japs. I could volunteer for the Navy and serve on a ship."

"I won't say that the Navy don't have their share of rough times," Charlie chimed in, "but I will say that I wouldn't care to be out in the middle of an ocean with no control over what's gonna happen to me. Them ships is just floatin' coffins, if you ask me."

"Now look here, son," Ray said, "what's the point of bein' in a war if you ain't gonna fight? The Marines will train you to be the best fightin' man on earth and you'll get to go to the Pacific and pay those bastards back for what they done at Pearl Harbor."

Franklin looked over to his grandfather who simply nodded in agreement. "Well, like I said, the Marine Corps is what I've always wanted."

"OK," Ray jumped from his chair to shake his nephew's hand. "You'll have to go to Cincinnati to report for the draft on Tuesday, but we'll talk to the Marine recruiter beforehand and have it all fixed up."

After Franklin had filled out about 1000 forms and signed his name at least as many times, the Marine recruiter, Captain Alvin Busse, glanced over the paperwork one more time. Rising from the desk, he smiled extending his hand, "Welcome to the United States Marine Corps," he said, "You'll be a part of the best."

"Am I a Marine now?"

"Good Lord, no," Capt. Busse exploded. "You ain't even a boot yet. There's a long way between now and you getting' to wear the globe, eagle and anchor that identifies a U.S. Marine. You'll have to prove yourself worthy."

"No problem," Franklin stated his confidence. "How long am I signed up for?"

"The duration of the national emergency," the Captain said.

"What does that mean?"

"Well, in theory, it means you'll be in the Marine Corps until the war is over. In actual practice, though, it means that you'll be in until they damn well decide to let you go."

"Oh," Franklin sighed, realizing that it was too late to worry now. "When do I get started?"

"Oh, glad you reminded me." He extracted a card from a desk drawer and stamped something on it. "Recruits from east of the Mississippi generally do their boot training at Parris Island down in South Carolina, but what with so many men joinin' up they're swamped down there, so you'll be going to the recruit depot in San Diego. The train don't go until the 19th, so this certifies your date of service as today and makes you a member of the inactive Marine reserve until then." He handed over the card.

"So, I'll be goin' to California?"

"Yep. You'll be what your Parris Island counterparts call a 'Hollywood Marine.'"

"What will I need to bring along?"

"Not a thing, son, not a thing. From the minute you step on that train, you're Uncle Sam's property and he will supply everything you need. Just make sure you don't screw up once you get to boot camp."

The young man wondered just what Capt. Busse meant by that, but let it pass. "That's two weeks away. What'll I do in the meantime?"

"Well, you've got a two-week vacation. Go home, kick up you heels a little, kiss all the girls goodbye and report to the train depot in Flemingsburg on the 19th.

"Weather's always worst at this time of year," Charlie Mitchell observed, just making conversation.

"Yep," Ray agreed, "mid January to mid February is as bad as it gets." Indeed, the weather on this January night was bad. Snow poured from the sky in sheets driven by an arctic blast. The ground had been covered when they left Hilltop; several additional inches had accumulated during the eight-mile drive to Flemingsburg.

"Y'all should go on home, the roads are gettin' bad." Franklin said, glad to find something he could say. The mixture of emotions welling within him: anxiety, excitement, fear of the unknown and a sense of adventure had sealed his lips as securely as a child's "tick-a-lock."

Goldie clung to her son's arm, her face twisted in agony mixed with a twinge of pride. "You'll be so far away in California," she said. "I'll worry myself to death."

"How long will it take you to get to California?" Julian wondered aloud.

"Three days on the train," Franklin informed. "I should be in San Diego by the 22nd. Please don't worry, Mother. I'll be in the lovin' arms of Uncle Sam."

"That's right," Ray chipped in. "I guarantee that the Marine Corps will keep him out of trouble."

Whatever she was about to say was interrupted by the wail of a train whistle. Everybody pressed to the window to watch the steam-snorting locomotive slide by the platform followed by several brightly lit passenger cars filled with young men, some in uniform. A smart-looking Naval officer stepped through the waiting room door. "Sousley?"

"Yes, sir." Franklin answered, leaping to his feet.

"Let's go!"

Franklin shook hands with Charlie, Ray, Hense and Julian then gathered his mother in his arms. "Don't worry, Mother. I'll send you my address as soon as I get there."

"Let's go, son," the officer demanded. "Uncle Sam ain't gonna wait for you."

The salty taste of the tears on his mother's cheeks would stay with the young man for a long time. As bravely as possible, he stood up straight and followed the officer out the door. They were no more than on the car when the engine sounded two short blasts on the whistle. The train lurched into motion, nearly throwing the young man off his feet. He grabbed at a strap just in the nick of time. The officer, hanging from another strap, smiled slightly. "Your first lesson in train ridin'," he said, humorlessly. "Come along." Franklin had not even had time to wave goodbye.

They walked through the smoke-filled car toward the rear, then out onto the platform between cars and finally into the last passenger car. The officer pointed to an empty aisle seat. "C37A, he announced. That's you."

Franklin sat. Seated next to him was a blond young man dressed in a green uniform that identified him as a Marine. The two ignored each other for a short time. Finally the young man turned. "Billy Simms," he said, offering his hand.

Although Franklin had already identified him as a Marine, he could not help asking, "You're a Marine?"

With obvious pride, Billy smiled broadly. "Just barely. I graduated from boot camp at Parris Island yesterday."

"I'm on my way to boot camp at San Diego. Tell me about it."

The grin covering Billy's face could be understood only by those who had finished the course. "Well, I'll tell you this. For the first three days, I was afraid I was gonna die and then for the next two weeks, I was afraid that I wouldn't die."

"That bad?" Franklin's anxiety level ratcheted up a bit.

"It's very demanding in several ways. Needless to say, they'll drive you physically far beyond what you think you can stand. You've a lot to learn, too; how to handle guns, discipline, personal hygiene and all manners of stuff." Billy sank back in his seat before adding, "I guess it'll all pay off when I get into combat."

Franklin studied the puzzling look on his companion's face. When he was talking about boot camp, he conveyed supreme confidence. While that confidence was still there, he could also see some uncertainty. He has the same fear of the unknown as me, he concluded. "Where you goin'?" he queried.

"Camp Pendleton, near Oceanside, California, for additional training."

"Oh? I understood that you got leave when you finished boot camp."

"Sometimes. It just depends on what's goin' on, I guess. The first thing you learn about the Marine Corps is to just do what you're told, don't volunteer for nothin' and don't never ask no questions. They don't run the thing for convenience of the troops. Maybe there's an operation comin' up that I'm slated for, who knows? I'll get to go home for a spell when there's time, I guess."

"Where you from?" Franklin had wondered about the accent so different from his Kentucky twang.

"A little town in upstate New York. And you?"

"Back where I got on the train."

"That don't tell me nothin'. I been on this train since early this morning with no idea of where I've been or where I'm at."

"Oh. Well, central Kentucky. Hilltop, to be exact."

"Hilltop? You're makin' that up?" He was laughing.

"No, that's the name of the place." Franklin did not see the humor.

"Well," Billy said. "One of the things they teach you is that while we all might come from different places and different backgrounds, we're all pretty much the same once you put on the uniform. We're all Marine green, is the way they say it."

The two lapsed into silence for a few moments. Eventually, they felt the train slowing. "What's goin' on?" Franklin wondered

Peering out the window, Billy observed, "Depot sign says we're at Lexington."

"Everybody just sit tight," one of the sergeants shouted. "Just takin' on some supplies. We'll be out of here in a few minutes."

A man came walking down the aisle with a number of little blue booklets in hand, offering one to each seat occupant. "Would you like a Bible, son?" he asked Franklin, offering a small New Testament.

"Sure." He accepted the paper covered book.

"Write your name – nothing else – in the front," the man advised. "In the back there's a spot that you can confess your sins and accept Jesus Christ as your personal savior, if you like." When Franklin didn't answer, the man said, "Keep that with you and it will always be a comfort to you. God bless and protect you." The man moved on. Holding the small blue book in his hand, Franklin Sousley realized for the first time that he was actually on his way to war.

When the train was underway again, Franklin opened the Bible to note that it had been presented to him by the "Gideon Camp, Lexington, Kentucky." He signed his name at the top of the page and scribbled the date on the line at the bottom. At that point, he noticed that his companion had done the same. He considered making some comment about carrying it into combat, but decided that some things were better not discussed. "I'm a might hungry," he offered instead. "Will they let us off for supper sometime?"

"I could eat myself. Come with me."

Billy led the way through the rear of their car into the next. Most of the seats had been removed from this car to accommodate a military kitchen. In one corner of the car was a rectangle, eight feet wide and four feet long, built of two-by-tens and filled with white sand. On top of the sand was a cook stove not unlike the one in Goldie's kitchen. A blue steel stovepipe – damper and all – poked through the roof of the car. An ample supply of stove wood lay on the floor beside the box. In the opposite corner was a counter covered with the most bountiful array of food Franklin had ever seen; fried chicken, baked ham, cold cuts of all varieties, five different kinds of cheese, milk in half-pint glass bottles and orange juice. The end of the table was covered with oranges, apples and bananas, banana pudding, chocolate cake and, wonder of wonders, light bread! "What do we get," Franklin asked in wonder.

"Whatever you want, dive in." As Billy led the way to the buffet counter, Franklin followed in absolute awe.

"This is all for us?"

"Another thing about the Marine Corps, they work the hell out of you, but they sure do feed you good."

To a country boy who had grown up through the great depression, this spread bordered on the unbelievable. Franklin loaded a plate with more food than he'd ever seen at one time and walked over to one of the tables that filled the remainder of the car. Jerking a thumb over his shoulder at several men wearing white smocks at the end of the car, "Who are those guys?" he asked as Billy joined him.

"There are four enlisted Army men, a couple of sergeants and a Naval officer on the train," Billy answered through a mouthful of ham. "They help keep everybody in line and also do the cooking and clean-up, stuff like that."

By the time they returned to their seats, darkness was obscuring the view out the frost-covered windows. Warm and full, Franklin decided to engage in one of his favorite pastimes – he'd tell a story. He lit a cigarette, leaned back in his seat and started talking. Soon, a crowd of young men clustered about where he sat, listening intently. "So see, a couple of years ago, my mother's Aunt Corie died. Well, it wasn't hardly no time at all before the lady from across the road was comin' over to help Uncle Jim with supper and all. Why, before you know it, they was sittin' out on the porch rockin' and holdin' hands and all manner of things.

"They had two adult daughters, you know, and it wasn't long at all before they showed up to give their Daddy a taklin'. 'You ain't doin' Momma's memory right at'll,' they told him. 'She ain't hardly cold in her grave yet and here you are carryin' on like this – we think you ought to wait a year or so before you go takin' up with that woman.'

"He said, 'Now girls, I knew you wasn't gonna approve and I've give the matter serious thought. In the first place, at my age, I might not have no year or so to wait. In the second place – like I said, I've give the matter some thought – I believe your momma is as dead right now as she's ever gonna be.'"

Franklin did not realize that the men clustered about him, representing a cross section of American society, were as entertained by his accent and folksy terminology as by the story he was telling. He was still basking in the laughter when a black porter in a stiff white uniform walked up. "Would you gentlemen step into the aisle while I fix your beds?" he asked.

Knowing that it was also his friend's first night on the train, Franklin asked, "Did you ever see such a thing?"

"Never," Billy replied. The two boys observed in wonder as the seats on which they had been sitting were converted into a double bed complete with feather pillows and starched, sparkling white pillowcases and sheets. Above where they had sat, another similarly equipped compartment attached to the roof and side wall appeared. "You want the inside or outside," Billy asked.

"I'll take the inside if you don't mind," Franklin replied. "I can look out the window."

"An option the ones in the upper berth don't get," Billy observed stepping aside to allow Franklin access to the bed."

"Hold on a minute." He lowered his voice, slightly embarrassed. "Where does a fellow go to pee around here?"

Billy pointed to the front end of the car. See that little room up there? That's the head."

"Head?"

"That's Marine talk for the bathroom," Billy informed, laughing. "I might as well tell you that the floor is the deck, the ceiling is the overhead and the wall is a bulkhead. To the left is port and to the right is starboard. The Marines got their own terminology for everything." He did not recall that someone had had to explain the same things to him a short six weeks ago. Come to think of it, he decided, there was nothing at all short about those six weeks in boot camp.

Franklin walked to the room his new friend had indicated. Blue lettering on a white ceramic plaque tacked on the door proclaimed it to be the "Lavatory." I wish they'd make up their mind what to call the toilet, be mused to himself. Inside was a mirror, sink and a gleaming stainless steel commode. Puzzling was a sign on the lid that advised, "Do not use when train is standing in station." When he lifted the lid, he saw why; crossties, gravel and steel rails were whizzing by below.

Billy was sitting on the edge of the bed when he returned. "What do you think of the accommodations?" he asked, standing.

"Seems like the lap of luxury," Franklin said. "Although I'm a little surprised at the flushing facilities."

"Wait 'til you have to sit on that thing," Billy said with a laugh. "The breeze takes some getting' used to."

"I guess there would be a slight under current." Franklin slid into the inside berth.

One of the sergeants came down the aisle, "Lights out in ten minutes," he shouted.

"You better get used to going to bed early and gettin' up early," Billy advised.

The porter made his way down the aisle closing the curtains to each berth. When the interior lights went out, Franklin could see the snow-covered landscape outside clearly in the moonlight. Thoughts swirled through his head as rapidly as the snowflakes flew by outside the window. At this moment, he was probably farther from home than ever before and getting more distant by the minute. Where he was at this instant was as unknown as what tomorrow would bring. And what lay at the end of this journey? Lonely, scared and homesick, he thought sleep would never come, but visions of Marine boot camp eventually gave way to sleep.

Dull gray light was filtering through the window when a racket jerked him awake. Waking in a strange place is always a bit uncomfortable, but what was that noise? The officer jerked the curtain open while banging on the bed rails with a baton. "More effective than an alarm clock, ain't it?" Billy said, rubbing his eyes.

"You got ten minutes before breakfast," the officer yelled, moving on down the car. "Let's go, Let's go!"

"What's the rush?" Franklin asked.

"Hurry up and wait is a fact of life in the Marine Corps," Billy advised. Franklin had not heard that phrase before but quickly grasped the concept.

The officer in charge of the train had everything timed to the minute. He woke the men in each car allowing just a few minutes for each in the "head" before everyone in the car went to the kitchen for breakfast. Bacon, sausage, ham, eggs, melon, toast, biscuits, butter, jelly, coffee, milk and juice in ample quantities filled the buffet – or, as Franklin had just learned, "mess" – tables. Seeing the wonder in Franklin's eyes, Billy said, "Take all you want; eat all you take," repeating the phrase from the Parris Island mess halls.

When everyone had eaten, they returned to their cars to find the beds converted back into seats. Plopping down in his seat, Franklin asked, "What now?"

"A long day of sitting here smoking cigarettes and watching the country slide by, I suppose," Billy answered.

Looking out the window at the flat, snowy fields, Franklin could clearly see that he was no longer in Kentucky. The rolling hills and valleys of his experience had given way to vast open plains. Huge herds of Angus cattle filled some of the spaces, but the scenery was mostly just open snow-covered ground. In a moment, everyone was lurched forward as the train began to slow. Franklin could see nothing out the window – no town or reason to stop. One of the enlisted men of the military complement came down the aisle shouting, "Exercise period, ever'body out. Ever'body out now!"

"I hate takin' orders from these Army turds," Billy observed as he clambered down the iron steps to the ground.

"Well, I guess the government does the best they can. We've got men from all the branches of the service on this train, looks like, and somebody's gotta be in charge."

"All right," the sergeant bellowed, "You blockheads run up there to where the Corporal is and back here as fast as you can. Move it, Move it, Move it!" After three running trips everyone was herded back onto the train for an afternoon and evening of watching the country pass by the windows interrupted only by occasional stops to take on supplies and for exercise.

On the next day, the landscape changed drastically. Somewhere south of Denver, another engine was attached to the rear of the train for the run through the Rocky Mountains to Salt Lake City. Here the Kentucky boy had his first opportunity to observe the difference between the Appalachians and "real" mountains. The speed of the train dropped as it struggled over trestles and through tunnels running uphill, always uphill. Sometimes on the curves, Franklin could see both the engine at the front and the one in the back expelling black smoke into the air as they pulled and pushed to get their burden through. The left side of the track was piled high with a snow bank while on the right, far below, a narrow stream of water bounced from one side to the other against the boulders. The young man marveled at scenes he'd only seen before in magazines and movies and gained a new appreciation for the hardy pioneers who had traversed this territory in search of a better life in California.

Eventually, the train reached the Golden State. Franklin saw seemingly endless orange groves and vineyards sail by in the bright sunshine, but was disappointed that they all had been pruned back at this time of year and were not very pretty.[3]

At Los Angeles, everyone was ordered off the train. "Marines to the left," a Marine officer shouted. Franklin and Billy moved in that direction until another officer shouted, "Camp Pendleton over there," as he pointed to a bus in the parking lot. "San Diego, stay here with me."

"Well, thanks for the companionship," Billy said. "You sure made the trip a lot easier, but I guess this is where we part company."

Franklin was searching for words to express his appreciation but before any came to his lips, the officer standing by the bus yelled, "Camp Pendleton, let's go!"

"Well, Semper Fi, "Billy said. Franklin did not yet know that the phrase was shorthand for the Marine Corps motto, "Semper Fidelis," Latin for "always faithful" and was the standard Marine "goodbye." "Good luck and don't get caught screwing up in boot camp." He hastily shook hands and watched his short-time friend disappear inside the Navy bus.

A crowd of perhaps 40 young men milled around the lieutenant who called for those going to San Diego. Suspiciously eyeing them for a friendly face, Franklin saw none. The only consolation he could find was that every one of them seemed just as anxious and isolated as he. "All right, gather round and listen up," the Lieutenant shouted above the din. "Follow me." The whole group moved to the far side of the parking lot where another Navy bus waited. Flourishing a clipboard, he instructed, "Get on the bus when I call your name." Four or five boys had already answered and boarded the bus when the Lieutenant called, "Sousley!" Franklin shouted, "Here" as he stepped onto the bus into an unknown world.

Chapter 7

Saturday, January 22, 1944
San Diego, California

In the darkness of the bus, each man could sense others all around him, but could see no one, hence all were sharing the experience, yet each was isolated in his own world of fearful uncertainty. As soon as everyone was on board, the Lieutenant said, "Let's go, Corporal," before taking a seat behind the driver. The bus lurched into motion and each passenger's distress deepened with every revolution of the wheels.

What a long day it had been. They had been jerked out of bed at daylight on the train. Doing little but sit around and talk all day had certainly made the time drag. Additionally, body systems had not yet adapted to being in the west – the term "jet lag" hadn't been coined yet – but they suffered from it just the same. Everybody looked forward to arriving at the barracks or wherever they were to spend the night and sleeping in a bed that was not moving.

As the bus droned on through the darkness, perhaps each man remembered that he'd been warned several times "not to get caught screwing up" at boot camp. Now, in a few quiet moments, maybe he had occasion to ponder just what that meant. As he turned the phrase over in his mind, he probably did not realize that this particular subtle part of the Marine Corps psychological makeover actually began at the recruiter's office.

"Thirty minutes," the Corporal at the wheel sang out. Each of the 40 passengers on the bus sat up and peered out the windows. Although tired, sleep was not an option now. As he contemplated what was happening and what was about to happen, he began to wonder if he had the stuff Marines were made from after all. Well, he'd soon start finding out.

"Twenty minutes," the driver said, causing the knots in the stomachs' of his passengers to tighten just a little more. That guy is some kind of sadist, the men thought. Why the hell can't he just let well enough alone and tell us when we get there? Nobody realized that this, too was just a part of the treatment: the Lieutenant sitting behind the driver could have interfered had he so desired.

"Ten minutes!" Now everybody sat up straight in their seats. Fingering the Bible he received on the train, the young man started thinking about the combat that lay beyond boot camp. A man could get killed, you know. Best get through boot camp before I start worrying about combat, he decided. He'd heard somebody say that he wouldn't give up the experience of Marine Corps boot camp for a million dollars, but he wouldn't do it again for a million, either.

"This is it," the driver announced as the bus slid to a stop. Forty young men leapt to their feet just as the door popped open. From out of the darkness outside, a tall, solid figure of a man wearing a flat brimmed hat bounded onto the front of the bus. "SIT DOWN!" the silhouette screamed. The bus was filled by the sound of 40 butts plopping into their seats. "STAND UP!" His voice was raspy, loud and left no room for one to doubt his authority. Forty young men nearly bumped their heads on the ceiling – overhead – of the bus as they leapt to their feet. "OUT! Everybody out! Move it, move it!" The man in the flat-brimmed hat jumped out the door followed by an avalanche of terrified young men. "Find a spot on the yellow footprints," he demanded. "Everybody on the yellow footprints. NOW!"

Thirty yards to the left, another group of young men poured off a Navy bus. Another group of flat-brimmed men were yelling at them in exactly the same way. In a moment, these two groups would merge to form Training Platoon 81.

The pairs of yellow footprints painted on the concrete, heels together and toes pointed out at a 45-degree angle, created a military formation. Everyone scrambled to find a place. "Stand up straight!" Flat-brim demanded. In the brightly lit assembly area, the silhouette became a man at least six-feet-three inches tall and weighing no less than 220 pounds – all solid muscle. A pair of steely gray eyes glaring from above his protruding square jaw provided the perfect complement to the upper plane of the hat. Moving to the front of the formation, he addressed the group: "I am your drill instructor. My name is Ryse, Gunnery Sergeant Ryse. In the Marine Corps, a Gunnery Sergeant is traditionally addressed as Gunny, but you WILL call me sir. Do you understand me?"

"Yes," a few of the boys mumbled.

From out of nowhere, two assistant drill instructors appeared. All three flew into the formation, screaming at the top of their lungs. Sometimes all three shouted into the face of one terrified recruit. Everyone soon came to understand that a recruit did not speak unless spoken to and if he did speak, the first word out of his mouth had better be "Sir." Another lesson some learned the hard way was that a recruit had better not refer to his drill instructor as a "DI."

The assistants backed off as the drill instructor spoke again. "Now then. Stand up straight and look straight ahead. Life, as you have known it, is over. Your soul might belong to God, but your ass belongs to me. I will tell you when to get out of bed, I will tell you when to go to sleep, I will tell you when to eat, I will tell you when to piss, I will tell you when to blink and I will tell you how you feel. I will not tell you what to think as there will be no necessity for you to think. Do you understand me?"

"Sir, yes sir," the group answered in unison.

"I cannot hear you!"

"Sir, yes SIR!" The response was louder.

"I am not here to teach you to fight for your country; I am here to teach you to fight for your life. As of now, you ain't got no Momma, you ain't got no Daddy. You ain't got no name. You are a United States Marine Corps "boot" and that's the lowest form of life in the known universe. You will be assigned a serial number and you will memorize it. In the unlikely event that there be any need for individual identity, you will recite your serial number. Do you understand?"

"Sir, yes sir."

"I cannot hear you!"

And so it went. The drill instructor was right: these boys had neither time nor need to think. Had one had time to think about it, he might have realized that the way his time was being managed left no option for him to be either lonely or homesick during those first hours of boot camp. But there were plenty of occasions to be scared. After several hours of the three drill instructors all yelling at the same time, the environment became somewhat familiar and, finally, some became only dully aware of the light streak in the eastern sky. They'd been standing there on the yellow footprints all night!

"All right," the drill instructor screamed, "turn left." The whole group made a 90-degree turn in response. The drill instructors instantly swarmed on the two unfortunate souls who turned the wrong way. Faces so close as to curl up the flat brim of their hats against the "boots" forehead, they did their best to ensure that their charges would henceforth know left from right. "Run to that building over there," he ordered, pointing to a building about a quarter mile away. "GO!"

The out-of-shape young men were gasping for breath after the run. The panting boots stopped outside the building where one of the assistants waited. "Line up in front of this door here," he ordered. The boots scrambled into a single file. Yanking the door open, he shouted, "Inside. Now!"

Clambering inside the building, they were met with iron hand rails which channeled them out before a long table marked with a stripe every 14 inches. When each boot claimed his 14-inch space, the drill instructor ordered, "Empty your pockets on the table. Do it NOW!" Feeling like a criminal, each boot scrambled to get the contents of his pockets onto the table. Some money, combs, cigarettes, lighters, keys, a few pocket knives and other common items made up the bulk, but some more ominous objects such as brass knuckles and switch blade knives showed up, as well. The drill instructors came along throwing the latter type objects into a bucket. These items would be seen by their owners no more. The order, "Pick up what's left. Out that way," segued into the next phase.

Outside they were directed to run again to the next building. Inside it, each man was issued a cardboard carton and instructed to address it to his next of kin. "All right, strip and stuff your clothes into the box," came the command. Many parents reported that the arrival of that box, signaling as it did that their son was actually in the Marines, was one of the more traumatic war-time events. After the boxes were finished, the boots were herded into a "head." Across the room, on a shelf above a row of urinals, specimen bottles awaited filling. When the DI, pointing, ordered "Everybody piss in a bottle," one boot innocently inquired, "From here?" Joking or not, he soon wished he'd kept his mouth shut.

Inside the same building, the next stop was the quartermaster's for clothing issue. Green utility blouses, dungarees, "boondocker" boots, socks, web belts, sea bags, blankets and underwear – "skivies" – passed over the counter in two sizes – too large and too small and that size was chosen by the clerk. Again, woe unto the man who made so bold as to voice a complaint. Each boot was beginning to understand the warnings against "screwing up." At the end of the line, each man's name and serial number was stenciled onto his sea bag and blanket. As suddenly as they tended to materialize, the drill instructors disappeared allowing a brief lull for the men to get dressed in their new duds. Some brave soul instituted a swap fest in which a man could swap a "too large" for a "too small." Still, though, nothing really fit.

Each boot was heartened when they were ordered to run to the barracks. The thoughts of sleep and rest that filled each head were soon dis-

Malcolm and Franklin Sousley. Price family collection.

Franklin Sousley. Price family collection.

Ready for squirrel hunting. Price family collection.

Duke and Goldie Sousley. Price family collection.

Ray Mitchell, shown here in later years, provided a father figure for his nephew. Price family collection.

Franklin Sousley. Price family collection.

The house where Franklin grew up is typical of rural 1930's homes. Price family collection.

Franklin and little brother Julian. Price family collection.

Fleming County High School Class of 1943. Price family collection.

Aside from the handicap ramp, Neal's Hilltop General Store is much the same as when Franklin last saw it. The ramp, added when the building was used as a polling place, would have aided getting cows on the porch. Author photo.

The employment application Franklin completed at Frigidaire also provides some details of his job. General Motors Archives.

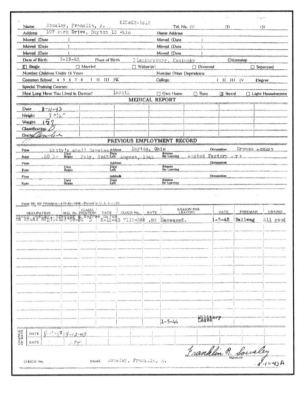

The front page of Franklin's service record gives his enlistment data. National Archives.

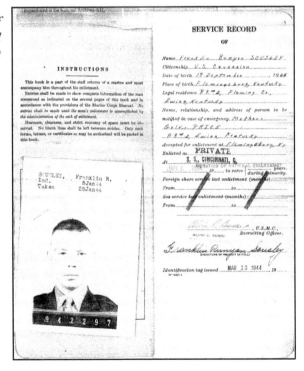

Marine Corps issue clothing only came in two sizes: too large and too small. USMC photo.

Franklin's boot camp mug shot. USMC photo.

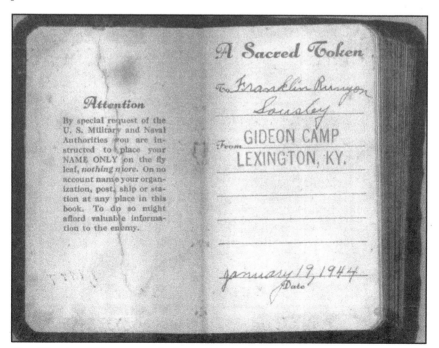

Franklin signed his name in the front of the Bible the day he received it. Price family collection.

Training Platoon 81. Franklin is second from left in the second row down. National Archives.

Marines on the rifle range, USMC photo.

Graduation from boot camp is a big event. USMC photo.

The impish grin in this picture reveals much about Franklin; the proud Marine loved his mother. Price family collection.

Franklin's Aunt Florine Moran recorded Joe Rosenthal's death on the front of the magazine Franklin sent her. Courtesy of Florine Moran.

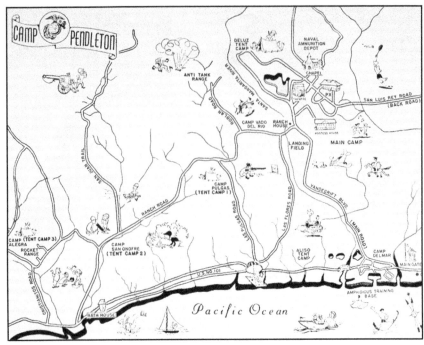

Sketch of 1944's Camp Pendleton. USMC photo.

Welcome to the Fifth Marine Division. USMC photo.

Tent Camp #1, Easy Company's home at Camp Pendleton. USMC photo.

Many Marines found descending a cargo net to a landing craft a harrowing experience. USMC photo.

The first step in combat swimming. USMC photo.

Franklin (right) sparing with Joe Senoracke at Camp Pendleton. Both men were killed on Iwo Jima. USMC photo.

President Franklin Roosevelt observed this assault on Pendleton Island. USMC photo.

Franklin's Dress Blue coat. Courtesy of John Snell.

Goldie and Hensley Price with Franklin and Julian Sousley on his last day at home. Price family collection.

Goldie somehow came up with the money to buy his dress uniform. Price family collection.

Hilltop Christian Church. Author photo.

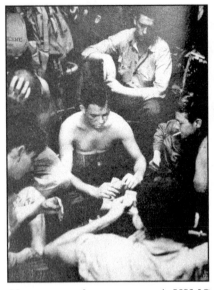

How young those men were! USMC photo.

Those in the lower bunks hope no one gets sick in this sea-going barracks. USMC photo.

This marker at the site of the front gate and some rusted metal huts are all that's left of Hawaii's Camp Tarawa. Courtesy of Carol Elliott.

In training, these volcanic cones served as a substitute Mt. Suribachi. Courtesy of Carol Elliott.

BLACK JAM CAKE

(Favorite of Franklin Sousley, by Goldie Price)

2 c. white sugar	1 tsp. each of allspice,	2 c. sour milk
2 Tbsp. cocoa	cloves, cinnamon	1 tsp. soda
1/2 c. lard	1 pt. jam	4 c. flour

Mix sugar, cocoa and spices together. Add lard and mix well, then add jam, and mix again. Add sour milk. Sift together flour and soda and mix all together good. Nuts can be added if wanted. Bake in oven 350 degrees for about 30 minutes.

At sea, the true identity of "Island X" is revealed. USMC photo.

Merry Christmas from "The Spearhead." Price family collection.

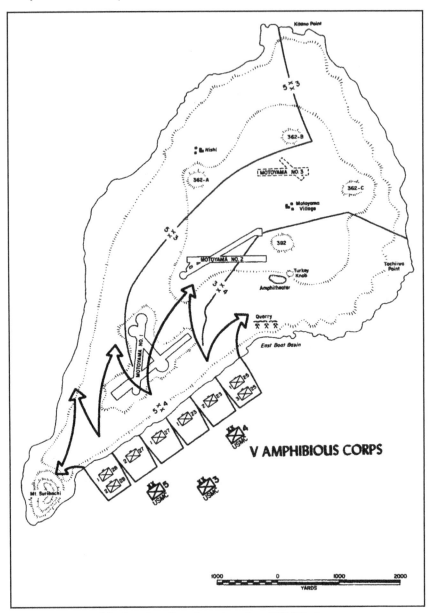

Marines Iwo Jima invasion plan. USMC photo.

The strategic importance of Iwo Jima's location is obvious at a glance. USMC photo.

Just as there are no atheists in fox holes, there aren't any on attack transport ships, either. USMC photo.

Eight square miles of misery. USMC photo.

A 15-foot terrace was the first beach obstacle. USMC photo.

pelled as they learned that the only purpose of the stop here was to dump the newly issued gear on a newly assigned bunk inside the barren wooden structure. Sleep and rest would have to wait.

Inside the next building eight wooden stools manned by stone-faced enlisted men sat in an imposing row. A line on the floor marked off the first eight boots. "First group onto the stools," the drill instructor demanded. These boots raced to the stools while the next group replaced them past the line, as ordered. Soon the room hummed with the sound of electric clippers and the floor was covered with different shades and textures of human hair as each man was shorn very close to his scalp. There was no mirror, but each could easily imagine the contrast as the whiteness of his scalp was exposed as sheets of his hair bounced off the apron onto the floor. The process was repeated until every boot was close-clipped.

The mess hall was a welcome relief, the opportunity to sit being as welcome as the food. And the food! For these men who had grown up all over America during the Great Depression, the abundance and variety of food was as if they were in a scene from a fantasy movie. The food was great – all you could eat in five minutes.

Herded like so many newly-shorn sheep into the next building the boots, who had spent most of the last ten hours on their feet, were finally allowed to sit for an extended time. The respite thus afforded was brief, however. Soon enlisted men swarmed along the tables depositing a tall stack of forms in front of each man. The drill instructors took up each form in sequence, explaining what information was to be entered. All had pity for the man who was caught sleeping during a lull in the action. By the time all forms were completed three hours later, each man had signed his name – accompanied by his newly assigned serial number – times too numerous to mention.

When the forms were completed, a visit to the Post Exchange (PX) provided a little entertainment. Instead of being allowed to shop, each man was issued a two-gallon galvanized bucket filled with such items as a toothbrush, razor, scrub brush, shoe polish, tooth powder, shoelaces and other assorted treasures. The thought of this booty at Uncle Sam's largess was dispelled when the first payday arrived and they discovered that they'd been docked $10 for this treasure. Also, at that time, each boot would be chagrined to learn that he'd been charged fifty cents for his stylish haircut.

In the waning glow of afternoon, not many left any footprints in the dust on the way back to the barracks. Inside, they were instructed in how to make up the rack and stow their gear. Each was also shown how to snap to attention and subjected to a lecture on just how lucky he was to be allowed the opportunity to try to become a United States Marine. Just as evening shadows started to creep like timorous mice from the corners of the huge room, these young men were ordered to sit on their racks. "One more little chore and we'll call it a day," fell on glad ears. "Write a letter home, tell 'em you got here OK and are having the time of your life. Then get undressed, stow your utility uniforms and get in bed. Lights out in ten minutes." Despite sheer exhaustion, with time now for loneliness and homesickness and uncertainty to reemerge, many may have had some difficulty in falling asleep. Perhaps a last groggy thought caused one to wonder if the second day in boot camp could possibly be any worse than the first.

Each of the boots would have sworn that he had no more than closed his eyes when he was jolted awake by a clamorous racket in the barracks. As his eyes popped open, he was aware that the drill instructor had entered the room, snapped on the lights and tossed a metal garbage can down the aisle between the bunks. The din it created careening off the floor and the ends of the metal bunks rudely jerked everyone from sleep. "Let's go boys. The war won't wait!"

As instructed the previous evening, the men jumped to the end of their bunks and stood at rigid attention while the drill instructors, shouting all the time, encouraged any slow-movers to action. When all were standing, he yelled, "Port side, head call!" The men on the left side of the barracks ran to the toilet facilities at the end of the long room while the drill instructor eyed his wristwatch. Exactly two minutes after the last man had disappeared around the corner, the instructor shouted, "Clear the head."

Immediately, an aloud count-down began; "10-9-8…." Every boot understood that he had better be back at attention at the end of his bunk before the count reached zero. When the head was clear, the command, "Starboard side, head call," began the process over again for the other half of the platoon.

When the second half's two minutes had elapsed, all were assembled at the foot of the bunks. "This floor is filthy," the DI advised. "It will be clean before we go to chow." At that, each man retrieved the galvanized bucket and scrub brush he'd unknowingly purchased yesterday and set about scrubbing the white pine floor. Thirty minutes or so on their knees brought the floor to an acceptable state, so the boots were allowed 10 minutes to shave, don their utility uniforms and assemble outside. A short run brought the group to the mess halls.

Before they entered, the drill instructor advised the men that they were to be back outside, in formation, when he exited the mess hall. Thus instructed, they were allowed to scramble up the steps for a small head start on eating. Although the ethnic and economic background of Training Platoon 81 represented a cross-section of segregated American society, each of these young men had grown up through the Great Depression and hence was impacted by it to some degree. Whatever the conditions of his youth may have been, each was impressed, once again, by the quantity and variety of the government's food tables. Scrambled eggs, bacon, sausage, ham, French toast, pancakes, gravy, biscuits, grits, coffee, milk, juice, what they called SOS and hash-brown potatoes filled plates to the brim. A wary eye was kept on the drill instructor, who sat at the end of the room. When he made a move toward the exit, everyone grabbed a last, quick bite before bolting outside. The DI did his charges the small favor of not hurrying; the platoon was assembled in formation when he exited the building.

The morning began with a round of vaccinations which simply added to the misery of already aching muscles. At the armory, each man was issued his "best friend," a brand-spanking new Garand M1 .30 caliber rifle. In addition to its serial number, he memorized that its weight was 9.6 pounds, its range was 440 yards, its muzzle velocity was 2800 feet-per-second, and that it was a "gas operated, clip fed, semi-automatic shoulder weapon." The first man who committed the unpardonable sin of referring to his rifle as a "gun" was made to sleep with his rifle beside him that night. If another was so silly as to repeat the offence, he would stand before the company headquarters with his penis exposed for a couple of hours. When anyone walked by, he would point to his M1 and recite, "This is my rifle." Then, pointing to his crotch, "This is my gun." Repeating the indication process, "This is for shooting, this is for fun."

Until this point in the war, Marine recruits had been issued the beloved Springfield Armory Model 1903 .30-06 caliber bolt operated rifle. Both the U.S. Army and the U.S. Marines had effectively utilized that reliable and accurate weapon since before the Great War, but in recent Pacific actions against the Japanese, the M1 had demonstrated similar accuracy and reliability characteristics, proved easier to clean, and established a faster rate of fire. Old timers reluctantly traded in their '03 Springfields, but the men of Training Platoon 81 readily accepted the weapon they would be using in combat.

The new rifles were covered with a gooey, stinking, substance the instructors called "cosmoline," the stickiest substance know to man. As soon as the rifles were issued, the platoon moved to an area where long benches and troughs filled with gasoline allowed instruction on how to field strip and clean the weapon. Now the boots found out why there were so many brushes and rags in those buckets they'd purchased. The several hours consumed rubbing, scrubbing and brushing the goo from the innards of the rifle convinced each man of the effectiveness of the gooey compound: with cosmoline on the job, there was simply no possibility of rust or corrosion.

Lunch, and every other meal, at the mess hall provided a repetition of the previous experience. Dismissed to enter the building, the boots scrambled inside, moved down the line filling their plates and gobbled the food before dashing out to assemble in formation before the DI appeared at the door.

Despite all the warnings and constant attention from the instructors, boots still managed to "screw up" in various minor ways. Although sleep deprivation was a planned part of the program, sleeping during a lecture was an offence that met with harsh punishment. Sometimes the individual offender would suffer alone. One particularly humiliating technique was to have a man stand in the barracks, wearing only his skivvies with a bucket over his head. In response to the DI's frequent rap on the bucket with a swagger stick, the offender would recite in a headache-inducing scream, "I am the platoon shit head and a miserable screw up."

Close order drill is a major time consumer and opportunity to "screw up" in boot camp. In platoon formation, the boots learned to march in step and execute all the "evolutions:" column left, right flank, about face and so on. On one occasion when a boot had faced in the wrong direction one time too many, the drill instructor rammed his rifle down hard on the man's foot. "Now, maggot," he yelled into the boot's face, "your right foot is the one that hurts." Performing the manual of arms while in formation claimed its share of time. Responding to "Right shoulder arms," "port arms" and "order arms" soon became as automatic as breathing.

Near the end of the second week of Training Platoon 81's existence, a particularly onerous offense by one of its members resulted in punishment for the entire group. At the end of the day of drilling, the boots were allowed to eat and return to the barracks for a cold shower and a brief rest. Just after dark, the drill instructors herded everyone outside and into formation. After a few minutes of close order drill, the group moved out, marching in formation. A couple of miles into the hike, the drill instruc-

84

tor recited an ancient Marine taunt; "If anybody is tired of walking, we can run for a while." After they'd marched some ten miles, the platoon executed an "about face" and marched back, arriving back at the barracks well after midnight. No one objected to the order to go to bed.

A seeming few minutes later, the lights flicked on to the sound of a garbage can careening down the aisle. "This floor is filthy...."

Chapter 8

Wednesday, February 16, 1944
San Diego, California

"All right, listen up," the drill instructor barked. Franklin noted that in the three weeks he'd been in boot camp, the DI's voice had become raspier – due, no doubt, to all the yelling he'd done – but at the same time somehow a bit softer. After the first ten days or so, most of the boots had stopped "screwing up," and progressed toward becoming "squared away" and hence life had become a little more bearable. All the men were actually looking forward to the next training phase; they were going to the rifle range where they'd actually get to load and fire the M1 rifle they'd been lugging around on their shoulders for the last three weeks. "Get your gear packed up for inspection tonight. We'll be leaving out of here early in the morning. Lights out in 30 minutes." With that, he exited the barracks, leaving the boots alone. The young men stared at each other for a few moments as if they'd suddenly been transported to an alien planet. Although they'd been together night and day for more than three weeks, they'd had virtually no time to themselves and hardly ever spoken. Looking around, they realized that they did not know one another at all.

"I'm Graham," the slight, dark-haired young man who occupied the bunk adjacent to Franklin said, extending his hand. After the scalping, his hair had recovered somewhat; now a half-inch stubble covered his head.

"Sousley," Franklin answered, glancing around to ensure no DI was lurking about. He felt as if he was engaged in some criminal activity by talking to his bunkmate. The two busied themselves stowing away their gear. Finally, Franklin ventured, "Do you have any idea where we're goin'?"

"Yeah, I do. My brother went through boot camp last year. He told me all about it. There's a rifle range camp up around La Jolla. We'll be up there for two weeks."

"I'm from Kentucky and don't know much about California, where is that?"

"Well, we're pretty far south here in 'Dago," Graham replied, "almost to Mexico. The rifle range is at a place called Camp Matthews, about 20 miles up the coast. Kentucky, huh? Is wearin' shoes strange for you?"

Having endured many such comments in his short time in the Corps, Franklin had learned to just let it pass. "Oh, I'm slowly getting used to it. How 'bout you?"

"I'm from Kansas," Graham said with a grin. "We wear clod hoppers there, so these boondockers are just like home." Each realized that the smile they were sharing was a rarity in boot camp. "Say," Graham continued, "do you know anything about shootin'?"

"Me and Sergeant York are first cousins," Franklin said with a smirk while licking his thumb to wet the front sight of his M1.

Graham started to make some reply but "Taps" followed by lights out interrupted further conversation.

Jolted awake in the usual fashion at 05:00, the boots endured the morning ritual one more time. After physical training and chow, Platoon 81 hefted their sea bags and marched to a bus dock where the men were loaded into a Navy bus for the trip north. Franklin and Jimmy, as he'd learned Graham's name to be, sat next to each other, rifles between their knees. The presence of the drill instructors prevented any conversation, so they simply enjoyed the spectacular scenery along the California coast. Perhaps each man gave some thought to his future that conceivably lay on some Japanese controlled island beyond the line where the sky limited their view of the vast Pacific Ocean.

At length, the bus arrived on the edge of a vast encampment with some permanent buildings and a huge tent camp. The command, "Fall in" caused the men to arrange themselves into platoon formation. "My brother says life will be a little easier here," Jimmy whispered to Franklin standing beside him. Before Franklin could make a reply, the proximity of the DI silenced him. As they marched down a wide aisle between rows of pyramidal tents, the men were halted at intervals where they were assigned eight to a tent. Inside, each tent had a wooden floor, eight canvas "army" cots arranged around the octagonal center pole, and a kerosene heater. Stopping in front of one of the tents the DI called out eight names to occupy it. "Sousley," he barked, "as of now, you're assistant squad leader. You'll be in charge of this tent." Franklin and Jimmy were assigned with six other men they had seen back at the recruit depot, but had never spoken to. Introductions all around followed: the small dark man introduced himself as

Frankie Maccio from the Bronx, New York, the lanky Texan was Howard – call me "Tex" – Bolton, Joe Miller was from Michigan, Billy Smather was a studious Philadelphian, Phil Marcy hailed from Northern California and Marv Thjorn was a pale, blond Minnesotan. They set about getting acquainted while making up their bunks and stowing their gear. "Anybody know anything about the program here?" Frankie asked.

"I do, a little," Jimmy answered. "My brother told me about it. We've got two weeks; the first is what they call 'grass week' when we learn about range safety and dry fire our rifles, it's what they call 'snapping in.' Then during 'firing week,' we actually get to shoot at targets and qualify."

"Should be a piece of cake for me," Tex opined. Back home, if I didn't get a jackrabbit or two, we didn't eat. I'm a pretty good shot."

"Me too." Franklin chimed in. "But there may be a difference between an M1 and the old .22 I shot squirrels with."

"So, which end does the bullet come out of?" Frankie asked, turning his rifle over and over in his hands. His smile did not betray whether he was joking. "Say, what happens if you don't qualify?"

"Ain't no such thing as not qualifyin'," Jimmy informed. "Training platoon 82 is coming along right behind us. If you don't qualify, they just tag you as 'unq' and you just stay here and join that platoon. Then there's 83 and 84 and 85 and 86 and...."

"So, if a man plays his cards right, he could stay here for the duration of the war," Tex joked.

"Maybe. Some might want that," Franklin said, thoughtfully, "but, as for me, I want to get out there and shoot some Japs."

"You said it," everyone chimed in unison.

When the others returned to the tent following mail call that evening, they found Franklin sitting on his cot with his head in his hands. From the fingers of his right hand, a letter fluttered in the ever-present breeze. "What's goin' on?" Frankie asked.

For a long moment, Franklin seemed not to hear. Finally, he raised his head to reveal red, tear-swollen eyes. "My mother's in the hospital," he choked.

Although these men had had little occasion to discuss their pre-boot camp lives, it was known in the tent that both Franklin and Tex had lost their fathers at a young age. Tex moved to the cot and sat beside Franklin. "What's the problem?" His voice was low and soft.

"She's had appendicitis," he managed to say, his voice cracking.

"Did they operate?"

Franklin's face returned to his hands. "I've done told you all I know about it," he said through his fingers.

"Appendicitis ain't that big a deal," Frankie advised, trying to be consoling.

None of his tent mates knew, of course, that one of Franklin's most vivid childhood memories was of his mother's distress in the wake of Malcolm's death. He immediately took offense at the other's remark. Rising to his full height, he got in Frankie's face and shouted, "It might not be to you, asshole…." His voice trailed off in rage and anguish. He could only hope that the state of medical care had advanced in the 16 years since his older brother's death as a result of the same malady.

"Calm down," Jimmy stepped between the two. "Let's go to HQ and get permission for you to call home."

"They got no phone," Franklin sighed as he sank back to the cot.

"If we contact the Red Cross maybe they'd get you an emergency furlough," Tex suggested.

"No good," Jimmy said. "Whatever is gonna happen may already be over by now and surely would be over by the time he got there and that's even if the Red Cross did manage to arrange an emergency leave."

All considered the situation for a moment. "Well," Tex finally said in his slow Texas drawl, "somebody will let you know if there's a problem. In the meantime, sad as it is, there ain't a damn thing to do 'cept suck it up and get on with what's got to be done." The group was silent for a moment before Jimmy added, "That is what Marines do, ain't it?"

The first half day of "grass week" was consumed with "sighting in" the rifles. Assigned in pairs, one man took a prone position behind his M1 which was resting on a low, wooden saw-horse type bench pointed at a target. His partner took a small metal disk with a hole in the center to the target 25 yards away. As the "shooter" directed, he moved the disk up or down and left or right until the shooter, looking through the sights, holding but not moving the weapon, determined that the hole in the disk was over the cross-hairs marking the exact center of the target. At that time, he'd yell, "mark" and his partner would mark the location of the hole with a pencil point. Repeating this procedure three times produced three points on the paper target. Connecting these points was supposed to produce a triangle less than one-half inch wide. When it did, the rifle was "sighted in" so that any subsequent misses were due to the shooter, not the sights.

In the afternoon came instruction on how to properly ensnarl oneself in the rifle's sling. If anyone thought that the sling's purpose was for carrying the rife, he was soon advised that, while carrying the rifle slung over a shoulder was an issue, its real function was to provide stability while firing the weapon. After the demonstration of how to form the loop and wrap the left arm through and around the sling, Franklin leaned over to Jimmy sitting on the ground next to him and whispered, "So, a Jap's comin' at ya, see? You just say, 'Please wait a minute here Mr. Tojo, while I wrap myself into this sling so's I can shoot you according to the book.'" Jimmy nearly choked trying not to laugh out loud.

The men soon discovered that given their proximity to the ocean, while the days were warm and sunny, the nights could be bitterly cold. The kerosene heaters, intended to help ward off the chill, were cranky and difficult to light. When they were successful in getting the heater lit, it filled the tent with a vile odor. The wind, which never stopped whistling under the sides of the tent, invariably managed to blow away most of the heat but not the smell. The two thin wool blankets each man had been issued at San Diego were the only reliable source of warmth.

Each day at Camp Matthews began with a head call followed by policing up the tent area. Sweeping the tent floor and the rock-lined walkways and raking the dirt all had to be done to the DI's satisfaction before the boots were marched to the mess hall. The days were filled with endless lectures on rifle safety, the firing positions: prone, sitting, kneeling and standing, physical training and exercises to strengthen the muscles used in the various firing positions. Franklin cracked at some point that he'd "done so much duck-walking that he was beginning to enjoy standing in the rain."

After chow one evening during grass week, the men were in their tent cleaning their weapons when someone entered the tent and shouted, "Sousley?"

Somewhat startled as it was not a drill instructor's voice, Franklin answered, "Yole," as he spun around to face the door. There, to his amazement, was one of his Fleming County High School classmates. "Ralph! Ralph McRoberts what the hell are you doin' here? Damn! You're a long way from home, son."[4]

"Don't I know it?" After they shook hands, Ralph rubbed the red stubble on Franklin's head. "I see you've got Uncle Sam taking care of your groomin'," he said, ignoring the half-inch growth on his own skull. "I'm a week ahead of you," he answered, "fired my rifle for the record just today."

"Yeah? What'd you shoot?" Everyone was always eager to learn another's score.

"I fired 302," Ralph said, pride evident in his voice. "That makes me a sharpshooter, damn near expert."

Both men knew that when one fired for the record, he shot 70 rounds, each of which could possibly score five points, so a total of 350 was possible. A minimum score of 240 was required to qualify; 240 to 289 classified one as a "marksman," 290 to 305 was a "sharpshooter," while above 306 brought the coveted title of "expert." A sharpshooter rating brought an extra $3 in one's pay while an expert earned an additional $5 per month. "Not too shabby," Franklin mused before adding, "I hope to qualify as expert."

The two launched into an extended conversation about the home folks and their friends in the military and their boot camp experience. "I'm going back to San Diego tomorrow," Ralph informed, "after another week there, I'll be a real Marine and I think I'm gonna get a furlough."

"I heard they've quit givin' leave after boot camp," Franklin said, a bit envious of his friend's both finishing boot camp and going home.

"Oh, there's nothin' certain about it one way or t'other." Ralph said. "It all depends on what's goin' on in the world. I've been told that it's probable that I'll get a furlough, though. I'm savin' up my money."

"Money?" Franklin was puzzled. "What for?"

"You got to have $80 in your hand or they won't let you go. Didn't you know that?"

"Wow! That's a pot full of money. How much leave will you get – if you do get it?"

"Ten days," Ralph said with a sigh. "That ain't long to get to Fleming County and back, but it beats the hell out of stayin' here."

"Sure does," Franklin agreed, wistfully. "I'll write Mom and tell her to be on the lookout for you."

"Well, I'd better be getting' back to my tent," Ralph said, turning to leave.

"Say," Franklin halted him. As Ralph turned back to face his friend, Franklin hesitated then requested, "When you get back," then, after a pause, he went on, "if you happen to see Marian, tell her I'm thinking about her, will ya?"

"It's extremely simple," Tex was telling Frankie in answer to the latter's question about the similarities and differences among the firing positions. "Take the sitting position, for example. You simply plant your foot," he stamped his right foot on the tent floor for emphasis. With no hint of a smile, he went on, "Then you simply compress the rest of your body directly and compactly onto that same spot."

Everyone laughed, but for Franklin and Tex, the comment was humorless. The firing positions they had been practicing seemed awkward, unnatural and totally opposite to everything they – who considered themselves excellent riflemen – knew about firing a rifle. Additionally, the aching in previously unused muscles was a constant reminder of how unnatural the positions were. Franklin readily embraced the idea of holding his breath and "squeezing off" a round with slow, steady pressure on the trigger as that was just as his Uncle Ray had taught him. But the instructors said that closing both eyes and flinching when the weapon actually fired was a fact of human nature that had to be overcome by practice. That whole idea was foreign to him as he'd been taught to keep both eyes open. Well, he'd been told more than once that "there's the right way, the wrong way and the Marine way." He was eager for firing week to begin so he could load a clip into his M1 and actually find out how his ideas stacked up against policy and just how good a marksman he really was.

On Sunday morning, the entire platoon marched to church just as they had done back at San Diego. The non-denominational service, just as at the Recruit Depot, was fairly brief and featured a sermon aimed particularly at men in the military. It always ended with a prayer for the safety of the men fighting in the field and the preservation of the American way of life. This was an idea that every man present solemnly endorsed knowing that the time for him to become a personal beneficiary of such prayers was undoubtedly coming.

After chow and a couple of free hours to visit the PX, write letters or read the Sunday paper to see what was going on in the outside world, the platoon marched to an empty soccer field while another platoon marched in from the other side. One group was required to strip to the waist for a game of "shirts versus skins" played with a six-foot diameter hard rubber ball. The object of the game was to push, pull or drag – by any available means – the ball over the opponent's goal line. The game was a "no holds barred" affair designed as just one more rung on the ladder of transforming these boys into real Marines. Everyone understood that the drill instructor would not be happy if his platoon lost the game and everyone definitely understood that an unhappy drill instructor was, to say the least, not a desirable thing.

Firing week began with a practice round from the prone position with a sand bag supporting and steadying the shooter's left forearm and wrist. Franklin was acting as coach while his friend Jimmy fired his first clip with the target at 200 yards. Before the rifle was loaded, Franklin shaped the sand bag and placed it under Jimmy's hand. Then he moved around, assuming a position so that his body was parallel to the shooter and his head was near Jimmy's. Throughout the shooting, Franklin helped Jimmy remain in the proper position and quietly admonished him to "squeeze" the rounds off. Jimmy was relieved when the clip was ejected with the characteristic metallic "ping" which indicates all eight rounds have been expended.

Then the two swapped roles as Franklin prepared to fire his first rounds. First he adjusted the elevation knob on the rear sight to 200 yards. Then, as they'd been taught, he eyed the range flag fluttering in the slight breeze. "I make the wind to be left to right about 4 miles per hour," he said.

"I agree," Jimmy said and watched as Franklin adjusted the windage knob accordingly. Then he assumed the prone position and waited while Jimmy positioned the sandbag beneath his left hand. Loading the clip into the rifle, he ignored Jimmy's advice that he did not have his cheek hard against his thumb and the rifle stock as the instructors had taught. "I've been shootin' since I was two, and I generally hit what I'm aimin' at," Franklin said. When the target was retrieved, Franklin was disappointed to note that he had hit the bullseye with only four of the eight rounds he'd fired.

When the weapons were cleaned and the other chores were finished that evening the group sat around the tent chewing the fat. During a lull in the conversation, Franklin decided to tell about a man in Fleming County. "His name is Dub and he's a real smart ass, busy body, so nobody likes him," Franklin explained. "Well, Dub walked in the blacksmith's shop one day and, of course, had to comment on whatever was goin' on. Walter, the brawny blacksmith, happened to be workin' on a horseshoe." Here he paused briefly to let that sink in on his attentive audience. "You know how hot they have to get them things to bend 'em. Well, old Dub picked up the horseshoe and 'course he flung it right to the ground real quick. Ever'body laughed at him and said, 'Ha, burned yourself, didn't you?' 'Naw,' old Dub said as cool as he could, 'it just don't take me long to look at a horseshoe, that's all.'" Everyone in the tent knew that there were plenty of laughs to be had when Franklin Sousley was around.

Firing week flew by in a haze of shooting practice. Firing from 200, 300 and 500 yards, clips for the M1 rifles were expended from the prone, sitting, kneeling and standing (which the instructors sometimes called "offhand") positions in slow-fire and rapid-fire sessions. The men were interested to note that the Marine Corps instruction worked: in many cases, those who had never seen a rifle before enlistment scored better than those who, like Franklin, had been shooting since a young age. Firing for the record, each man fired 70 rounds each of which could score five points, hence a maximum of 350 could be scored. As a case in point, Frankie, the Bronx youth who'd wondered which end of the M1 the bullet came out of, shot a 310 which qualified him as an "expert" and earned him an additional five dollars per month, while the Texas boy who had to shoot jack rabbits to eat, shot 250, a mere ten points above the minimum qualification score. Jimmy, the Kansas clod-buster, failed to qualify and so would remain behind while most of the platoon returned to San Diego to finish their boot training. Franklin Sousley, the Kentucky boy who'd heard about "barking" squirrels, fired a disappointing 289, making him a "marksman," a single point shy of sharpshooter.[5]

Merriment prevailed on the bus ride back to the recruit depot in San Diego. Through with firing week now and qualified to wear their marksmanship badges on the breast of the uniforms they'd soon be donning, these men were beginning to feel like real Marines. The last week of boot camp would prove as physically demanding as the previous ones, but the instructors toned down the psychological harassment and concentrated on honing their skills acting as a combat group. The men were divided into "fire teams" consisting of four or five men and practiced acting in concert assaulting various types of fortified positions.

One evening when the men were left alone in the barracks, Franklin called to those around, "Hey guys gather 'round I got something to show ya." Those in earshot clustered near his bunk expecting to hear a story. Instead, Franklin picked up his rifle. Holding it across his waist, he began to strum it as if it had strings. "Back home," he said, "we listen to the Grand Ole Opry ever' Saturday night." Some in the group nodded understanding. "One of the biggest hits is Roy Acuff's Wabash Cannonball." Again, some nodded. Then Franklin, strumming away on his rifle, burst into the Roy Acuff standard, but singing "From the Hall of Montezuma to the shores of Tripoli...." Everyone got a big laugh as they noted that Franklin had observed that the words of the Marine's Hymn fit the country melody perfectly. "That'll land his ass in the brig if the DI hears it," someone commented.

At last the big day came – graduation day. A final inspection by the biggest brass on the base was followed by a huge parade where each training platoon passed in review before the assembled brass on a reviewing stand. As Training Platoon 81, short a few members who failed to qualify with the M1 and marching in formation for the last time, passed in front of the reviewing stand, the Drill Instructor commanded "Eyes Right." He almost smiled when he heard many sets of eyeballs "click" in response. As they passed, the band positioned in front of the stand, burst into The Marines' Hymn. One could almost see every chest swell with pride as the men realized that they'd successfully completed boot camp. At the end of the parade, the DI called the platoon to a halt, eyed his charges for a long moment, ordered them to attention and then solemnly announced, "Dismissed!" Instantly the group, joined by their instructors, burst into celebration with hand shaking and back-slapping all around. Moving together to the PX to share a few GI beers and some much coveted ice cream, the men discovered that the Drill Instructors, who had been the objects of so much loathing over the past six weeks, weren't such bad guys after all. "When the Japs come over the hill screaming 'Bonsai!' at you, just remember what I taught you," was one DI's final advice.

Back at the barracks, the men were allowed a few hours of free time after their gear was squared away. Every few minutes, a sergeant would appear at the door calling out names. The men so summoned were ordered to follow the man to waiting transportation to their "line camp" assignments. Eventually, a tall, blond sergeant walked in and shouted "Sousley!"

"Yole," Franklin answered, leaping to his feet.

"Come with me," the man said.

Franklin picked up his sea bag and bid a quick farewell to the Recruit Depot barracks, scene of so much anguish. In company with several other men who joined up along the way, he followed the sergeant out of the company area to a large parking lot where a truck waited. "Get in," the sergeant instructed, "some more men will be along in a few minutes." Seated on a bench in the back of the truck, Franklin turned to the pimply faced youth beside him, "Any idea where we're goin'?"

"None," the young man said. The others seated nearby who had overheard the question shook their heads to indicate that they too, had no idea of what was to come next for them. Finally several more men showed up to claim their seats on the bench and the truck began to move slowly across the concrete ramp.

Near the front gate, every man in the truck felt his stomach tighten a little when they drove by a Navy bus disgorging men in civilian clothes. Around them swarmed three men in flat-brimmed hats yelling, "Find a place on the yellow footprints. Move it, move it, move it!" The men on the truck eyed each other knowingly and each smiled inwardly. Those boys on the yellow footprints were mere boots, the lowest form of life in the known universe. But each man on the truck had endured the physical and mental torture, had mastered the military fundamentals and had learned a few survival tricks. Yes sir, he was a full-fledged United States Marine. On his uniform he proudly bore a globe, anchor and eagle emblem to prove it.

Chapter 9

Friday, March 3, 1944
Ewing, Kentucky

Mildred May leaned into the stiff wind which seemed determined to keep her from reaching her sister's new Fleming County home. Finally gaining the porch, she firmly gripped the doorknob so that the wind would not whip the door from her grasp, pulled it open and scurried inside. The blast that followed her inside caused the flame in the fireplace to flicker and admit a puff of smoke into the room. "How are you likin' this weather?"

"In like a lion," Goldie replied with a smile quoting the old adage about March.

"Are you gettin' back to full strength yet?"

"Oh, I guess," Goldie said, resuming her seat in a rocker. "With this old body, it's a slow process. I was pretty sore for a few days after the operation, but it's about gone now."

"Shufflin' all these heavy boxes around probably doesn't help you any. Are you gettin' settled in?" Mildred glanced around the room piled high with boxes filled with clothes, dishes and assorted other household items.

"It takes a while to get everything situated," Goldie sighed. "Movin' is a mess under the best of circumstances. Such as it is, Hense ain't hardly ever home and Jake is always busy with something at school, so I have to do most of it by myself. Take off your coat and sit a spell."

Removing her coat, Mildred moved across the room to stand before the fire. "How come Hense ain't never here?" She held her palms out to the warmth.

"He's always workin'," Goldie replied. "This war causes plenty of work to go around while there's less and less men home to do it. His milk business is going great guns but he's havin' to work about 36 hours a day. It's what's allowed us to get this new farm and a bunch of cows to milk, though."

"Can't have it both ways, I reckon. Does Jake have any interest in helpin'?" Mildred rotated her back to the fire.

"No more than he can wiggle out of. He ain't but eleven, you know, so naturally his main interest is in the girls. Franklin's the one that wants to be a dairy farmer."

"Yes, I know." Mildred crossed the room to take a rocking chair facing her sister. "He'll be pleased with all this when he gets back. By the way, is he still mad at you for not telling him you were in the hospital?"

"Oh, he was just upset because it was appendicitis. He remembers…." Both women fell silent knowing that she'd decided to leave mention of her oldest son's death unsaid.

After a few moments, Mildred broke the spell. "Where's Franklin at now?"

"I don't know," Goldie answered, wistfully. "In his last letter, he said that he'd have shot his rifle for the record by the time the letter got here. He said he'd then have one more week back at San Diego and he'd be finished with boot camp. I guess he's done with it by now."

"Why can't he write and tell you where he is?"

"Oh, he writes as often as he can. I suppose sometimes they're so busy that he simply doesn't have time. He said they'd be sendin' him to a line camp after he finished boot camp."

"Well, I wish somebody would send me to sunny California. Comin' up here, I had to lean so far into that wind that sometimes my nose touched the ground."

Goldie laughed at the image. "Yeah, I had to load my pockets with rocks to get to the barn this mornin'. Franklin said that 'sunny California' is pretty much of a myth, at least wherever he is – or was. He said that it was cold and foggy ever' morning and while it might be sunny and hot during the day, lots of times the rain just poured."

"Oh? I heard it never rains in California."

"Well, what his letter actually said was that it was just like pouring blank out of a boot."

"Blank?" She was laughing.

"He left a blank space. We both know what he meant. Anyhow, I don't even know that he's still in California. They may have sent him overseas already, for all I know."

"We'll find out in God's own good time, I guess. Does he say he needs anything?"

"Ha," Goldie spat. "He always wants us to write more often, send some candy and cigarettes and make sure he gets the *Fleming Gazette* so he can keep up with what's goin' on around here."

"You don't need a newspaper to tell you what goes on around here," Mildred said with a grin.

"Oh, it's hard for us to imagine what it's like for Franklin bein' nearly 3000 miles from home." As the ladies meditated on that thought, each concluded that, indeed, they had no idea, neither having ever been more than 50 miles from home. "The paper allows him to keep up with his high school friends in the service, where they're at and all."

"I guess I could send him some candy." Mildred suggested. "He wants homemade?"

"I'm sure he'd be grateful for whatever he gets, but hold off until he writes and tells us where he is now. There's no point in sendin' anything to the wrong address."

Suddenly the door flew open to admit a fresh blast of cold air along with the ladies' brother Ray Mitchell. "Hello girls," he greeted while leaning against the door to close it. "What's goin' on?"

"Oh, just local gossip. What brings you around?"

"I've got a couple of weeks worth of papers and magazines Ma saved up for you." He pulled a bundle of papers from beneath his arm.

"Well," Goldie pretended indignation. "Just what good are they gonna do? You've done read 'em and got all the information out of 'em, ain't you?"

Ray laughed. "Well, I guess I'll just have to give you the summary." He took a chair facing his sisters. Picking up a magazine, he began, "This one shows the situation in Italy. The Germans have counter-attacked the beachhead at Anzio." He shook his head, "I reckon that's a mighty rough place to be."

"No worse than the Pacific," Mildred opined. "What's doin' on that front?"

Ray laid the magazine aside in favor of a newspaper. "You already know that the Marines took Kwajalein Island a couple of weeks ago?"

"Where's that?" Goldie's interest was more than academic.

"Hell, I don't know," Ray said. "There's a whole pot full of tiny little islands between Hawaii and Japan. The Navy's probably got somebody busy full time porein' over a map deciding which ones they'll try to take away from the Japs and which ones to bypass." He paused to shuffle through several newspapers before adding, "On that latter score, more recently, the Navy bombed the hell out of Truk – that's in the Caroline Islands and Rabaul on New Guinea. Those are both Japanese strongholds. Says here that both bases were destroyed."

"Then there's two places that Franklin won't have to go, ain't it?"

"Maybe they'll just keep flyin' over those places and droppin' bombs and the Marines won't have to go ashore." Mildred tried to sound hopeful.

"That's just wishful thinkin'," Ray said. "Like I said, there's a pot full of islands out there, the Japs control all of 'em. If you ask me, the Japs could have all 'em but it ain't up to me and some of 'em will be strategically important. In some cases, we've got to keep the Japs from having 'em as an observation post or a point for launching raids, in other cases there's reasons why the Americans have got to control a specific island. For Franklin's sake, I'm sorry to say it, but this war in the Pacific has a long way to go and the Marines will have to take plenty more real estate away from the Japs." He started to add that plenty of blood would be spilled capturing that real estate but decided to leave that unsaid.

"How'd the Japs get control of all those islands?" Mildred was also more than curious.

"Well," Ray began, pleased that he was asked to share the knowledge he'd studied so hard to acquire since his nephew had joined the Marine Corps. "Some of it is a result of the Great War – Japan was our ally back then, you know. Anyway, as a part of the Treaty of Versailles, the League of Nations gave 'em control – Japanese Mandates it was called – of some Pacific Islands. Then, early in the war, before we got involved and nobody was lookin', they simply took control of some more islands. Then, right after the Pearl Harbor attack, they occupied a bunch more. Since then they've been fortifin' 'em against the time when somebody, probably us, might want to take 'em back. Now there're what they like to call 'unsinkable aircraft carriers.' All those little islands are loaded with Jap troops and planes just waitin' for the Marines to show up."

"In some of his letters," Goldie chipped in, "Franklin says that Marines recently back from fighting the Japs come to his camp and tell all about it. According to him, they're really mowing 'em down out there."

"Yeah," Ray agreed, "from what I read, I reckon they are. But, you know, the Japs will not ever give up. Evidently their religion requires them to fight to the death, regardless."

"I hear it's an honor for 'em to die for their Emperor," Mildred added.

"That's what I hear," Ray said. "For them, death is much preferable to being captured. Everywhere we've fought 'em; at Guadalcanal and Tarawa and at Kwajalein they've proved that they'd rather die than surrender. I also hear that the Marines are quite willin' to help 'em die for their country."

"I've read about that," Goldie added. "The Marines have had to kill almost all of 'em. I fact, I read that one reason for those Bonsai charges is it's a quick way for 'em to die and get it over with. They say that many of the Jap soldiers chose to kill themselves when it looks like there's no way out. It just makes no sense." She shook her head in disbelief.

"I got no sympathy for the little yellow bastards," Ray said. "But like you said, it makes no sense to us. We ain't gonna understand them and they surely ain't gonna understand us. If they understood the American character at all, they never would have attacked Pearl Harbor like they did."

"But why?" Mildred wondered. "The Japs don't really think they can win the war do they?"

"No, I don't reckon they do," Ray opined. "Seems to me that what they're tryin' to do is make it so costly that we'll give up and negotiate a peace."

Goldie rocked thoughtfully for a moment. "Do you reckon we'll have to invade Japan itself?"

"I'm sorry to say, I think we will," Ray said shaking his head. "I hear that they're arming every old man, woman and child with a rock and a sharp stick if that's all the weapons they have left. The invasion of the home islands will be a real blood bath."

As that comment hung in the air, no one spoke, each lost in their own thoughts of what the future might hold. At length, Ray asked, "Say, Goldie, what do you hear from my favorite nephew?"

"Nothin'," she said. "Ain't had a letter in ten days."

"Pa had a letter from him a couple of weeks ago asking if we could loan him some money."

"Yeah, I know," Goldie responded. "He says he has to have $80 in hand before they'll let him come home and then he wants another $63 to buy a dress uniform."

"A fellow needs a dress uniform to wear when he comes home," Ray laughed.

"Seems to me Uncle Sam would supply that," Mildred commented.

"Not unless your duties require it for some reason," Ray informed. "But he'll surely need that for parading down the street in Flemingsburg. One's got to impress the girls, you know."

"He made that pretty clear," Goldie said. "He said he'd give his right arm for a set of dress blues."

"Let's see. That's nearly $150 – that's a lot of money," Ray spoke thoughtfully.

"Well, he does have some war bonds he bought while he was in school and there's one calf that belongs to him. We could cash in the bonds and sell the calf."

"What with Hense doin' so good, will he help out?" Mildred ventured.

Goldie gave her younger sister a hard look but softened before she spoke. "Hense and Franklin aren't close." That comment seemed to close the discussion on her husband chipping in any money.

"Is he through boot camp yet?" Ray asked.

"I guess so. His last letter seemed to indicate that he'd be moving on to a line camp assignment pretty soon."

"Will he get leave?"

"He didn't seem to think he would right after boot camp but he's mighty concerned about the money. If his name does come up for a furlough, he doesn't want to have to say he can't go because he doesn't have the money. Maybe the fact that he gets no leave after boot camp means that he'll be assigned to serve stateside."

"More wishful thinkin'," Ray said. "In the Marine Corps they say there's two kinds of Marines; those who are overseas and those who are about to go." Then, thinking to change the subject slightly, he picked up one of the newspapers. "On that topic, here's something interesting," he said. "You know the Marine Corps has been expanding over the course of the war. Says here that two new divisions will be formed this year. One of 'em, the Fifth Marine Division, was officially activated at Camp Pendleton – that's in California – late in January. They'll join with the existing Third and Fourth Divisions to form the Fifth Amphibious Corps."[6]

"Amphibious?" Goldie laughed. "Franklin wouldn't fit in there at all."

"Why not?" Ray noted the twinkle in his sister's eye.

"He's strictly right handed," she giggled. "Doesn't 'amphibious' mean you can write with either hand?"

Mildred caught the spirit. "Naw. It means that the Marine Corps is gonna teach 'em to breathe underwater."

Although Ray was sure both already knew, he thought he'd explain anyway. "It means, of course, that they are 'specially trained to invade islands from the sea. I'll bet Franklin gets assigned to that. Camp Pendleton is only a couple of hundred miles up the coast from where he's at." Ray nodded knowingly.

"Where he was, anyway. We don't know if he's still in California. Anyhow, they can't build a new outfit out of raw men just out of boot camp, can they?"

"Says here," Ray said, thumping the newspaper, "that the VAC ranks will be filled about half and half with new men and combat veterans. They've broken up the Marines First Parachute Regiment and the Marine Raider Battalion to furnish the veterans.[7] Those men fought at Vella Lavella and Bougainville. Anybody who survived those two rough campaigns is bound to be a tough customer."

"VAC?" Mildred asked, "what's that?"

Ray smiled. "Using the Roman numeral V for five, that's what they're calling the Fifth Amphibious Corps. And they've nicknamed it 'The Spearhead.'"

"That sounds like they intend to get there first," Goldie mused. "Well, if they do assign Franklin to, what did you say, VAC?, sounds like there'll be some old hands around to help him."

"Like everything else, there's no substitute for combat experience. If you're gonna hit the beach on one of those Pacific Islands, having a veteran who knows a little something about Japs and jungles around wouldn't hurt anything," Ray said.

Mildred had remained quietly thoughtful throughout this last exchange. As Goldie digested Ray's comment, Mildred was still thinking back to "VAC." "'V' stands for victory, too, you know," she softly observed.

Chapter 10

Wednesday, March 15, 1944
Near Oceanside, California

Huddled beneath a flapping canvas cover in the back of a truck rolling north on Highway 101, USMC Private Franklin R. Sousley (949927) did not realize, of course, that he and his truck were just a trickle in the veritable river of men, machines and supplies pouring into Camp Pendleton. The camp, located on the former Rancho Santa Margarita in Southern California, was the home of the newly formed Fifth Marine Division. Like the other divisions, the Fifth consisted of three regiments which consisted, in turn of three battalions, which were further subdivided into three companies. The company, which is made up of about 250 men, is the division's basic element. The men in a company all know each other and engage in a constant struggle not only to take objectives but to gain and maintain each other's friendship and respect. By truck, by rail and on foot men poured in from the boot camps at Parris Island and San Diego, from training centers at Camps Elliott, Lajeune and Pendleton, from post-campaign furloughs, from recuperation hospitals and from schools at Quantico. These were the men who would fill the ranks of the fledgling 26th, 27th, 28th (infantry) and 13th (artillery) Marine Regiments which composed the Fifth Division.

While the peace-time Marine Corps consisted of just three divisions, war-time demands had created the Fourth a year before and now, with no end to the Pacific war in sight, the Fifth Marine Division had come into being by official order on November 11, 1943. The official activation date was January 21, 1944 and by mid-February, Division Commander Major General Keller E. Rockey had appointed his key staff officers and roughed out a training schedule aimed specifically at utilizing the lessons learned in prior battles to perfect amphibious assault techniques.[8]

Shortly before noon on this early spring day, the truck rolled through the front gate, turned onto a dirt road before eventually skidding to a stop in front of the headquarters building. Hefting his sea bag on his shoulder, Franklin grasped his rifle in his right hand and, with the other men, jumped to the ground. The first thing they noticed was a welcome message sign tacked on the side of the building. The Division Commander's signature at the bottom lent a certain gravity to the message. They eyed the picture of a Marine sporting the Spearhead patch on his shoulder and solemnly took in the printed words:

To the officers and men of the Fifth Division:
You are now members of a division that is destined to play an important role in winning the war. To wear the 5th Marine Division insignia on the sleeve of your uniform is an honor.

The insignia means:
- That you will conduct yourself with dignity at all times.
- That you are well disciplined and that you know only discipline will win a war.
- That if you disgrace yourself you are disgracing YOUR division.

A sergeant bearing a clipboard appeared from inside the building. Calling the formation to attention, he announced, "Listen up for your assignments." Franklin noted that this man's voice had none of the raspy quality of a drill instructor. He said a small prayer, once again, that he'd survived boot camp and was now a real Marine. As the Sergeant called out names, corporals appeared to escort the men to their respective company headquarters. He heard "Sousley," along with several other names, called to go to Company E – Easy Company – of the Second Battalion of the 28th Marines. "Let's go," the corporal ordered, turning to walk away. Ambling along, Joe Rodriguez, Bill Ranous, and Lowell B. – call me L.B. – Holly introduced themselves. After walking for some time the group arrived at Company HQ. "You're all assigned to the second platoon," the guide announced. "Lieutenant Pennell is in charge, but Captain Severance, Easy Company's boss, will want to talk to you first." With that, he ushered the men into the building.

Captain Dave Severance was a tall, straight Marine who had come to the Spearhead as one of the veterans from the parachute marines. After the military formalities, he spoke with a soft mid-western Wisconsin accent. "Glad to have you men here," he began. "Our training will be rough, but you'll readily see the value of what you'll learn here. In boot camp, you learned by the book, but in combat, there ain't no book, so here, you'll learn in other ways. Lt. Pennell and I will be right there with you in the field, so just let us know if you have any problems. Now, let's get to work, we've got a war to win." Following a similar pep talk from the Lieutenant, the new men were led down a steep slope to vast array of tents – the same kind Franklin had lived in at Camp Matthews – situated in a valley between steep hills. "Welcome to Tent Camp #1, home of Easy Company," the guide intoned as he led the men into the company street. Stopping in front of a tent, he announced, "This is second platoon, move your gear inside and find an empty bunk."

In the dim light inside the tent, Franklin saw the darkest-skinned individual he'd seen in the Marine Corps sitting on a bunk. He was pulling whiskers from his chin with a small coil of wire.[9] "Is this second platoon?" Franklin asked, even though he knew it was.

"Yeah," the dark man answered, flinching slightly as he extracted a hair from his cheek. "That's your rack there." He indicated a metal bunk with a rolled up mattress next to where he sat.

"I'm Sousley. Franklin." He extended his hand.

The other shook hands but did not smile. "Hayes," he said, without looking up. "Name's Ira, but you might as well call me 'Chief.' Everybody does."

"You're an Indian!" It was more of an exclamation than a question.

"Well, ain't you the observant one? Yeah, I'm an original American." The dark one made that statement with pride, but still he did not smile.

Ignoring the comment, Franklin asked, "Are you one of the code talkers?" The Native American code talkers were already legend in the Marine Corps. Speaking over the radio in their native language, they provided communications which were totally indecipherable to the Japanese. In instances where the Japanese had attempted to broadcast false and confusing transmissions, the code talkers had the added benefit of being unquestionably authentic.

"Naw," Hayes answered, his attitude seemingly softening a little. "They're Navahos."

"What tribe are you?"

"I'm a Pima and one of three Indians in the company."

"Wow! I ain't never met no Indian before. Where are you from?"

"Arizona. And you?"

"Kentucky," Franklin answered, his state pride showing as well.

"Well," Chief said, "I ain't never met no ridge runner before either, so I guess we're even."

On the other side of the tent, Franklin met a small, dark, very handsome young man. "I'm Sousley," he announced.

"Yeah, I heard. My name's Gagnon. Rene."[10] Franklin thought he said "Rainey" only later did he learn the spelling. "So you're a barefoot hillbilly?"

"That's me," Franklin answered good-naturedly. "How 'bout you?"

"I'm from New Hampshire," Gagnon said, smiling. "I worked with my mother in a shoe factory, so we always had shoes."

Over the course of the next several weeks as Franklin became acquainted with the men with whom he was serving, he learned that Easy had men from all 48 states and every conceivable background. While the officers, who were generally older, and may have had a profession in civilian life, most of the enlisted men had, like Franklin, come into the service straight from high school. In the "bull sessions," every kind of accent would be heard and the Kentucky boy soon discovered that his distinctive "twang" was no more idiosyncratic than many others. Given his penchant for telling stories however, his voice was judged more entertaining than most.

One of the first orders of business in the amphibious training was learning to climb down a vertical cargo net while fully loaded with battle gear. From a 40-foot high wooden mock-up of a ship, the Marines went over the side, climbing down what amounted to a rope ladder. In the first practices, the objective was the ground, later a bobbing landing craft would be the receptacle. Some of the men found this particular exercise terrifying, but in the midst of one climb, Franklin was heard wondering aloud if there weren't easier ways to get off a ship.

Another part of the amphibious training was called "combat swimming," and nearly everyone found this exercise frightening. It began with a simulated exit from a ship: a feet-first leap from a high wooden platform into a swimming pool. Clad in swimming trunks, the men were advised to hold one hand over their crotch while pinching their nose with the other. Anyone who was a non-swimmer had that obstacle to conquer before he moved to the next phase: swimming in full combat gear, backpack, boots and all. Knowing that under the best of battle conditions they would wade through the surf to get ashore helped all to understand that what they were doing was preparation for the worst conditions.

Franklin was assigned to the first squad which was led by Sergeant

Mike Strank. Strank was a Czech born Pennsylvanian who had been in the Marine Corps since 1939. Mike was a Bougainville veteran who had proved his leadership in battle to the extent that even platoon leader Lt. Pennell sometimes deferred to Strank's judgment. Cool in all situations, Strank was an ideal Marine leader who exhibited genuine concern for the men in his charge. At the first squad meeting, he advised, "Each fire team is gonna learn to think and act as one man. All you guys just do as I tell you and I'll get you home to your momma." Franklin could see in Mike's eyes that he meant what he said.

Within a squad, the men were divided into two fire teams, each consisting of four or five men. Franklin's fire team consisted of himself, Chief Hayes, Bill Ranous and Lewis Hesse and was led by Corporal Harlon Block. Block, a tall, rangy Texan, had been in the Marines for a little more than a year and was a former member of the Marine Parachute Regiment, as was Ira Hayes. Sgt. Strank, Cpl Block and Pfc Hayes had all fought on Bougainville, but did not know each other there. Franklin, Lewis and Bill represented the men fresh from boot camp and were glad to be able to benefit from the experience of the veterans. This fire team was typical of the entire division in that nearly 40 percent of the Fifth's men were combat veterans. Strank's other fire team, led by Cpl. Dayton Russell consisted of Casimer Doran, Dick Mathewson and Don Short.[11] Together, these men hiked up and down the steep hills that made up Camp Pendleton and learned to follow Mike's direction acting as a team assaulting fortified objectives. Every fire team had one Marine assigned to carry the Browning Automatic Rifle, a hand-held machine gun that could fire bullets singly or in a continuous burst. The BAR fired the same ammunition as the M1, but weighed about twice as much and used a twenty-round clip. Franklin Sousley was proud when he was assigned to be the BAR man in his fire team and even prouder when he qualified as expert with that weapon.[12] As the BAR represented considerable fire power, the man who wielded that weapon was a popular guy in combat.

As the men in a tent got to know each other better, Franklin learned that when Ira Hayes had served in the Marine Parachute Regiment, the men there called him Chief Falling Cloud. Ira had seen combat not only on Bougainville but also Vella Lavella. Although Chief Hayes was quiet, shy and sensitive while Franklin was a gregarious jokester, the two struck up an unlikely friendship. Indeed, as the training progressed, if the reticent Pima had a true friend, it was Franklin Sousley.

Franklin made friends with other members of Easy Company outside his squad: L.B. Holly was Franklin's BAR counterpart in the 2nd squad, Rolla Perry and Ken Milstead were friends, too. Of the men in Easy's weapons squad, which worked with all three rifle squads, he liked Joe Rodriguez and Art (Tex) Stanton and got along very well with Joe Senoracke, a quiet Wisconsin farm boy.[13] These men were together all day every day, worked together, played together, drank together and became family. Sometimes they fought among themselves, but if an outsider threatened one, he would have to deal with them all.

Easy Company, like all others, had its characters and Franklin Sousley was one of them. Since his Marines Hymn/Wabash Cannonball was such a hit, he'd added a few new verses which he was happy to perform for any audience. One evening in his tent, he asked all to gather around. Now plucking imaginary strings on his BAR, he introduced his latest composition: *If I'm Really Lucky, I'll Make It Back to Old Kentucky*. His singing voice would win no prizes, but his stage presence won everyone over. Then, while he had everyone's attention, he announced, "There was this time Tea Run Baptist Church got a new minister, see?"

"Tea Run?" Bill Ranous quizzed, "you're makin' that up."

"You ain't been to Tea Run?" Franklin replied in wide-eyed innocence. "It's just right over the ridge from Big Bone Lick." Ignoring the laughter, he continued, "Anyway, it bein' his first Sunday and all, the preacher prepared a super sermon. Well, I'm dad-gum if on Saturday night it didn't come a big snow storm, so on Sunday mornin' just one ole farmer showed up."

"I didn't know it snowed in Kentucky," Chief said.

"Well, you're just a dumb ole Indian, what the hell would you know about anything in general or snow in particular?" Franklin, along with Harlon Block and Mike Strank, was one of the few who could tease Ira without incurring his wrath. "So, the preacher asked the farmer if he wanted to go ahead with the service. The old boy answered, 'Well, all I know is farmin' and I ain't one to advise the clergy, but I can say that if I went out to feed the cows and just one ole cow showed up, I'd feed her.'"

"I didn't know they had churches in Kentucky," Doran chimed in.

"Now that just goes to show just how damn ignorant you actually are," Franklin said, unfazed. "Over at Possum Trot, they've only got six houses but there's four churches." Ignoring the howls the mention of that name precipitated, he continued his tale. "So the preacher decides to go on with it and proceeds to whup his carefully prepared 90-minute sermon on the congregation of one. Then, it bein' his first Sunday and all, he ran out to ask the farmer how he liked the service.

"'Like I said,' the farmer replied, 'all I know is farmin' and I still ain't one to advise the clergy, but I can tell ya that if I went out to feed the cows and just one ole cow showed up, I wouldn't feed her the whole damn wagon load of hay.'" As Franklin basked in the laughter, he realized that all of his popularity did not stem from the fact that he was the BAR man.

Another of Easy Company's characters was a small, cocky Montana kid named Don Ruhl. Everybody found the pronunciation of his name ironic in that Don had no respect at all for the Marine Corps' rules. The young man refused to wear his helmet during training, preferring a simple baseball cap, showered with his boots on, resisted most attempts at personal hygiene – he insisted that brushing one's teeth simply eroded the enamel – and generally distained all training exercises. Whenever he was dressed down for his various transgressions, he'd simply say that no one had any right to judge him until he'd had the chance to show what he could do in battle. Perhaps on that basis, Captain Severance tolerated Ruhl's behavior.

Rene Gagnon was, in a different way, considered another of the company's characters. Nothing ever suited the New Hampshire man; neither the food nor the equipment nor the living arrangements nor the USO shows nor the liberty nor the orders for the day were ever to his liking. Those who had to live around him soon learned to ignore his grousing just as they generally ignored him in total. Gagnon was, in most estimates, not a very good Marine; nobody trusted him and hence, no one wanted to serve with him. Given that, Sergeant Strank rode Gagnon pretty hard, but no amount of Mike's effort seemed to get Gagnon "squared away." On liberty, however, was a different matter as the handsome Gagnon attracted the girls. Then, every man was his friend.

As spring crept in, the men of Easy Company put in their days with amphibious training and assaulting pillboxes. In all cases, the emphasis was on teamwork – one fire team would lay down suppressing fire while another maneuvered and then the teams would reverse roles. The live ammunition expended in the assault training tended to set the grass afire, so a goodly amount of time was also consumed fighting fires. Night hikes were worked into the training schedule, so they also got in some practice climbing hills in the dark. Clearly, the brass intended for the men of VAC to be in top physical condition. Living in tents and showering in cold water may have been operational necessities, but the brass was not upset that these factors added an extra touch of toughness to the training.

Given the boom town expansion of Camp Pendleton since the Fifth Division's creation, there was a shortage of nearly everything except rattlesnakes. The reptiles were everywhere and the sight of a Marine frantically beating the grass with his rifle butt was not uncommon. In fact, one memorable night, a rattler had infiltrated Sousley's tent. The discovery was made when "Tex" Stanton reached up to brush a bug from his neck only to discover that it was the snake. Little sleep was had in the tent the rest of that night.[14] Another encounter was had in the field one day. Joe Rodriguez rushed to where his fire team was huddled. "A rattler bit somebody over there," he announced, excitedly. "Get a corpsman."

"What happened?" Mike Strank, ever the cool one, asked.

"It's Billy," Joe said. "He pulled out his pecker to piss and a rattler jumped up and bit him right on the end of it."

Amid the laughter, Mike pointed to the left. "There's Doc Bradley over there. Franklin, go get him." John "Doc" Bradley was Easy Company's chief Navy Corpsman and although he was attached to the Third Platoon, he usually seemed to be everywhere. The Corpsmen, while remaining part of the Navy, were trained to treat the Marines' battle injuries and so dressed like Marines, ate the same food, endured the same training and participated in every exercise.

Informed of the snakebite, "Doc" told Franklin, "You don't need me. There'll be two little red circles where the snake's fangs penetrated. Use your Ka-bar knife to cut an 'X' over each of those marks and then suck the poison out. If you get that done quickly, it's not serious but otherwise he's in trouble; it could prove fatal."

When Sousley returned to the fire team, Mike asked, "What did he say?"

Straight faced, Franklin reported, "He said Billy was gonna die!"

One evening as the men relaxed in their tent, Rene burst in. "The PX is openin' tonight," he announced excitedly. "They've got beer!"[15]

"No kiddin'?" L.B. asked.

"On the level. The thing is, though, there's somewhere in the neighborhood of 25,000 men in this camp, so we'd better get there early."

"They'd better have a hell of a lot of beer," Don Ruhl said.

"Well, let's go." Ira Hayes jumped to his feet.

Just at that point, Mike Strank walked in. "What's all the excitement?"

"The PX is open and they've got beer," Don informed, moving toward the door.

"Hold on," Mike said, eyeing Hayes with a gleam in his eye. "Ain't it illegal for Indians to drink alcohol?" Sgt. Strank was another of the few in Chief Hayes small circle of friends.

"I'll drink my ration and any other man's that don't want his," Ira said. There was no hint of humor in his voice. "Let's go."

Ira, Joe, Franklin, Rene, L.B., Harlon, Tex and Mike walked to the PX and each received his allotment of the GI beer. After each had consumed one, a game was got up. "Any man who can't chug the whole can ain't got a hair on his ass," Mike suggested. The "John Wayne," Marine slang for the GI can opener they'd seen the "Duke" use in a training film, made the rounds as each man punctured a metal can and attempted to down the entire contents without pausing for breath. For some of the boys, such as Franklin, who had had little previous drinking experience, this was quite a sensation.

"This stuff tastes like they dissolved a cake of yeast in a glass of weak tea," Franklin observed, a slight slur in his words.

Swirling a sip of beer around in his mouth as if to savor the essence, Tex smacked his lips. "With just a dash of horse piss for flavor." As everyone laughed, he asked, "Am I right, Chief?"

Ira thoughtfully savored a sip. "Five-day-old clabbered horse piss, I would say." Amid the giggles, Ira said, "Let me show you how a real American drinks beer," as he took the opener. He punctured one end of the can and held his thumb over that hole while he cut an opening in the opposite end. Then, with a thumb over each hole, he shook the can vigorously before moving it to his mouth. In a flash, he removed his thumbs allowing the whole contents of the can to shoot down his throat. With a satisfied grin and a belch, he said, "Any man who can't do that ain't got a hair on his ass," as he handed the opener to Mike.

Franklin Sousley was one of several woozy and sick young men by the time he returned to his tent that evening.

"Heard the latest scuttlebutt?" Joe asked, bursting into the tent.

"No. What's doin'?" Franklin, always eager for the latest rumor, replied as he brushed a spot of rust from his BAR.

"Well, seein' as how the veterans got a furlough after their combat tour, all of us who came here straight from boot camp are gonna get a furlough in the next month or so."

"Where'd you get that?" Franklin inquired.

"Oh, I know a guy who knows a guy who's a clerk in battalion HQ. The guy who knows the guy said that the clerk cut the orders himself just yesterday." Joe was serious.

"Seems to me," Franklin said, reassembling his weapon, that we'd at least get a weekend liberty sometime before we'd get a furlough. Anyhow, do you have the money for a furlough?" Even if one was approved for a furlough, the fact that he would be required to have $80 before it would be granted was a topic of much discussion.

"Almost." Joe turned serious. "How 'bout you?"

"I've been asking ever'body back home to help out in any way they can," Franklin said. "I've got the $80 squirreled away, but I ain't going home without a dress uniform. I hope my mom is workin' on the money for that."

"Are you goin' home with a missing front tooth?" Joe teased. In addition to all the required physical activities, the men were encouraged to participate in boxing matches, basketball, volleyball and baseball games. Those who proved best at those were organized into teams to compete against men from other outfits. Franklin had lost a front tooth proving that he was no boxer.

"They said they'd fix it for me," Franklin replied, his spirit dampened slightly. "I really don't want to go home lookin' like the big bad wolf." He wiped a light coat of oil over the barrel of his BAR.

Sergeant Strank strode into the tent. "Say, Mike," Joe said, "do you know anything about us ex-boots gettin' a furlough?"

"Nope," Mike answered. "But I'd advise you to be standin' by for it anyway."

"How 'bout a liberty?" Franklin asked, stowing his weapon.

"Strange you should ask," Mike said with a slight grin. "The reason I came in here is to alert you to the fact that you're on liberty tomorrow."

"All of us?" Joe enthused.

"Yep, everybody." As the grins broke all around, he went on, "Before you get too excited, Sousley, be advised that you're spending your liberty in a dentist's chair."

"You're jokin'?" Franklin was hopeful.

"Do I look like I'm foolin'? The bus is leaving at 07:00. Everybody is goin' to San Diego."

Folly reigned on the bus carrying the young Marines to San Diego for their weekend liberty. For many, this would be the first time away from the authority of parents or officers and the boys were laughing it up, bragging of all the women they were going to get and all the alcohol they'd drink. The normally dour Ira Hayes sat in a rear seat displaying his usual grim attitude and ignoring the party atmosphere. Next to him sat the normally cheerful Franklin Sousley. Franklin was sullen; not ignoring the others, but eyeing them enviously. "It just ain't right," he told Chief, "for all of you to be goin' on 'skirt patrol' while I get to go to the dentist." Staring straight ahead, Hayes simply said, "I'm gonna get rip-roaring, commode-hugging drunk."

Even though he'd put in his boot camp at the San Diego Recruit Depot, Franklin had seen little of that city. Spending this liberty there did not alter that fact. He spent the entire day in a Marine Corps dentist's office getting fitted for a bridge for his missing tooth. Additionally, the Major removed 21 old fillings and replaced them with new silver ones.[16] Franklin wrote his mother, "Only a Marine could stand up to all that time in a dentist's chair." In answer to her letter saying she had been ill, he wrote, "Mother, you said you were awfully sick. I want you to stay in out of that field and look real pretty when I come home. You can grow a crop of tobacco every summer, but I sure as hell can't grow another mother like you. So, please, take care of yourself and look real pretty when I come home. Won't you?" Six months in the Marines and away from home had not diminished his love for his mother. When a letter from her arrived containing enough money to buy him a set of dress blues, his heart nearly burst with affection for Goldie Sousley Price.

"Pack up your gear," Lieutenant Pennell ordered, "we're goin' on a little trip."

"This is it," Chief Hayes said, "we're goin' overseas, sure as hell."

"Great," Franklin gushed. "I'm tired of trainin'. It's time to go shoot some Japs."

"You'll not be so eager when you get there," his friend Ira advised. "Shootin' at 'em tends to make 'em mad. Encourages 'em to shoot back, you know."

The Marine Corps food and training had done well by Franklin Sousley. He'd learned to stand straight with his shoulders back and now he stood six-feet tall and weighed in at 185 pounds of muscle. Stretching to his full height, he bragged, "No near-sighted little yellow bastard is gonna get this ole bluegrass boy, I guarantee you that."

"Listen to the voice of somebody that's been there," Ira advised. "The

Japs are clever, tough fighters and they will not give up under any circumstances. On Bougainville, they'd lay on the ground all day and all night pretending to be wounded until somebody approached. If a Marine got close, they'd suddenly jump up and shoot him."

"You'd soon learn not to try to help, wouldn't you?" Franklin wondered.

Ira was about to answer but was interrupted when Sergeant Strank entered. Mike shot a look at Sousley out of the corner of his eye and then faced Corporal Harlon Block. "Block," he began, "this may well be our ticket overseas. Make sure everybody in your fire team has his masturbation papers in order and ready for inspection. They won't let you board the ship without 'em."[17]

Franklin Sousley, ever on the alert for scuttlebutt, picked right up on it. "Masturbation papers? What's that? I ain't never heard of that."

Mike Strank spoke as seriously as he could manage. "What? You ain't got your papers? Don't you want to go overseas?"

"Why, hell yes, of course I do." Franklin was frantic. "Nobody told me, honest."

"Well then, you better get your ass up to Company HQ and report right now." As Franklin started for the door, Mike added, "and don't waste no time. We'll be movin' out soon."

When Franklin returned, red-faced, neither his ire nor the derisive laughter of his mates lasted long. In only a few minutes, Easy Company's men were in trucks headed south. Seated on a bench with sea bags stowed beneath and holding their rifles between their knees, these men once more had occasion to eye the vast Pacific and contemplate what lay beyond the horizon. The trucks soon arrived at the San Diego docks where the men jumped off the trucks and carried their sea bags up a gangplank onto a transport ship. Other trucks disgorged similar cargos all around; the whole Fifth Division was moving onto four troop transports. As soon as everyone was on board, the ships moved out of the bay. As Franklin and Ira stood at the rail watching the dockside facilities fade into the distance, Franklin said, "Looks like goodbye to the good ole USA for a while."

Ira, deep in his own thoughts did not reply for a moment. Finally, he asked, "How eager are you to get at the Japs now?"

Like every other man on board, Franklin tried to sort out his mixed emotions. He felt himself to be a part of the finest fighting force ever assembled on earth – goodness knows they'd been told that often enough – but still, uncertainty and fear of the unknown gnawed at his guts. These were emotions no Marine would speak aloud, but every man had his own fears; failing his buddies in combat headed that list. The training they'd endured had taught them that every man depended on every other man, every squad depended on every other squad and so on right up to the division level. While the Marine Corps warned that forming too many close relationships would lead to sorrow in combat, they also encouraged each man to adopt a "buddy." One buddy would sleep while the other kept watch; they would share whatever ammunition they had; they would even share their last cigarette and carry each others' last letter to be sent home "just in case." A Marine's buddy would be close at hand to lend help or comfort no matter what happened. With these thoughts running through his mind, Franklin turned to Ira. With a sigh, he said, "I'll be there for you."

The men were pleasantly surprised – and silently relieved – when the ship slid to a halt after a couple of hours out. Ordered into full combat gear, the men went over the side on cargo nets just as they'd done so many times on the mock-ups. This time, though, the target was a small landing boat – what was officially termed a "landing vehicle, tank" or LVT in military parlance – bobbing up and down at the water line. Occasionally, the landing craft would bang against the side of the ship with a loud report. Tex Stanton, beside Franklin, said, "I sure hope I ain't between that thing and the ship when they decide to smack together." The already tight knot in Franklin's stomach ratcheted up another notch as he swung a leg over the rail with Ira Hayes right behind him.

Bearing in mind Tex's warning, about three feet above the LVT, Franklin pushed himself away from the side of the ship to fall the last few feet. Heavily laden, he landed hard with a little prayer that he was intact. When the landing craft was fully loaded, it moved away from the ship to make way for the next one. Franklin's boat wallowed away from the transport ships to where it joined in a grand ballet of LVT's sailing in a huge circle. On one arc, the men could see a barren island some 1000 yards distant. "What is this place?" somebody asked.

"San Clemente Island," Lieutenant Pennell informed. "We're gonna assault it."

"Ain't never heard of it," Joe said. "Any women there?"

That brought a laugh from everyone. "Nope," the Lieutenant answered. "It belongs to the Navy to be used for training purposes." After a moment, he added, "We're liable to be goin' plenty of places you've never heard of."

When all the landing craft had assumed their assigned positions, the small armada fanned out in a line and made for the island's beaches. The boat's bobbing in the water caused several of the men to vomit and so find a new use for their helmets. Given the foul odors in the boat, no one was unhappy when it ground to a halt on the sand and the ramp fell. Following their training, the men jumped down the ramp to find themselves chest deep in seawater. Holding their weapons over their heads, they started for shore. When a wave swept over them, Franklin and the others learned the value of their combat swimming practice and the utility of the condoms they'd placed over the muzzles of their rifles to prevent water from getting down the barrel.

Ashore and exhausted, Joe, Ira, L.B., Tex and Franklin flopped down on the sand. "Well, that wasn't so bad," Joe observed.

"Kinda reminds me of swimmin' in the Licking River back home," Franklin said with a laugh.

"Get off the beach," was the order. In all the practice runs, getting inland as quickly as possible had been stressed. As the fire team began to move, L.B. pointed forward. "Look. Look at Ruhl!" Far ahead of all others, even his own fire team, the non-conforming Montana boy, a baseball cap instead of a helmet on his head, was running inland for all he was worth. "I wonder how he gets away with that?" Joe said.

"I'll tell what I wonder," Ira muttered, "is will he do that for real."

When they reached the objective point, Harlon Block's fire team sank to the ground. "Well, that was kinda fun," Franklin said to no one in particular.

"Wasn't nobody shootin' at you this time," Ira commented, sullenly. "It ain't nearly as much fun when machine gun bullets are kickin' up the water all around." For once, no one had any bantering reply.

Back aboard the transport ship, after supper, the men retired to their quarters. Far below the water line, canvas hammocks strung on steel frames five tiers high provided a sea-going barracks. If the men thought they'd endured the cornucopia of odors in the landing craft, the crush of bodies in this cramped space proved them wrong as several new sensations assaulted their noses.

"Do you suppose we're allowed up on deck?" Franklin asked, turning up his nose.

"They let us go up whenever we wanted on the way to Bougainville," Ira said.

"Allowed or not, I'm goin,'" Don announced, jumping to the deck. The trio made their way to the top deck where they basked in the fresh air in an unoccupied, out-of-the-way nook they managed to find. As the lumbering ship moved through the soft summer night, the conversation died off and soon the men were snoozing away. Despite his exhaustion, Franklin was kept awake by his emotions. Looking at Don and Ira sleeping beside him, he began to truly understand what the Marines called *esprit de corps*. His last thought before sleep was how much at home he felt in the company of these men even though he was, at this exact moment, farther from Hilltop, Kentucky than he'd ever been before.

A gray light was streaking the eastern sky when the bustle of the ship awoke the Marines. In the semi-darkness, the men could barely make out the California coast before they scrambled to breakfast. Again ordered into full combat gear, they assembled on deck for a briefing. "This is 'Pendleton Island,'" Captain Severance announced, pointing to the land mass on the east. "It's a strongly fortified advance Japanese base in the Western Pacific."[18] Again, the banter that was usual among Marines ceased to exist as the Captain spoke of the island's defenses and the Spearhead's mission. "This particular island," Captain Severance went on, "is a threat to American operations and we WILL overcome all opposition to take possession of this real estate. Is that understood?"

"Yes sir," the entire company shouted in unison.

As the men climbed over the rail onto the cargo net, the banter returned but no one made mention of the fact that they were actually just returning to their training base. As the Captain had indicated, this was serious business. When the LVT's ramp fell, they saw just how serious. From behind barbed wire obstacles, rifle and machine gun fire poured from concrete pillboxes. The fact that the ammunition was blanks detracted little from the combat realism created by the din and confusion. As Franklin and Ira waded ashore side-by-side, an explosion of a simulated mine a few yards to their left caused them to dive to the sand. Covered in mud and wet sand, Franklin rolled to face his buddy. "Damn!" he exclaimed, slightly dazed. "The real thing can't be any worse than this." His face was pale and grim.

"I done told you," Ira muttered, "the Japs shoot real bullets."

"Look!" Franklin cried. Ira rolled over to note that the defending force was falling back to prepared positions farther inland.

"Let's go," Mike Strank yelled as he ran by. "Let's go, let's go. We gotta get off the beach."

All of Harlon's fire team leapt to their feet to follow Sergeant Strank. They raced 100 yards inland where they fell to earth in front of a pillbox. "Harlon," Strank ordered, "wait until I get over to Russell's team and then keep the enemy pinned down while he moves forward."

"Right," Harlon said as the Sergeant scrambled away. "Franklin," Block ordered, "when Mike gives the signal, you pepper the firing port of that pillbox with your BAR. Ira, you and Bill and Lewis, be ready to take up the slack when Franklin runs out of ammo."

"Go," Mike yelled above the din. Franklin, his BAR on full automatic, took aim on the slit in the concrete bunker and fired away. When the clip was expended, he dropped down to load another while his team-mates fired with their M1's. Corporal Dayton Russell, leader of the other fire team in Strank's squad, led his men toward the pillbox. When Russell's team reached a sheltered position, at Strank's signal, his team fired away while Block's men advanced. If these men had had time to notice, they would have seen Spearhead's commander, General Rockey, observing from a bluff high above the beach. Had they been closer, they would have noted a pleased smile on the General's face. Beside him was another observer, President Franklin Roosevelt, draped in a black cape watching from a black limousine.[19] General Rockey knew that the months of hard training were paying off. He had done all that he could to ensure that The Spearhead was ready for the battle that could not be long in coming.

Back at Tent Camp #1, Franklin was kept busy cleaning his BAR. "I never knew that salt water could cause so much rust," he told Joe.

"Me neither," Joe agreed brushing away at the metal of his M1. "Seems everywhere the water touched causes a rust spot.'

"Yep, and it spreads, too. I ain't done a thing except clean this weapon since we went to San Diego."

Lieutenant Pennell's entrance into the tent halted the conversation. "Sousley," he announced, "get your gear squared away."

"Yes sir," Franklin said, jumping to his feet. "What's up?"

"You're on a fifteen day furlough starting tomorrow."

Having dreamed of leave and suffered through so many rumors in the months since he'd come to Camp Pendleton, Franklin could hardly believe what he heard. "On the level, sir?"

"Get those dress blues pressed, son. You're going home."

Chapter 11

Tuesday, August 8, 1944[20]
Flemingsburg, Kentucky

Amid screeching brakes and hissing steam, the locomotive ground to a stop along the station's wooden platform. In the second car, Private Franklin Sousley peeked out the window to see if he could discover who was waiting. Because of the short notice he'd received that his furlough had been approved, he was not certain that the air mail letter he'd sent announcing his arrival had beat him home. Momentarily distressed because he saw no one, his heart skipped a beat when he finally spotted his mother and Hense, brother Julian, friend J. B. Shannon and Marian Harding standing far down the platform. He jumped to his feet before the train came to a full halt and nearly fell when it did lurch to a stop. Tugging at the tails of his dress blue jacket, he made sure that the red stripe on the side of his trousers was centered and placed the white hat on his head. He did not know how his mother had managed to come up with the money to purchase this dress uniform, but at this minute he was more than glad that she had. Just before stepping into the doorway, he adjusted his hat to the proper jaunty angle and fixed a noncommittal expression on his face.

That expression gave way to a mischievous grin the instant Goldie saw her son step to the open doorway. Franklin had just managed to descend the single step to the platform, when she threw her arms around him, embracing him in a huge hug. Grinning widely, he managed to free a hand to greet his little brother Jake. "I cannot begin to tell you how good it is to see you," he whispered in his mother's ear.

"You look so frail!" Goldie exclaimed, stepping back to admire him. Placing her hands on his shoulders, she held him at arm's length. "Just wait 'til I get some home cookin' into you."

"Gee, Mom," Franklin said, laughing, "I weigh 30 pounds more than when I left." Untangling his arms, he shook hands with J.B. "How you doin', young man?"

"Wow," J.B. cried, "you're lookin' straight as a string and you ain't lyin' about puttin' on weight, are you?" He playfully punched the Marine's stomach.

Franklin, pretending to wince, said, "The Marine Corps does that to you." Eyeing Marian standing behind the others, a demure smile on her face, he let go of Goldie and J.B. to step between them. A bit self-consciously, he put his arms around the girl's waist and drew her to him. "Thank you for being here," he said.

"Oh, I wouldn't have missed it for anything," she cooed. With a side glance at Goldie, she whispered, "I've missed you," as she pulled away.

Finally, he turned to his stepfather. "I hear you're takin' over supplyin' milk for the whole county," he said , extending his hand.

"Well, I ain't exactly got the whole market cornered just yet," Hense answered, "but I'm workin' on it." His demeanor disclosed no emotion.

The noise of the train pulling away from the station suspended the conversation for a few moments. When the train was gone, Hense suggested that they go back to his home in Ewing. "I'm anxious to see it," Franklin said.

As they walked toward the car, J.B. shook Franklin's hand. "I've got business here in town, so I'll see you later. I want you to tell me all about the Marines."

"I will," Franklin assured. "See ya."

Hense slid behind the wheel as Julian opened the passenger's door. Marian gently slipped her hand in Franklin's and in a quiet voice said, "I'll see you tomorrow night."

"You cannot imagine how I'm lookin' forward to it," Franklin whispered, a huge grin covering his face. She gave his hand a little squeeze and he thought he saw her wink before she turned to walk away.

Goldie and Franklin climbed in the back seat. She clung to her son's hand during the entire eight mile drive to Ewing. Just as the car pulled up in front of the house, Franklin's grandparents, Uncle Ray and Aunts Florine and Mildred burst from the door. Encircling the car, they swarmed over the young Marine with hugs and handshakes. Grinning broadly, he spoke what was in his heart, "Damn it's good to be home!"

The women had gone all out in preparing a "welcome home" dinner. On the farm where meat rationing had little effect, a center piece featuring pot roast, pork chops and spare ribs was surrounded by the garden's bounty: tomatoes, potatoes, salad, okra, radishes and various kinds of beans. Additionally, Goldie continually shoved her from-scratch biscuits slathered in hand-churned butter in front of her son. "Marine Corps food is good," he commented, "but it ain't nothin' like this." Finally Goldie and Mildred retreated to the kitchen. When they reappeared, Goldie carried Franklin's favorite dessert, a jam cake, and her sister had a pineapple upside-down cake. "We've been saving our sugar ration for months," Goldie announced slipping the treats to the table. "Gee, Mom, I don't think I can handle another breath of air right now," Franklin said, pushing his chair back from the table. "I'm gonna have to wait a while for that cake."

"Why, you oughta eat," she opined, "you're lookin' so thin."

"He looks pretty healthy to me," Mildred observed, laughing. "What do you weigh now, Franklin?"

"Almost 190, mostly muscle," he said, standing to stretch. "And I've grown about an inch taller."

"And I see the Marines have taught you to stand up straight," Ray said.

"Nothin' like good food, fresh air and plenty of exercise," Franklin replied, laughing. "It could be that livin' in a tent and cold showers have something to do with it, too."

"Cold showers?" Jake shivered.

"I haven't seen a drop of hot water or slept under a roof since I arrived at Camp Pendleton."

Hensley Price stood. "Well, I reckon we've sat around here long enough. Jake, you wanna help with the milkin'?" It was more of a demand than a question.

"Aw, Hense...."

"I do," Franklin interrupted. "Tell you what, Hense, you just relax and let me and Jake take care of it tonight. Come on Jake, let's me and you go milk some cows." His offer had less to do with helping his stepfather than it did an opportunity to spend some quality time with his little brother.

Jake agreed much more readily than he would have had it been his stepfather asking. Walking to the barn, the brothers stopped to admire the soft summer evening as darkness gathered along the ridge line. "I'd forgotten how beautiful Kentucky actually is," Franklin said, leaning against the top board of the fence.

"I can't wait to get out of here," Julian muttered. "I'm ready to see something besides weeds and hard work. I wish I was graduatin' this year."

"Don't rush it, buddy. Or, as Mamaw says, 'Don't be wishin' your life away. It'll go fast enough.' That's good advice."

"Well, when I'm old enough, if the war's still goin' on, I'm gonna be a

Marine, just like you." The young man spoke with the confidence of inexperience. The he added, thoughtfully, "Tell me about it."

They herded the cows into the barn where each sought out her accustomed stall. Franklin pulled a stool up to the first while Julian moved to the next. "Well," the older began, "it's a couple of things. Boot camp ain't a bit of fun, but I didn't have the trouble with it that some of 'em did."

"How's that?" Jake interrupted.

"Oh, some of the guys there just didn't know how to respond to authority, I guess. The Marines push you as far as they can, questioning your manhood and parentage and physical stamina, and some boots can't take it and try to take their frustrations out on the instructors."

"How's that work out?" The younger man was enthralled.

"Not well, as you can imagine," Franklin answered with a wry laugh. Rising, he dumped the contents of his bucket into the ten-gallon milkcan stationed midway through the barn and moved to the next cow. "If you just do what they tell you, it's not really any trouble. Then, when you come out, there's nothing in the world like how you feel."

"What do you mean?" Julian dumped his pail and moved on.

"When you survive boot camp and become a full-fledged Marine, you have a sense of pride at having accomplished something and being a part of the best fighting force on the face of the earth. There ain't nothin' like it. Nothin'."

When the milking was finished, the pair picked up the milk can and walked toward the spring house. Franklin sat the can inside and scooped a dipper of the cool spring water. Smacking his lips at the refreshing taste, he looked at his brother. "Seriously, Jake, don't be in a hurry. Life here in old Kentucky is pretty damn good. I'm looking forward to goin' off to whip the Japs, but once that's done, you can bet that I'm comin' right back here. Then, after I milk the cows ever' evenin' I'll sit on the porch holdin' my wife's hand while we rock and watch the grass grow." Jake noted a wistfulness in his brother's voice.

"On that whippin' the Japs business, don't you ever think about the fact that there's a chance you might not be comin' back?" That possibility often filled the young man's thoughts.

This was a subject Franklin was not eager to discuss with his family, but here was an opening for some information he needed to supply his brother. Leaning against the fence, he began, "Jake, when our father died, you were too young to know anything about it."

Sensing his brother's mood, Jake turned serious. "Yeah?"

123

"Well, ever since then Mom has given me to understand that as we had no father, I was to help her look after you and I've always tried to do so." Franklin heaved a sigh, then continued, "I aim to keep right on lookin' after you, no matter what. Now, she's got Hense and I have an insurance policy that'll pay her some money if anything happens to me, so she'll be OK no matter what." He paused a moment, then went on, "But, you know, me and you can't depend on Hense." With a wry laugh, he added, "Me and you are the proverbial red-headed step children, you know."

Having lived in Hensley Price's house all the time his older brother was gone, Julian knew the truth of Franklin's words better than the speaker. He simply nodded understanding.

"Well, the government has what they call a 'gratuity pay' program," Franklin continued. "If a man has no wife and no children, then he can designate someone to get some money if he gets killed in combat. In that case, whoever he named gets six months worth of his pay. I hadn't been sure until now, but when I get back to Camp, I'm gonna name you as my beneficiary."

Jake was stunned. Although several thoughts raced through the eleven-year-old's mind, "How much would that be?" came out of his mouth.

"Oh, it depends," Franklin said with a smile. "There's extra pay for bein' out of the country and combat pay and I might be gettin' promoted soon, but I expect it'd add up to somethin' in the neighborhood of $350."

The younger man was silent for a moment. "I'd a whole lot rather have you back," he finally said.

"Well thanks," Franklin said, laughing, "I'll do my best to see that the government don't have to send you no money. I just wanted you to know." The brothers stood silently for a moment. "We'd better get inside before they start wondering what's become of us."

Walking toward the house, Julian returned to what he wanted to know about. "Franklin, ain't there a lot of things out there in the world to see? I mean other that what's between here and Flemingsburg."

"Yeah, there are, and I'd encourage you to go see 'em." They paused again to lean against the porch railing. "But, when you've seen a lot, you'll find that the view from right here on this porch is just about as pretty as anywhere on God's green earth."

Much to Franklin's dismay, the days flew by in a whirl of visiting with friends and relatives and catching up on activities. The Sunday service at Hilltop Christian Church was very emotional and he nearly lost his composure when the minister specifically asked God to protect him. He was not surprised to learn that many of his friends and classmates were in the service and flung to the far corners of the earth, but also dismayed to hear that some would not be returning. Of his fifteen days leave, the train ride in each direction consumed four, so his time at home was short. On the afternoon of his last day at home, he considered asking Hense for the use of his car, but thought better of that idea and arranged to borrow his Aunt Florine's car for his date with Marian.

He walked to Florine's house and drove home to carefully don his Marine dress uniform which Goldie had pressed for him. Arriving at Marian's parent's home, he bounded from the car and up the walk. Before he could knock, she opened the door and stepped out on the porch. She was dressed in a red and white polka dot dress with a full skirt and matching shoes. "Wow," he exclaimed, acknowledging that she had dressed to the nines for the occasion. He failed to notice that she'd spent the afternoon in the beauty salon having her hair done.

"Wow yourself," she said with a huge smile. "You look so handsome in your uniform." She slipped her arm through his as they walked to the car. "Where are we going?" she asked as he opened the passenger's door for her.

He closed the door and walked around the car. "I thought we'd stop by Aitkin's Drug Store," he said, sliding behind the wheel. "The kids do still hang out there, don't they?"

"Some things haven't changed," she said with a smile. "The jukebox still works, too."

Several high school girls were gathered inside the small building that served as the local teen hang-out. Several young people sat in the booths sipping Cokes. Franklin knew everyone, of course, although his high school days seemed so far in the past. The effect of the war on Flemingsburg was evident as there was only one other boy in the room. That young man eyed the Marine's uniform with obvious envy as the couple walked in the door, but he, along with the girls, greeted them warmly. "Let's get this party going," Franklin said, slipping a quarter into the jukebox. "What kind of music do you like to dance to?" he asked Marian before he made a selection.

"Let's have some Benny Goodman," she giggled. From past experience, she knew that her date was an excellent dancer and she was eager to show off the steps she'd been practicing since he'd been away. The music was appropriate for the jitterbug, but he also selected some slower tunes which offered the opportunity to hold her close as they glided around the

125

floor. While he really didn't want to let Marian go, he was obligated to dance with the other girls as well, but made special effort to ensure that Marian noticed that he did not hold them in the same way.

All too soon, the hour had grown late. "I'm gonna need some new shoes," he joked as they walked back to the car. "What do you wanna do now?" He already had a plan.

Her non-committal reply, "I'm to be home by eleven," brought a smile to his face as he assumed she was deferring to his plan.

"Well, I know a nice quiet little spot out in the country," he suggested, trying to suppress his grin.

"I thought you might. I'll bet it's dark out there, too." She slipped her hand in his as he started to drive away.

The spot he had selected high on a ridge was indeed quiet and dark and also offered an excellent view of the farms spread out below sparkling in the moonlight. "Well, this is it," he said, switching off the engine. "I brought a blanket to sit on," he suggested, again suppressing a grin.

A sky full of twinkling stars seemed to put on a show just for the young couple as they enjoyed the soft summer night. Franklin started to speak as he slipped an arm around her waist, but found that his voice did not want to cooperate. "Marian," he managed to choke out, clearing his throat.

"Yes." As she turned to face him, the fullness of her lips almost made him forget what he was going to say despite the many times he had played this moment in his mind.

"Well," he began hesitantly, "something's been on my mind for a while now."

"I'll just bet it has," she replied with a giggle. She moved a little closer.

"This war ain't gonna last forever, you know," he began just as he'd rehearsed. "A fellow needs to make some plans for what he's gonna do when it's over."

"What do you want to do?" Her voice was soft.

"I want to come back here, get me a little piece of land, about 15 head of Guernsey cows and be a dairy farmer." That was the easy part of his speech.

"That will be nice. Your Mom has a start on that for you." She was waiting.

He cleared his throat again and squeezed her a bit tighter. "Well, and umm...." Choked with emotion, he could not continue.

She waited, then observing his difficulty, she suggested, "A man is probably gonna need a good woman for a wife to help him around the farm." Her voice laced with sweetness.

Franklin's mouth dropped open in total amazement. "Not to mention that a wife is a necessity for a passel of kids," he finally opined, recovering his composure somewhat.

"Yeah," she said, leaning toward him to place her head on his shoulder. "Not to mention."

In the pale moonlight, he placed his fingers beneath her chin to raise her face. How her hair glows in the moonlight, he thought as their lips met to seal the deal.

After he dropped off Florine's car, he was much too keyed up to sleep, so he just wandered aimlessly down the road. In a while, he realized that he was approaching the Hilltop General Store. As he neared the store, a voice called through the night, "That you Franklin?"

Peering through the darkness, he finally made out J.B. sitting on the liar's bench on the porch. "You ain't got any cows penned up on there, do you?" That incident was far enough in the past that he could tease about it.

"No," the reply came with a laugh. "That was just a one-time thing. What the hell are you doin' out wanderin' around at this time of night?"

"I've been out with Marian," he explained. "Just on my way back to the house. What about you, what are you doin' sittin' out here in the dark?"

"Oh, you know," J.B. said with a sigh. "There ain't a whole hell of a lot to do around here."

"Yeah." Franklin joined his friend on the bench. "I ain't been gone so long that I forgot everything about life in Fleming County. But, you know, that ain't necessarily all bad."

"Actually, I figured you'd be comin' by here so I've been waitin'. I've been wantin' to talk to you, Franklin. I'll be a senior this fall, you know. If the war's still goin' on next spring, it'll be my turn. Tell me about life in the Marine Corps."

Franklin related some of the same things he'd told his brother, but felt free to go into a little more detail about his feelings with his friend. "It's hard to explain," he began, "but it's kinda like knowing that you're where you're supposed to be in life. Coming back here has cleared that up for me."

"How's that?" J.B. was intrigued.

"Jake and I were just standin' at the fence the other night, just lookin' over the valley. It came to me there that the Germans and the Japs are tryin' to take away our right to do things as simple as that. They'd take away all the things we learned about in school: our freedom of speech, the right to live how we want and for a man to earn a livin' at whatever profession he can do. They'd take away a man's right to get married and run a little farm and go to the church of his choice on Sunday if they could. I'm so proud to be a part of the force that's gonna see to it that they don't do that. I know that's kinda dopey, but am I makin' any sense?"

"Yes, you sure are," J.B. said. "It's already been a long war, though. How come you're so sure we're gonna win and stop 'em?"

"That's part of what I was sayin' is hard to explain," Franklin added, thoughtfully. "It's partly the way the Corps teaches you to think – I guess 'feel' is more accurate than 'think' – but it's also the faith that you develop in the men around you. The men I'm with in Easy Company, for example, come from all over the country and we're all different, but somehow, at the same time, we're all the same. When we go into battle, we'll whip the Japs, there ain't no doubt about that."

"I don't mean to be fatalistic," J.B. said, "but ain't some of you gonna get killed?"

Franklin fished a package of Lucky Strikes from his pocket, pulled a cigarette from the pack, slowly tamped it against his watch crystal and lit it before he spoke. "Yeah, no doubt some will. But there's plenty more – you're one of 'em – comin' right along behind us. The Japs started out thinkin' we wouldn't fight but they soon found out that they cannot beat the United States Marines. Now they think we'll get tired of all the killin' and give up. I guess they hope so, because they know they cannot beat us." He leaned back and exhaled a long stream of smoke.

The two sat in silence for a long moment, each considering his future while the crickets chirped around them. Finally, J.B. broke the quietness. "Franklin, are you scared?"

Franklin did not answer for a moment. He took a slow puff and flipped his still-lit cigarette into the darkness, thinking about the fact that the Marines, among themselves, never discussed such things. "Well, yeah, a little," he confessed. "I suppose I am. It ain't so much fear of gettin' killed, but I am scared that I might get mangled and come home missin' some parts." He started to speculate on what that prospect would do to his marital plans, but decided to leave that unsaid. "I guess the thing that scares me most is that I might fail my buddies in battle, though." As that thought soaked in on his friend, he decided to lighten the mood. "Missin' parts would make it hard for a feller to keep up his reputation as a dancer, so I plan to be extra careful about that."

Again, the ladies went all out for Franklin's last meal while on leave. Up long before daylight, Goldie and her sisters prepared fried chicken, sausage, bacon, eggs, gravy and, of course, plenty of made-from-scratch biscuits for his breakfast. During the course of the meal, Franklin steered every conversation away from the war and where he might be going, preferring to discuss what he was going do when he got back after the war. While he did mention that he and Marian had "made plans," he did not find occasion to give any details.

When everyone had finished eating, Franklin helped his mother wash the dishes despite her protest. "It's the least I can do after all the effort you've made," he explained.

After everything was cleaned up, Goldie said, "Go put your uniform on, I want to get some pictures. When he emerged from the bedroom dressed in his summer service uniform, they moved to the back yard where pictures were made of all the family members standing by Hense's car. At one point, Uncle Ray Mitchell took Franklin aside for a few minutes. No one could hear what they were talking about, but Ray did all the talking while Franklin simply nodded agreement. When they came back to the group, Goldie heard her son say, "Yes sir." As the morning wore on, everyone who lived in the neighborhood stopped by to say goodbye and see the young man off.

As Franklin walked to the door with his sea bag on his shoulder, Julian came running carrying Franklin's dress uniform on a hanger. "You forgot this," the young man shouted, happy that he was contributing something to the event.

"Well, thanks Jake," Franklin said with a smile, "but I didn't forget, I'm leavin' that here."

"Won't you need it?" Goldie inquired.

"No. I'm pretty sure that we'll be goin' overseas relatively soon and there won't be any need for a dress uniform there. I'll get a leave when I get back so I'll just leave it here so I'll have it when I come home."

At last the time to head for the train station arrived. Hense, Goldie, Franklin and Julian piled into the car for the short trip to Flemingsburg. Franklin was mildly surprised to see J.B. and Marian waiting on the platform. Their timing was good, they had hardly arrived when the train was heard rounding the bend. Franklin shook hands with Hense, Julian and J.B. He put his arms around Marian. Ignoring the lump in his throat, he whispered, "It's a great big war out there, but I'm gonna do something to make you proud." He kissed her as passionately as he dared given the circumstances. Then, turning to his mother, he embraced her in a long tearful hug. As the engine's bell signaled departure, he stepped onto the car and said, "I'll see you all soon." Just as the train started to move, he looked into Goldie's eyes and predicted, "When I come back, I'll be a hero."[21]

Chapter 12

Tuesday, September 19, 1944
San Diego, California

"A hell of a way for a man to celebrate his birthday," Franklin groused to no one in particular. Easy Company's men were lined up on the San Diego dock alongside a troop transport ship, the *Sea Corporal*.[22] The anxiety of this time being "for real" was enough to set nerves on edge and the fact that they'd already been standing on the dock for three hours did not help anyone's humor. "Hurry up and wait" has always been a facet of military life.

"I'm tellin' ya," Rene Gagnon said, "we're just goin' to assault San Clemente again. We'll be back at Camp Pendleton before dark."

"Oh, put a sock in it, Gagnon. What the hell do you know? You think they had us pack up all our gear and come down here just for fun?" Harlon's voice was a growl. "We're goin' to the Pacific, for sure!"

"How the hell would *you* know? We've done it just for fun before, ain't we?" Tex asked, teasingly.

"You think they made me a corporal for nothin'?" Block snapped. "I know about these things."

"I got the straight scoop," L.B. Holly chimed in, "I know we're goin' to China."

"Tokyo Rose says we're goin' to Hawaii," Joe added, referring to the honey-voiced woman who played popular music and propaganda on the radio.

"Well," Strank opined, "that certainly makes it official."

"All I know," Franklin said, "is that it ain't lookin' very good for me to get any birthday cake and ice cream like I would if I was still back in Kentucky."

"Maybe next year," Holly laughed. "It ain't likely that you're gonna get anything else like you did on furlough back in Kentucky, either, is it?"

"Maybe next year," Franklin replied, a smug grin on his face.

"If you're alive for your next birthday," the dour Hayes commented.

"Speakin' of your furlough," Joe said, drawing Franklin aside. "Can I ask you a personal question?"

"What's that?"

"Well, I know it's private, but I was on furlough at the same time as you and I find that I came back with a different attitude."

Although Franklin thought he understood, he answered hesitantly. "How so?"

"I had a serious talk with my girl while I was home and when I got back here, I started thinkin' about how it ain't gonna be much longer before…."

Thinking of his plans with Marian, Franklin realized that he had gone through the exact same thought process. "Yeah, I got ya," he interrupted.

"Well, I noticed you writing in your Bible a few days after you got back. If you don't mind, tell me why."

Franklin thought for a few moments before answering. The matter was very private, but Joe was his best friend in the Corps and seemed to be in the same spot, so he decided to share. "I also had a serious chat with my girl while I was home; she and I made some plans…."

"Yeah, that's it," Joe interrupted, "that's why I was curious about the Bible."

"Well," Franklin went on, "when I got back to camp, I just got to thinkin' about her and the future and the fact that we might be standin' here on this dock gettin' ready to go to war pretty soon, so I just decided to sign my name in the Bible where it gives me the opportunity to confess that I'm a sinner and accept Jesus Christ as my savior."

Joe nodded understanding. "Does that make you feel better? Less anxious? More at peace?"

"Well," Franklin said with a sigh, "it certainly can't hurt anything."

Lieutenant Pennell's voice booming down the ranks ended all conversation. "All right, let's move. Up the gangway." At his command the men, aligned four abreast, surged forward eager to end the wait. Franklin somehow sensed that those who predicted that "this is it" did, indeed, know what they were talking about. They'd engaged in this exercise before, full battle gear and all, but somehow this time seemed different. He sensed the feel of actual combat. "Hell of a way for a man to spend his birthday," he repeated.

Like a giant green and brown snake, the line of helmeted men moved up the gangway onto the deck of the wallowing ship. Then the head of the snake disappeared as the column of Marines entered a hatch and climbed down endless ladders to their quarters far below the water line. Five tiers of hammocks created by lacing canvas unto steel frames greeted them in the crammed compartment already filled with the odor of too many men. A few hours were consumed getting equipment and gear squared away before the men sensed the ship getting under way. Franklin, Ira, Joe, L.B. and Tex rushed topside where they joined hundreds of other Marines lining the ship's rail to watch the San Diego docks slide away.

"You think this is it?" Tex asked of no one in particular.

"Yeah, I do," L.B. answered.

The ship maneuvered around North Island and seemed to settle into a rhythm as the bow pointed down the channel. Up and down the line of men, speculation on the destination dominated the conversation until the ship eventually reached open water.

Franklin, the wind ruffling his hair observed, "It does feel a little different this time, somehow."

"It is different this time," Ira stated, matter-of-factly.

"How's that?" the others asked, almost in unison.

With a glance at the sun, the Indian observed, "We're heading southwest. San Clemente is northwest of here. We're moving out into the Pacific and that's a fact."

Conversation fell off as the men digested that information. In a few minutes, Harlon Block squeezed in with them. "Chief can tell by the sun that we're moving out into the Pacific," Tex informed. "Do you know anything?"

"Yeah," Harlon muttered. "I know I ain't comin' back."

"Oh stop that kind of talk," Franklin said. "You don't know no such thing."

"He might," Ira added in his usual humorless voice. "I'd just as soon I don't come back, either. I got nothin' to live for."

Following the morning exercise period on the second day out, some Marines were idly milling around the deck when, "Now hear this," boomed from the ship's loudspeaker. "All Marines report to your berthing compartment. Marines below on the double!"

A stab of excitement went through Franklin as he joined in the scramble of hundreds of men shuffling below decks. He knew that now that they were well at sea, the officers would disclose the destination putting an end to the constant speculation. This, indeed was "it." In the small open space between the tiers of bunks, Captain Severance stood, Easy Company's platoon leaders, Lieutenants Wells, Stoddard and Pennell standing behind him. Their faces betrayed no hint as to the announcement. When everyone was in place, the Captain began speaking. "We've had six months of hard training at Camp Pendleton, men and, I must say you've done well. Now, we'll be moving into advanced training and a lot closer to a combat objective." Looking at the men around him, he continued, "We're going to an advance base in the Hawaiian Islands, a place called Camp Tarawa located on the big island, Hawaii." The men who'd heard that destination from Tokyo Rose exchanged knowing glances. "I'm told we'll be at sea about six days before we arrive at the port city, Hilo, then we'll go by train to the camp. You can write letters, but you will not disclose where you are. The censors will check to ensure that you do not. Rumor has it that if you start a letter with 'Hello, how are you?' the censors will cut that out because it sounds too much like 'Hilo, Hawaii.' Anyway, you can say, "at sea," or, once we land, "on an island in the Pacific," but nothing else. We'll have physical training sessions on deck every morning and some lectures during the day. I think maybe there'll be some movies in the evening. The Red Cross has provided some books that you can check out but aside from that, you'll have to entertain yourselves. On that score, one word of advice; do not play any kind of card game involving money with a sailor."

Following the announcement, the tenor of conversation changed, but the speculation did not stop. What life would be like in "paradise" became a popular subject. Harlon, Franklin, L.B. and Tex were at the rail discussing that very item when Lieutenant Pennell approached. "What's doin', men?" he asked.

"We're wondering about Camp Tarawa." Harlon spoke for the group. "Are you in the know?"

"Well. It so happens I am, a little. It's on the Parker Ranch, the largest cattle ranch anywhere on American soil." Seeing Stanton's mouth start to open, he added, "Sorry, Tex but that's a fact. The place is over 250,000 acres and there's about 50,000 head of cattle on it. At the beginning of the war, the owners leased it to the Government for a dollar a year. They originally planned to house prisoners of war there, but a Red Cross inspection found the place unfit for human habitation, so they decided to make a Marine base out of it."[23] That comment brought a laugh from the group.

"Eleanor Roosevelt must have had a hand in that," Harlon said, referencing the scuttlebutt that the First Lady had once commented that Marines returning from combat were so rough that they should be housed in a special camp where they'd be isolated from society.[24]

"Could be," Pennell said. "I don't know that she said any such thing and if she did it makes no sense, all they'd done was bust up a couple of bars. At any rate when the Second Division – what was left of it anyway – got back from taking Tarawa away from the Japs last year, they went to the Parker Ranch to rest and refit. There wasn't a damn thing there, those battered men had to build everything themselves. They named the place Camp Tarawa."

"Wow," Tex cried. "If it's a cattle ranch, we ought to get plenty of steak. I ain't had a decent slice of cow since I left home."

"It bein' Hawaii, will we get pineapple?" Holly wondered.

"It bein' Hawaii, is the place filled with hula girls?" was Franklin's concern.

"I've told you all I know," Pennell said, "but it bein' the Corps, I wouldn't count on any of those things."

Just as Captain Severance had predicted, on September 24, a jade green island swam up over the horizon. Excitement coursed through the men lining the rail. "Look at that!"

"Wow."

"What? What is it?" Tex questioned.

"Hawaii," Franklin answered, "can't you see that land mass floatin' over there? It's bigger than Possum Trot and Hilltop put together."

"Naw, hell I can't see nothin' that far away." Stanton lamented.

"How did you pass the eye exam if your eyesight is that bad?"

"Well," Tex said with a wry laugh, I held the card so that I read the chart with my good eye both times. I can see well enough to shoot some Japs when the time comes, I reckon."

"You didn't see all those porpoises and flyin' fish?"

"Nope," Tex admitted. "Some guys I was standin' with said they saw a whale. I didn't see nothin', so I don't know whether to believe it or not."

The big island grew larger and more beautiful as they approached. Finally the ship nosed into Hilo harbor and the men were ordered below to get their gear in order. After six days on a rocking, pitching and rolling ship, no one needed any extra encouragement to get ready to disembark. The men readily formed up and walked down the gangway, happy to be on solid ground once again. Whatever expectations they had had for a reception quickly faded as only a few curious dark-skinned natives showed up to witness the arrival. A few flower leis were tossed and some of the

Marines tried to flirt with the girls, but the men were quickly herded into rail cars for the 65-mile ride to the camp located in the interior of the island.

From the windows of the train, the boys got a view of the "Big Island," southeastern-most of the chain of islands that composed the Territory of Hawaii. As the latest of the islands to thrust up out of the sea, much of the surface was simply black volcanic lava. Some of the landscape was covered with lush green grass implying fertile soil below, but plenty of areas covered in a volcanic ash similar to, but much more coarse than, sand existed. Many waterfalls and volcanic "cones" – simply mounds of the erupted ash – dotted the countryside, too. At length, the train stopped beside a Quonset hut which served as the head quarters building. "Everybody out," Lieutenant Pennell ordered. "Welcome to beautiful Camp Tarawa."

"Ain't a hell of a lot different from Camp Pendleton, is it?" Franklin observed as they marched down a valley into a virtual re-creation of their former home, Tent Camp #1.

"I see one thing different right off," Joe observed, wrinkling his nose. The air was filled with blowing volcanic ash, creating a haze as one looked into the distance. "I'll bet this stuff will gum up our weapons."

"Yeah, and probably your guts too," Tex commented. "I expect we'll get to eat plenty of it."

"I used to sprinkle sawdust on my steaks back home to give 'em a little texture," Franklin joked, rubbing the air between his fingers. "This grit ought to do about the same."

"I just hope we get steak to add some texture to," Tex said.

The island of Hawaii offers diverse weather patterns with eleven different climate zones. Camp Tarawa happened to be located in an area where rain is usually falling and adjacent to an arid-desert like region. "Only place I've ever been where you can stand in the rain and have dust blowing in your eyes," somebody commented.

The men were assigned the same tent mates as at Pendleton and settled right into the new training routine. Now the training took on a different theme as well as increased intensity. Included was the dreaded climb down a cargo net into a, in most cases simulated, landing craft, an exercise made no less terrifying by repetition. Also included was additional exposure to a training implement the Marines called the "infiltration course."

In that dreaded exercise, the men crawled on their backs beneath a grid of barbed wire strung about 14 inches above the ground. As the men followed a prescribed path through the course, live machine gun bullets whizzed through the air three feet above the ground while explosions rocked the ground near where they squirmed. In terms of sounds and feel, this training was as close to actual combat as could be produced in training and no one stuck his head up to see if the bullets were actually real.

Many, many times the men were arranged standing in a closely packed formation designed to simulate the confines of a landing craft. So situated, they marched to a line of tape on the ground marking the "beach," while dive bombers and fighters roared overhead. "Get off the beach. Move inland!" was the officers' constant cry. Easy Company was tasked to move a few hundred yards inland and then turn to the left where one of the volcanic cones loomed.

"We're gonna assault "Island X," Captain Severance explained. "There's a mountain just like this and Easy Company WILL capture it. Understood?"

"Yes sir!" two-hundred-fifty men roared in response.

One evening in the tent, Tex Stanton observed a strange odor wafting through. "What the hell is that smell?" he asked of no one in particular.

Joe, sniffing the air, wandered around trying to locate the source. "Smells like something crawled up in here and died."

Franklin sat on his bunk doing his best to appear unconcerned as the other men snooped around. Finally, they traced the origin to where Franklin sat. "All right, Sousley," his friend Joe demanded, "what the hell's goin' on?"

With a smug grin, Franklin stood. After looking around to ensure no authority was watching, he slid a metal tub from beneath his mattress. Pulling back the rubber poncho covering it revealed a dark liquid. "What in the hell is that?" Joe screamed recoiling from the increased intensity of the odor.

"Just practicin' a little Kentucky craft," Franklin announced, scooping the aroma toward his face with an open palm. "It's raisin jack. Oh, this gonna make some fine drinkin' whiskey."

"Yeah?" Tex asked, much less repelled now. "Where'd you get the ingredients?"

"Well, I was on KP last week, so I got to hang around the mess hall," he explained as the others gathered. "I stole the raisins and some yeast and there you go." The young man swelled with pride in his work.[25]

"Do you know what you're doin'?" Joe asked, eyeing the concoction suspiciously. "I've heard tales of people goin' blind from drinkin' such bathtub gin."

"I come from a long line of moonshiners," Franklin lied. "When it's ready, I'll strain it through gauze and we'll have a big party."

"I hope to hell it tastes better'n it smells," was Tex's final comment.

Fall melted away in a flurry of amphibious training, inter-company athletic competitions, field exercises, daily rain and an occasional liberty. "Liberty," as Franklin wrote his mother, "if you want to call it that." The only place to go outside the vast limits of Camp Tarawa was the town of Waimea, a tiny nearby native village. "If you want to call it that," was occasioned because Waimea offered little in the way of entertainment. Its major attraction was a hamburger stand operated by a native woman named Tsugi Kaiama. The Marines immediately dubbed her "Sue."

"I sure am lookin' forward to one of Sue's hamburgers," Tex said, licking his lips as he, Joe, Ira and Franklin exited the bus.

"Since Camp Tarawa is located on a cattle ranch, military logic would dictate that all we get to eat is mutton SOS," Joe commented.

"That ain't all we get," Tex disagreed. "Don't forget about the mutton stew and spaghetti with mutton meatballs we sometimes get. But you know, Joe, that 'military logic' is an oxymoron."

"I've ate so damn much mutton that I'm beginin' to bleat like a sheep," Franklin joked.

"I heard," Ira said, changing the subject, "that Sue grinds up the whole cow for her hamburgers, sirloin, ribeye and all."

"Could be," Tex agreed, "they sure are good."

Observing that Sousley was plodding sullenly along, Joe asked, "Say, Franklin," what's goin' on with you?"

"Yeah, you ain't said a word since we left camp. What's up?"

"Aw, nothin'. Leave me alone."

"Come on, let's have it. You're lookin' about as sour as Hayes."

"Go to hell," Ira growled.

"I saw your face fall over that letter yesterday. Bad news from your mother?" Joe was concerned about his friend.

"No," Franklin said, hesitantly. "It's my girl back home, Marian."

"Get a 'Dear John' did you?" Tex asked, trying not to smile.

"Not exactly, we just had a little misunderstanding. It's hard to carry on a romance by letter, you know."

"Ain't that the truth," Joe agreed.

The men walked in silence for a few steps before Franklin blurted out,

"I think she just fell in love with that dress blue uniform. I wish I hadn't worn that damned thing home."[26]

"Why you would have died seven deaths if you'd had to go home without that uniform," Ira exploded.

"Aw, go to hell."

Training continued into the fall. On November 22 after ten months in the Corps, Franklin Sousley was promoted to Private First Class (PFC). In a letter to his mother, he admitted his pride, but asked her not to tell anybody as he did not want it plastered all over the *Fleming Gazette* as he had seen done by some of his classmates.

As Christmas approached, Easy Company was settled enough into its routine that they got the day off to celebrate and were treated to a turkey dinner with, as Franklin wrote his mother, "all the assessories." He'd had a letter from his Aunt Florine saying that they'd had a big snow in Kentucky, so listening to Bing Crosby sing on the radio about a White Christmas made him more homesick than he'd been since boot camp. While they baked in the tropical sun, each man hoped that he'd be home for Christmas, white or not, in 1945.

Back in the routine after the day off, they may have realized that their training was complete; they'd assaulted "Island X" so many times that they could hit the beach, move inland and then turn left to take a mountain in their sleep. The high command hoped that the level of training would allow these men to perform their assignments by rote when all hell broke loose on the beach when they actually reached "Island X," wherever that might be.

On January 7, 1945, in the middle of the night for security, the Fifth Marine Division boarded a train and traveled back to Hilo. Standing in line waiting to board the USS *Missoula*, an attack transport ship, the usual rumors ran along the ranks. This time, though, no one doubted that this was the "real thing." Easy Company was on its way to war.

But not quite yet. A day was spent practicing loading into landing craft and assaulting a beach on the beautiful island of Maui. Then on January 10, the *Missoula* rounded Diamond Head and steamed into Pearl Harbor.

"My God, look at that," Joe exclaimed, standing at the rail, eyeing the vast armada of assembled war ships.

"This has got to be the whole damned Navy," Franklin said, awed by the array of transports, destroyers, cruisers, escorts, tankers and battleships.

"Hot scoop, guys," Tex said, joining the group. "We're gonna be here four days and each man is gonna get a day's liberty on shore. One-fourth of the Division's Marines get to go ashore each day!"[27]

"Yeah," Franklin scorned, "and the Easter Bunny is gonna bring everybody a hula girl."

For once, the scuttlebutt was correct – each company got a day of shore leave. "Where do we go?" Franklin asked walking down the gangway with his pals.

"Chinatown," the veteran Ira Hayes answered. "That's where the action is."

"I wanna see Waikiki Beach," Joe said.

"Well, you go right on," Tex advised. "You might as well take in the public library while you're out on such a wild spree."

"We only got a day, some choices have to be made," Gagnon suggested.

"Where are the girls?" Franklin wanted to know.

"Canal Street in Chinatown," Ira answered with authority.

All were disappointed when they discovered that the bars were closed, perhaps by arrangement with the brass. After several hours of aimless wandering in Honolulu's famous Chinatown, jostling among all the sailors and Marines crowding the streets and shops, the boys learned that they had little chance with what few females they did encounter. "Well, there's always the whorehouses," Ira offered.

"Where?"

The veteran Hayes took the lead. "Follow me, men," he ordered, turning a corner into Hotel Street, home to at least a dozen brothels.

"Are you kiddin' me?" Franklin asked, a look of disgust on his face. Across the street a line of perhaps 300 Marines and sailors stretched from the front door of a building down the street and around the corner out of sight.

"That's where the action is," Ira announced. "Let's go get in line."

"Not me!" Franklin announced. "No way."

"Me neither. There's a hamburger stand over there," Joe suggested pointing down the block.

"I saw a tattoo parlor back a few blocks. I think I'll go check that out."

"I'll go with you," Joe said. An hour later, young Franklin Sousley exited the building with a USMC globe, anchor and eagle emblem inked into his right arm.

"What do you wanna do now?" Joe inquired.

"You said you wanted to see Waikiki Beach," Franklin suggested, "let's go check it out." The pair walked to a city bus stop where they boarded a bus headed for downtown Honolulu. There they strolled along the famous strip of sand and eyeballed a few girls on the beach. "What's that pink building?" Franklin asked.

"I think that's the Royal Hawaiian Hotel," Joe guessed. "I heard the Navy's took it over for the submarine crews to party in when they come off a patrol."

"Maybe they'll let us stay there when we get back," Franklin hoped.

In a nearby curio shop, Franklin purchased a Zippo cigarette lighter and had it engraved with his name.[28] Back out on the street, they walked over to the beach where they observed the sun sinking toward the water. "We'd better get back to the ship," Joe reminded. "We've had an exciting liberty, wouldn't you say?"

Franklin considered his answer. "I'll certainly remember it for the rest of my life."

On January 22, the immense armada steamed past Diamond Head out into the vast Pacific. The rumors now did not even touch on if "this is it;" the true identity of "Island X" was the only topic of speculation. On the second day out, an hour after a sealed pouch had been transferred from another ship, the ship's loudspeaker once again blared, "All Marines below decks," indicating they were about to find out.

"OK, guys," Captain Severance said, his face set with grim determination. "This is our objective, Iwo Jima," he announced pulling back a canvas sheet covering a model of a pear shaped island. At the southwestern stem of the pear, a lump on the map indicated a mountain. "This is Green Beach," the Captain said, pointing to a stretch of sand on the eastern side of the island just north of the mountain. We'll be landing here and then, just as we've practiced, we'll move inland, turn left and take this dormant volcano, Mt. Suribachi. Now, the air forces have been bombarding this tiny little island since November and we'll get a few days of naval gunfire to soften it up even further when we get there." He moved back to let the men get a good look at the model. "It ain't gonna be easy, but we think we can take the place in four or five days.

"We're sailing to Saipan where we'll join up with the rest of VAC. All three divisions will be on the same tiny island, but we'll be fighting different battles. In fact, there'll be three battles going on. Our job, as I said, is to turn left and take Mt. Suribachi. The 28th's First Battalion will land on the same beach just before us. Their job is to move straight across the neck thus cutting Suribachi off from the rest of the island. Everybody else will hit the beaches northeast of us and turn right to take the remainder of the island. Our only D-Day assignment is move behind the First Battalion and maybe mop up anything they miss.

"Do not underestimate our enemy. They're tough, clever and determined fighters, and they know we're coming and they've had plenty of time to prepare. We've decimated the Jap Navy, so they know they have no hope of reinforcement or rescue,[29] so have no doubt that they're ready to fight to the death. In our favor, we're better trained, better equipped and while they do know we're coming, what they don't know is when. Also, there'll be a lot more of us; intelligence estimates about 22,000 Japs on the island, when we're all ashore, we'll number nearly 70,000.

"We'll be sailing for a few more days, so get all your gear in order. Sharpen your knives and bayonets and clean your rifles. I suggest you write a letter home. You can say that you're at sea headed for combat, but give no details. Do not mention the name of this ship or the name of any island. You might also say that you'll be pretty busy for the next few days, so they should understand if you're not able to write again for a while.

"It's a Jap island – although that's about to change – and they've designated it as a part of the home land. That means that we've gotta take Japanese soil, something that hasn't been done in 4000 years of Japan's history. Make no mistake, they will fight hard.

"Finally, remember that wars are not won by dying for your country, but making the enemy die for his. If these damned sons of Nippon are determined to die for their Emperor, I, for one, am willing to accommodate."

A great cheer went up from the men before they broke up for platoon level briefings. Second Platoon commander Lieutenant Pennell stood at the front of the compartment between two wall maps: one of the Pacific Ocean and another of Iwo Jima. "All right, men," he began, pointing to the map of the Pacific. "As you can see, the objective of our Pacific Campaign so far has been to gain bases close enough to Japan so that the fly-fly boys can bomb the home islands. As you may know, the Air Corps' B-29's are doing just that from bases here on Tinian and Saipan." He pointed out these spots on the map. Now, it's about 1200 miles from there to Japan." Tracing a line from Tinian to Japan with a pointer, he continued "and there ain't a damned thing between – except Iwo Jima." He slapped the spot on the map. "As you can see, Iwo is almost exactly half way."

"More importantly, there's three air fields and a radar station on this otherwise worthless island. The Jap planes based there can harass our bombers coming and going and the radar station allows them advance warning on the bombing. And finally, when it's in American hands, the B-29's will have an emergency landing strip when they're coming back shot up and we can base fighters there to escort the B-29's. So, you don't have to be no military expert to see that we have to have it and that the Japs are gonna do everything they can to keep it.

"We've got everything we need on this ship. There is no fresh water on Iwo, so we've brought plenty. There's also plenty of food, supplies, ammunition and cigarettes."

The discontented Gagnon leaned to Sousley and whispered, "I'll bet they brought plenty of bandages, plasma and grave markers, too."

"What's all these black dots on the map, sir" somebody asked, observing that the white map appeared nearly black with so many dots.

"Those are defensive sites; pillboxes, blockhouses, artillery emplacements and whatever else they can dream up. This map was made from aerial photographs, so we can pinpoint the Jap's defenses."

Ira Hayes let out a long low whistle. "And we're gonna land right under all those guns on that mountain. This is gonna be rough."

"One more thing," the Lieutenant said. "From now on, do not salute and do not call any officer 'sir.' You do not want to identify the officers to the enemy. Any other questions?"

"Sir," someone said, raising his hand. The military discipline drilled into these men was not easily dismissed.

"Do not call me 'sir'," Pennell reminded. "Just call me Ed or Pennell."

"Sorry, sir. I forgot."[30]

The *Missoula* was so crowded that the each man had to spend most of the time in his bunk lying with his rifle and pack on a sheet of canvas 18 inches below the one above. One just hoped nobody got seasick! Many squinted at the Red Cross-supplied novels in the dim light, but most just talked, tried to sleep or cleaned his rifle.

"Did you hear about the guy fallin' overboard?" Bill asked.

"No! Somebody went over the rail?"

"It happened during the exercise period this mornin'," Bill added.

"But we didn't stop," Franklin noted.

"Time and this armada wait for no man," Bill informed. "They signaled the next ship in line and I hear they just threw over a life preserver for him."[31] After a moment of silence, he added, "We've got to be on time for our date with Iwo Jima." The men fell silent for a time.

"Franklin," Joe asked, breaking the spell, "what's goin' on back in Kentucky?"

"Not much at this time of year. Tobacco's sold already and it's still too cold to break up ground for spring plantin'."

"Same in Wisconsin, but the cows still gotta be milked." he agreed. "What about your girl? What's her name? Mary Lou?"

"Marian," Franklin said. "Same there – nothin' goin' on. I ain't heard from her in two months. I don't want to talk about it." He wished he could at least turn away, but the cramped space offered no escape.

"Well," Joe said, "I wonder...."

"I do not want to talk about it," Franklin's voice was harsh. "Ain't you got other things to worry about?"

The fact that Joe did not bother to answer indicated that he did, indeed, have other things to think about. Combat was near.

On February 5, the armada arrived at the previously won island of Eniwetok, where it stopped for refueling. During the two-day hiatus, the men were allowed to swim in the lagoon. While the anxiety of pending combat lingered, it was a joy to get off the ship for even a short while.

Then the ships moved on to Saipan to rendezvous with another task force on February 11. The combination assembled the entire VAC at one location, evidence enough that the battle was eminent. Here Easy Company got a surprise: as they were to be the very point of the Spearhead, the first ten waves to hit the beach were transferred to smaller vessels the Navy called Landing Ship, Tanks (LST's) for the final leg to Iwo Jima. Easy Company would travel aboard the *USS Talladega*.

Although the LST's were much smaller than the transports, there was more room for each man and they could stay on deck during the day and stand at the rail at night. On the first evening as Tex, Franklin, Ira, Joe and L.B. stood awed by the phosphoresce in the ship's wake, the conversation turned to the possibility of getting killed. "Well, they might get you but they won't get me." Joe voiced the prevailing attitude.

"Sometimes I get the feelin' that none of us will make it," L.B. muttered.

"You guys knock it off," Tex commanded. "If your number is up, it's up. If it ain't, you'll be goin' home to your momma as soon as this is over.

Broodin' will do no good. Come on, Franklin, let's get away from these sad sacks."

The two men moved along the rail of the ship, slapping hands occasionally with friends along the line. Near the back of the ship, Franklin pulled up short. "What the hell is that?" he asked, pointing.

Tex followed the line of his finger to where a stainless steel trough welded perpendicular to the ship's rail sloped toward the water at a slight angle. On a wooden bench just above the trough sat two men, their pants around their ankles. Seawater gushing from a nozzle near the rail provided a continuous flushing action through the trough. "That, my son, is the Navy version of a good old-fashioned out-house," he informed.[32]

"You're kiddin' me?" Franklin was amazed.

"Nope. They build these tubs with only enough heads for the swabbie crew and the Marine officers. For the rest of us...." His voice tailed off as he nodded toward the make-shift facility.

Later that evening, the men had an opportunity to observe a sunset at sea on the Pacific Ocean. Franklin and Ira stood at the rail silently watching the orange ball of flame descend toward the water until it lingered a moment just touching the horizon. In another minute, the sun disappeared leaving only a pink and orange glow. "I've seen some beautiful sunsets in Kentucky but I never saw anything like that," Franklin observed, awe in his voice.

For once, Ira's grim mood was absent. "I've seen it before," he said, "sailing to Tarawa." After a moment, he added, "At sea, I saw it, but there ain't nothing like it in Arizona either."

Being aboard an LST offered another advantage that everybody considered a plus. In the bowels of the LST, they would load into amphibian tractors (amtracs) for the dash to the beach. The fully loaded amtracs would rumble down a ramp through a huge open door into the water, so the Marines would not have to descend the cargo nets.

After two days at Saipan, the LST's moved on to nearby Tinian where the men practiced landing one final time although they did not actually step onto the beach. While anchored at Tinian, the men could see the reason for their being here: the giant, bomb-laden B-29's lumbering off the runways headed for Japan. Their route was via Iwo Jima.

Chapter 13

Monday, February 19, 1945
D-Day at
Iwo Jima, Volcano Islands

G etting up at 03:00 was not really any problem as most of the Marines had been too keyed up for sleep anyway. A breakfast of steak and eggs was followed by an on-deck religious service and a final briefing. While they waited on deck, the gray sky gradually lightened to a pale blue. At 07:00 every gun on every ship in the vast armada arrayed around them suddenly began blazing away at the island which lay in the distance. Easy Company's men recognized the distinctive lump at its left end as the mountain they were to scale. Fighters and bombers roaring overhead contributed to the destruction being wreaked on the defensive positions and added their voices to the incredible loudness of war. Ten minutes later, the Marines, dressed in full battle gear, climbed ladders down into the bowels of the ship, loaded into the amtracs and waited some more. Although the mood was still casual, this waiting was made more difficult because each man knew that many of the 20 or so men packed in with him would be dead before the day was done. The suffocating fumes emitted by the amtracs' engines simply added to the misery.

"Somebody ain't got much of a sense of humor," Franklin observed, eyeing the words, "Too late to worry now," stenciled on the inside of the vehicle's ramp at the rear.

"Relax if you can," Pennell ordered. "We'll be in this boat for a while."

"I sure am glad we didn't have to climb down that net," Harlon said. "A man could get hurt fallin' from that thing." In view of the much worse danger looming, that comment brought a nervous giggle from those within hearing.

"That's good news and bad news," Ira opined. "Comin' here on this LST keeps us off the damned net, but it means that we're gonna be some of the first ashore."

"Hey Lieu… uh, Pennell," Franklin shouted, remembering how to address officers. "What wave are we in?"

The clatter of the amtrac's tracks on the metal ramp prevented an immediate answer. Franklin's watch read 07:25 as the amtrac waddled down the ramp and splashed into the blue water. "We'll have to form up and get our spot on the line of departure, so it'll still be a little while." Then the Lieutenant turned to Sousley. "In answer to your question, son, we're in the ninth wave. We'll hit the beach at 09:40."

Franklin turned to his buddy Joe. "This ain't nothing like February in Kentucky. Must be 70 degrees out this mornin'."

"This sure as hell ain't Kentucky. Welcome to winter in the north Pacific." Joe replied.

"A good day to die," somebody said, exhibiting a kind of bravado that wouldn't last much longer.

"Hey, Harlon, can you see anything?" Tex shouted to Block who was up front near the slits through which the machine guns fired.

"Naw, nothing but ships," he replied peering through the firing ports. "We're runnin' an obstacle course through all the Navy hardware floatin' around out here."

"Hey," somebody said, "Where's Gagnon?"

"The Captain made him the company runner," Pennell informed. Every man in the craft understood that the reason for the move was to remove the malcontent as a cog in Easy Company's combat machine. As a runner, Rene Gagnon would be attached to Company headquarters and thus not be involved in the Company's battle maneuvers.

As suddenly as the bombardment began, it ended leaving only the relatively quiet roar of the amtrac's engine. Franklin's watch read 08:35. "OK," Pennell shouted, "that means the first waves are passing the line of departure. Lock and load, we'll be goin' in pretty soon."

As the men checked their packs and equipment and shoved clips into their M1's, the mood in the craft turned serious. This, indeed, was "it." In a half-hour or so, the amtracs of the ninth wave would fan out along the line of departure and dash at full speed for the beach. Every man knew that when the ramp dropped, all hell would break loose and that shortly after that many of them would be dead. The cocksure "they can't hurt me" attitude began to give way to, "I hope they don't hurt me."

"You'll learn more in the first five minutes after we hit the beach than you've learned in a year of training," Ira informed. That news set grim determination in all who heard it.

At 09:10 the amtracs carrying the men of the ninth wave began their run to the beach. The next 30 minutes were a gut-wrenching hell as the tiny boat rolled and pitched over the waves. Fighting off seasickness at least took the occupants minds' off what was about to happen. Then the Marine Corps training began to take hold: each man looked at his buddy next to him and thought, if he can do it, so can I. At 09:42 – two minutes behind a timetable determined months ago – the nose of the amtrac scraped onto sand and the ramp dropped. Lieutenant Pennell's "Let's go," was totally unnecessary; each man instinctively lurched toward the surf with his rifle in his hands and his heart in his throat. Pennell stumbled just after he yelled so the entire 2nd platoon scrambled over his back in the rush to get out of the landing craft. Two surprises waited: no one was shooting and the beach "sand" was a coarse black volcanic ash similar to what they'd seen at Camp Tarawa. All around, men and machines struggled to reach the plateau beyond the 15-foot high terrace facing them just inland. Each step caused one's foot to sink ankle-deep in the ash making walking difficult and running impossible. The sheer number of Marines crowding the beach also caused difficulty of forward movement.

"Why ain't they shootin' at us?" Franklin wondered.

"Maybe the Air Corps poundin' and the naval bombardment killed 'em all." Tex opined.

"They tried to push us back into the water at Bougainville," Ira said. "If they couldn't do it there, they can't do it here, so maybe they're tryin' something new."

"If they ain't dead, they're too stunned to fight, I'll bet," Joe said optimistically.

As if in answer to the comment, suddenly all manner of gunfire opened up, accurately aimed at the men on the beach. Rifle fire, machine gun bullets, mortar shells and large and medium caliber artillery shells fired from protected, and in some cases invisible, locations raked the packed beach. As Pennell's platoon dove to the ground, Ira observed, "I think I'm beginnin' to see the Japs' strategy. They waited until we're packed on the beach so they'd have better targets." These men had been in combat less than Ira's predicted five minutes when they first heard the sickening 'thud' of bullets impacting flesh and bone and the anguished screams of horribly mangled men.

Franklin looked behind him to see more amtrac's coming in and more men crowding onto the already packed beach. Perhaps due to their push, perhaps due to training, he crawled forward thinking about how silly he'd been in believing that the infiltration course was an accurate simulation of real combat. As he inched forward, he saw a Marine lying in one of the many shell holes the naval bombardment had created. "Hey, Mac" he said, "you'd better get a move on." Getting no response, he nudged the man before he noticed that the entire back of the man's head was missing. Everything seemed to stop as Franklin sank to the ground. In total silence, despite the deafening noise, he stared at the blood stained ground and the flecks of black ash peppering the man's exposed brain. He was still vomiting when Ira Hayes crawled in beside him.

"Would ya look at that," Ira said, pointing to the left. If the veteran even noticed the dead man's mangled body sharing their shell hole, he ignored it.

Franklin pulled his face from the ground to look where Ira indicated. There, amid the bullets and shells, Sergeant Mike Strank sat fully upright on the ground, calmly dumping sand from his boot. Strank was casually looking around as if he was back watching the girls on Waikiki Beach.[33] "A cool customer, ain't he?" Ira observed as Joe and Tex joined them in the shell hole at the base of the terrace.

Suddenly Mike was standing above them. "Let's go," he shouted. "We gotta get off this beach. If we're gonna win this war, the first thing we gotta do is get up this little hill." He started running up the terrace, his movements made almost comic by the difficulty of lifting his feet in the ash. Sustained effort got him to the level ground atop the terrace. "Come on!" he shouted, waving for his men to follow.

The "if he can do it, so can I" mentality kicked in. The rest of the men scrambled up the incline, helping one another when necessary. The plain above was also pock marked from the bombardment and the artillery shells raining down from Mt. Suribachi. On level ground now, the men dove into a vacant hole.

Mike had raced ahead to the next hole, moving to the west, across the island's slender neck. There he waited for the others. "Don't bunch up in one hole," he commanded. The Japs have got all this registered so they can drop a mortar shell anywhere they want. Five or six of us in one place makes a dandy target."

Don Ruhl jumped into the hole with Ira and Franklin, a cloth cap on his head. He was also minus his backpack and most of the rest of his equipment. "Where's your gear?" Franklin asked.

"Why carry all that stuff around? I can just pick up anything I need." His expansive gesture indicated that he had a point – the surrounding area was already littered with dead Marines and their equipment.

Pennell came into the area. "They landed us in the wrong place," he announced.[34] "You guys stay put while I figure out where we're supposed to be." There was concern in his voice but no panic.

"If we're staying here, I'm diggin' in," Franklin said. Much to Ira's amusement, he started trying to expel the sand only to find that with each scoop, more flowed in than he threw out. "Kinda reminds me of tryin' to dig a hole in a bushel of shelled corn."

"I'm beginnin' to understand how the proverbial fish in a barrel must feel," Tex commented, gesturing to indicate the bullets flying all around.

"Anybody seen a Jap?" Joe asked.

Everyone paused. Nobody had thought about it but somebody had to be firing all the missiles flying at them. Not one of the men had seen even a single enemy soldier.

"I ain't seen none," Franklin said, "but I've heard 'em."

"How's that?" Joe asked.

"I heard 'em jabberin' in the ground underneath me a couple of holes back."

"That's right," Mike said, "they're in caves and tunnels and spider traps all over the place. Most of these defensive sites seem to be reinforced with concrete, too."

"Didn't the bombardment take any of 'em out?" Franklin was one of those who thought nothing could survive the pounding the Navy had given the tiny island.

"Oh, it took out some," Mike observed, "but there' still plenty left and we're gonna have to root 'em out one by one."

Lieutenant Pennell crawled back in with them. "I've found the rest of the Company. We need to be over there." He pointed to a spot of elevated ground to their west across the island's neck. "Let's go."

"Remember," Mike ordered, "don't bunch up."

Moving west, Franklin ran past a couple of structures that appeared to be simple mounds of dirt. He would have taken them for just that but for small white flags fluttering in the breeze. The First Battalion, crossing before them, had placed a flag to indicate that this pillbox had been neutralized.

Franklin and Ira ran to the next hole in the indicated direction. In it, they found another Marine with his lower jaw shot away. Franklin saw "help me" in his eyes. Beside him lay a dead Marine who had died in the act of trying to stuff his cascading intestines back into his abdominal cavity. "Corpsman!" Franklin screamed. Before the word was out of his mouth, "Doc" Bradley dove in the hole. Just as at Camp Tarawa, Bradley seemed to be everywhere.

"I'll take care of him," Doc said. "You guys just go on about your business."

In the next hole, Franklin said, "You gotta admire those Corpsmen. They're out here getting shot as just like us, but don't carry a weapon to fight back."

"What good has that weapon done you?" Ira asked. "Have you fired a shot?"

Franklin was embarrassed to admit that he had not even thought about firing his BAR. "Hayes, Sousley. Over here." Strank's voice rose above the din. "Get over here on the double!"

The pair stood to locate Sergeant Strank waving to them from the elevated location Pennell had indicated earlier. Reaching it, they were relieved to find that enemy fire was light. "They're shootin' at somebody else right now. Dig in and stay put," Strank ordered.

The ground here was more solid and soon Ira and Franklin were in a hole deep enough to provide relative security. Franklin had an opportunity to scrutinize Mt. Suribachi at a range of about 400 yards. "It don't look much like the ones we climbed on Hawaii, does it?"

"The view's more interesting back this way," Ira said.

Franklin turned to follow his buddy's gaze back to Green Beach. Despite the Marines – whole, dead and wounded – packed on the beach, landing craft were still coming in. Some brought more men and some brought supplies but all went back out carrying wounded. Some dead were lined on the sand covered with ponchos, other bodies rolled in the surf.

"Hey Chief," Bill yelled, "how's this stack up against Bougainville?"

"Rougher," Ira said, "but we had malaria and dysentery in addition to Japs to contend with there. At least we ain't got diseases here."

"Hurmp!" Franklin exclaimed. "That's no surprise 'cause any self-respecting germ would have sense enough to steer clear of this place."

After a couple of hours, Strank summoned from behind a huge rock about 10 yards closer to the base of the mountain. Arriving, they found the rest of the squad huddled in the shelter of the rock. "All right, it's time to start fighting back," Strank said. "If we have to take this island away from the Japs one pillbox at a time, that's just how we'll do it. That innocent looking mound of dirt straight ahead is a pillbox. If you look close, you'll see the machine gun firing ports on each side about four inches above the ground."

"Hey," Joe said, there's one of our white flags there. They already took it."

"Like I been tellin' ya," Mike said, "the Japs are pretty clever. "All these fortifications are connected by tunnels so when we kill one bunch, another just comes in to take their place. Now, Block, you take your fire team to the left; Russell, you take the right. We'll do it just the same as in training. Stay of the edge of their range of fire and watch for my signals. Let's go."

Harlon led Franklin, Ira, Lewis and Bill to a shell hole on the left while Dayton Russell led his fire team in the opposite direction. "Just like at San Clemente," Harlon instructed. "When I say, Franklin you pepper the firing slit on this side with your BAR. Lewis, you fire too. Both of you put your rounds right through the slit if you can. Chief, when they run out of ammo, you and Bill take up the slack while they reload." Corporal Block turned to watch for signals from Strank. When it came, he screamed "Fire!"

Although he could not see – and had not seen – any Japanese, Franklin found a sense of satisfaction in pulling the trigger of his weapon and feeling the familiar recoil. At the edge of the hole, he took aim at the narrow slit and held the trigger down. His BAR responded with its distinctive and gratifying chatter until the clip was empty. When he dropped back to reload, his mates fired their M1's.

"Good job, guys," Harlon said when the M1 clips were empty. "Russell got closer while we kept their heads down. Now we're gonna move while Russell covers us." At the signal from Strank, Harlon shouted, "Let's go" and the fire team sprang into motion. Twenty feet closer to the pillbox, they plunged into another hole. This process was repeated until Block's team arrived near the side of the pillbox. Chief Hayes pulled the pin on a grenade as he crawled to the mound. Releasing the pin when he was in position, he tossed the deadly missile through the firing port and ducked into a hole.

Immediately, excited Japanese voices were heard inside the fortification. An instant before the grenade exploded, the entrance to the pillbox, a steel door at the back, flew open and a lone Japanese soldier exited on the run. Franklin cut him down with a short burst from his BAR as the grenade finished off the other occupants. "That's the way it's done," Harlon said. "Strank's located the next one, let's move on."

As they moved forward, a racket to the rear caused everyone to look back. Another fire team was assaulting the pillbox they'd just cleaned out. "Damn," Bill said, "didn't we just kill those bastards?"

Still moving west, the squad encountered a series of Japanese antitank ditches that provided perfect cover. The First Battalion had taken out defenders moving through these same ditches earlier as witnessed by the wounded Marines along the way. Swathed in bloody bandages, these men had been treated by the corpsmen and were awaiting evacuation. Franklin tried not to make eye contact because they reminded him that he could join their ranks at any minute. He could not help but notice, however, that many of them had an "M" painted in blood on their forehead. The corpsmen marked them when they administered morphine.[35]

Two pillboxes later, dusk was setting in when Mike's squad reached the defensive perimeter established by the First Battalion. Franklin and Ira hunkered down behind a rock and lit their first cigarettes since landing. Before they finished smoking, they were ordered to gather for a platoon meeting. Franklin was saddened to note some missing men. "We've learned a few things today," Pennell began, "so tomorrow we'll use some new tactics. We'll attack in the same way, but we're gonna use the flame throwers more. When we get close enough, rather than try to toss in a grenade, we'll just let the flame throwers fry 'em. More importantly, since they've got all their positions connected by underground tunnels, once we neutralize a pillbox, or tank trap, we'll blow it up so they can't use it again. The Sergeants will show you where to dig in. Before you 'button up' for the night make sure you define your fields of fire. The brass thinks we'll get a few 'banzai' charges tonight and you can bet your ass the sneaky little bastards will be trying to slip into your foxhole with you. We're in reserve tomorrow, so just keep your heads down until further notice."

Ira and Franklin scooped out a hole in their assigned spot. "You hungry?" Ira asked.

"I don't know," Franklin replied absent-mindedly running his finger through a bullet hole in his trousers. "I've been too busy to notice." Neither took any note that they'd eaten nothing since their early breakfast.

Ira tossed him a K-ration carton. "You're the only guy in the whole Corps that likes these things," he teased, lighting a cigarette.

"This place sure does stink," Franklin said, tearing into the cardboard carton.

"I heard somebody say that Iwo Jima means 'sulfur island' in Japanese."

"Smells like rotten eggs to me," the farm boy said.

"General Sherman missed a trick on this place," Joe Senoracke commented from the next hole.

"Huh?"

"Well, you know that in the Civil War, General Sherman said, 'War is hell.' This place would be hell even without no war."

"If the bullets bouncing off these rocks ain't enough to spoil your appetite, the smell of the place is." Franklin said as he broke the metal key from the bottom of the tin can, inserted the tip of the sealing strip in the key's slot and rolled the key around the can, winding the metal strip into a tight coil around the key thus unsealing the lid. Inside was some kind of gooey pork paste.

Ira pushed the fiery end of his cigarette into the sand. "Who said this place was worthless? It's the world's largest outdoor ash tray." Turning up his nose at Franklin's meal, he added, "the odor of that stuff makes me sick enough."

"You know what?" Franklin wondered. "A man could push this can down in the sand, warm as it is, and have him a nice hot meal." He shoveled a spoonful of the paste in his mouth.

"That'll probably feel good later," Ira suggested, shoving his fingers into the hot sand. "The air's gettin' colder already. Did you hear what the Lieutenant said about banzai charges?"

"Yep. I've seen 'em in the movies," Franklin said as he and Ira enlarged their foxhole, "but it never made no sense to me."

"Well, I've seen 'em first hand. You don't understand it 'cause you ain't a Jap," Ira laconically noted. "If they're gonna die for the Emperor anyway, maybe they just figure that's a simple way to get it over with."

Impressed once again that his partner was a veteran, Franklin asked, "What about the infiltrators?"

"Huh!" Ira snorted. "On Bougainville, the sneaky bastards would crawl into a fox hole and feel around for a warm body."

"What? Why?"

"The cold-hearted sons of bitches didn't want to waste their time cuttin' a corpse's throat."

"Well, if one of them lemon-colored bastards should happen to catch me asleep – which is highly unlikely – and put a hand on me, he'll just draw back a bloody stub."

Darkness was setting in as the unlikely buddies settled down for the night. "I'll take the first watch," Ira offered.

"OK," Franklin said, trying to find a way to comfortably position himself in the hole they'd fashioned. Although it was not part of the formal training, he obeyed a tip the veterans had taught him as he positioned the BAR's stock between his legs to protect his most valuable assets. He closed his eyes for a moment and realized that he was bone weary. With his eyes closed, he fingered the small Bible in his breast pocket. Even though he did not have time to read it, knowing that it was there provided some small comfort. "What a day!"

"You're alive ain't you?" Ira was as humorless as usual. "That's more than a lot of Marines can say."

Franklin did see humor in that comment. "A lot of dead Japs can't say it, either."

Darkness fell suddenly, bringing a drop in the air temperature. In the dark, the ships offshore turned on searchlights to illuminate the island and started firing star shells. These phosphoric rounds burst with a "poof" high in the air, releasing a flare on a parachute. Descending slowly while drifting with the breeze, the flares cast an eerie yellow light over a wide area.[36] As the bright lights swayed back and forth suspended from their parachutes, they created moving shadow patterns that terrified the exhausted Marines. In those shadows, the American boys saw Japanese soldiers creeping in from every direction. Sometimes that really was what they saw, sometimes it was just imagination but, in either case, they fired at what they saw. With that racket and artillery booming, Franklin soon gave up on getting any sleep. Sitting with his back against the wall of dirt, he lit a cigarette as he spoke to his friend. "The First Division got all the way across, didn't they?"

"Sure," Ira replied. "You can see the western beach over there past their positions."

"Well, then. I don't know how many Japs are in that mountain, but we've got 'em cut off, ain't we?"

"That's right. Just accordin' to the plan."

Franklin reflected, eyeing Suribachi, illuminated by the searchlights. Occasionally a flash on the slope could be seen as an artillery piece embedded in the mountainside fired. With each flash, the thought that the mountain was winking at him went through the Kentucky boy's mind. "That mountain seems evil," he mused.

"It ain't the mountain that's evil," Ira responded, "it's those bastards in it."

Franklin let that sink in. "Well, I can't see them, but I can see the mountain."

"You might not see them, but they're there and you can bet they see us."

"Hey, Sousley!" came from the next foxhole in line.

"Yeah?"

"Did you hear about Ruhl?" Franklin recognized the inquiring voice as Tex Stanton's.

"Nope. Did he buy the farm?" The phrase "buy the farm" had a double meaning: in one sense, it simply meant "got killed," but as most of the men had a $10,000 GI life insurance policy, if one was killed in battle, the money would go home to his parents who could use the money to literally "buy the farm."

"Far from it. They were moving on a pillbox when a First Battalion squad flushed the eight Jap occupants. Ruhl and Lieutenant Wells happened to be in the right place when the Japs made a break. Wells got five of 'em with his Thompson, Ruhl shot two and bayoneted the other."[37] The disembodied voice was laced with awe.

"Well, I reckon nobody will fuss at him any more about not wearin' a helmet, then."

"Knock off the chatter," Sergeant Strank's voice commanded. "No use givin' our position away. Pay attention to what you're out here for. Get some sleep if you can."

"Like they don't know we're here," Ira grumbled.

Not much sleep was had by any Americans on Iwo Jima that first night. If the noise didn't keep one awake, the fear of banzai charges and infiltrators did. No banzai charges occurred anywhere on the island that night as the Japanese were trying to conserve their resources. As those who had earlier prayed for darkness changed their request to daylight, the long night slowly gave way to dawn.

Daylight on February 20, D-day + 1 in assault parlance, brought little relief, but it did bring a driving rain, a booming naval bombardment and an air strike. In reserve, Easy Company's men huddled and shivered beneath their ponchos as they waited to be ordered into action. They may have shivered more had they known that the first day's casualties amounted to some 2,500 Marines killed, wounded and missing.

"Wonder why they didn't treat us to one of those banzai charges," Franklin wondered aloud.

"I guess they ain't ready to die yet," Ira remarked. "I wish they had of charged us. The sooner we kill 'em all, the sooner we'll get off this miserable piece of rock."

The men of Easy Company merely sat and watched as units on both sides of them moved to the attack. In mid-morning, they were ordered to spread some white sheets in advance of their position to mark the line for air attacks. Later, they moved back to the east over the ground they'd bled for the previous day. Called to a halt on a patch of high ground, they spread out into existing shell holes. This vantage point provided an opportunity to observe the state of the landing beaches.

"Wow, what a mess," Franklin commented, observing the wrecked amtracs, jeeps, guns and tanks strewn all over the beach.

"There's an even bigger mess," Ira said, pointing to the line of bodies covered with ponchos. Behind them were wounded waiting for evacuation. As they watched, mortar and artillery shells fell among the dead and wounded, sometimes lifting mangled bodies high into the air.

"You know," Tex observed, "there ain't nowhere on this whole island a man is safe."

"Yep," Franklin agreed. "Who gets hit and who don't is just a matter of chance."

"It's like tryin' to sit out in the rain without gettin' wet," Ira observed. Everybody fell silent as the truth of that observation soaked in.

"Look! There's tanks over there!" Joe shouted, pointing behind them. "Why are they just sittin' there?" These men had no way of knowing that while the tanks had successfully landed, they were short of fuel and ammunition.

At that moment, the Second Battalion's Commander, Lieutenant Colonel Chandler Johnson walked by, striding confidently among the singing bullets as if out for a stroll, a cloth hat on his head.

"Hey, Colonel," somebody yelled, "How's it goin'?"

"Rougher'n hell, I'd say," he answered. "Who's in charge here?"

"If he ain't careful," Franklin whispered in Ira's ear, "somebody might mistake him for Ruhl. They're the only two Marines on this island not wearin' a helmet."

Despite the injunction not to identify officers, Colonel Johnson left no doubt that he was in command. The boys could not hear, but got the impression that he was chewing out Captain Severance and the platoon leaders for not saluting.[38] When the conference ended, Lieutenant Pennell informed, "The Colonel said the engineers found a two-inch cable running north from the mountain this morning. They cut it, so the bastards are isolated. Saddle up, we're gonna go get 'em."

The company moved south toward Suribachi which was still trembling under the pounding it had taken from ships and air assaults. The day's assault had moved the front lines about 200 yards closer to the base of the mountain. In position near the center of Iwo's slender neck, Easy

Company replaced a company who had participated in the day's battle. "Ain't too many of 'em left, is there?" Franklin asked, rhetorically as the decimated company crawled away.

"We've been shot to hell," one of the retiring men commented in answer to the unspoken question in Easy Company's men's eyes. At that moment, a mortar shell landed in a hole twenty yards from where Franklin and Ira huddled. The two occupants were blown into the air, arms and legs going one way while torsos, twisting like rag dolls, went another before falling back to earth.

"Look over there, boys," Pennell said, crawling into the hole with Franklin and Ira. "There's some wounded men out there!" He pointed toward the mountain to where five men lay in a heap about 50 yards away. One of the men was waving a weak arm in the air. "We gotta rescue them!" Despite the withering machine gun fire, he stood looking around. Back to the north, a couple of tanks, finally in action, lumbered toward them. Crouching low, Pennell ran to the nearest tank. Grabbing the handset that allowed communication with the tank's commander, he guided the machine back to the squad's location. "Come on," he shouted to Ira, Franklin, Harlon and Mike. These five men ran, some of the time in the lee of the tank, to where they could reach the wounded. The tank provided cover while they pulled the wounded Marines to a safer location.[39]

As darkness settled in, the men were ordered to "button up" for the night, now about 200 yards from the numerous fortifications at the base of Suribachi. Some 2000 Marines who had attacked that morning had become casualties and no longer needed to worry about tomorrow's attack. Easy Company had been relatively lucky so far with only two killed and thirty wounded. For those who remained alive and whole, Mike Strank advised, "Get some sleep if you can. It's our turn at bat tomorrow." Their good luck would not hold.

"I hope the bastards charge us tonight," Franklin said, positioning his BAR to cover his assigned field of fire.

"Them banzai charges are kinda scary," Ira informed, "but they give you a good chance to dispatch a bunch of 'em. I doubt they will, though. Looks like they've learned better."

Franklin leaned his back against the dirt. Bone weary, he realized that he'd had virtually no sleep in the last 48 hours. "I'll take the first watch," Ira offered. Despite the continual cacophony, the Kentucky boy was soon asleep.

The sky was illuminated by the star shells when Ira woke him a few hours later. "Look," the Indian said, pointing toward the base of Suribachi. The glare of an offshore destroyer's searchlight had illuminated a group of Japanese soldiers gathered perhaps with the intent of a banzai charge. The navy ship deprived them of the opportunity, however. Franklin and Ira watched in fascination as the destroyer's guns decimated the enemy.

While both were awake, a spectacular explosion occurred on the beach behind them. "What the hell was that?" Franklin wondered as they both spun around to see the show.

"Ammo dump," Ira replied. "Maybe one of those sneaky infiltrators got to it."

"Hell of a fireworks display. Could have been an artillery shell," Franklin guessed.

"Whatever," Ira muttered as he slid down in the hole. "Your turn," he said, asleep almost before the words were out. Franklin spent the remainder of the night huddled against the rain under the eerie light of star shells. Sometime during his vigil, he saw a man moving between him and Suribachi. As the Marines had been told not to move around, he knew it had to be an infiltrator. "Tree!" he shouted.

An American would have answered "Oak" or "Maple." The figure made no answer as he moved closer. "Car!" Sousley yelled, expecting to hear "Chevy" or "Ford."

He heard no response as the stranger moved to within 20 yards of his position. Franklin squeezed off a short burst with his BAR. The man went down. "What's goin' on?" Ira asked, rousing.

"I shot somebody. It might have been a Marine," Franklin was upset. Then, from where the man had fallen, they heard some shouting in Japanese. "The bastard's giving our position," Ira exclaimed, pulling the pin on a grenade. After the grenade exploded near the source of the sound, the talking ceased. Hayes slumped back into the hole and was soon again asleep.

Sometime during the night, reviewing the horrors he'd witnessed, the thought crossed Franklin's mind that he'd probably be willing to give up an arm or a leg if the sacrifice would get him off this island alive. He was glad when the dawn came, dispelling such ideas. Harlon slid into the hole with him and Ira.

"Did you hear about Ruhl?" That seemed to be the first question every morning.

"What now?"

"Oh, not much. He just killed the occupants of an artillery emplacement and then spent the night in there to make sure the Nips didn't reoccupy it. I hear he even went explorin' in some of the underground tunnels." Harlon shook his head.

"No kiddin'? What did he find?"

"Oh, he come out of there with a few Jap trinkets and a poster."

"Poster?"

"Yeah. It was printed in Japanese, of course. When intelligence translated it, it turned out to be a creed for the Jap soldiers. Each one swears to kill 10 of us before we get him."

"He also found out it was hotter'n hell down in there. He said he didn't see how the Japs could stand to stay in those underground rooms where the temperature must be 120 degrees."

"Well, I got no sympathy for 'em." Harlon spoke for all the men.

"Ruhl's gonna get himself killed," Franklin said, missing the irony of the fact that the same could happen to any of them at any moment.

"There's gonna be an artillery barrage at 08:00." Harlon informed. "That'll be followed by an air strike. The Colonel told 'em to fire all the rounds they got because there ain't gonna be any room for shells between us and them once we get over to the base of the mountain. Then we'll attack at 08:25."

"What about the Navy?" Franklin asked.

"Can't you hear 'em?" They're blasting an attack path for the other guys attacking to the north.

When the artillery barrage ended, carrier planes swooped in blasting the mountain with bombs and napalm. By the time the planes disappeared over the sea, it seemed the entire island was shaking. A relative quiet descended, portending the time for attack. Franklin stood up looking to the rear. "Where's the tanks?" he wondered. "We ain't gonna attack without tank support, are we?"

Men near both the east and west beaches started moving toward the mountain. Ira stood beside Franklin, waiting. On their right, Lieutenant Wells stood and looked around for a moment. Then, without a word, he started running to the south. His 3rd platoon followed, ducking from shell hole to shell hole as they advanced into the maelstrom.

"Let's go, boys," Pennell shouted following Wells' example. Franklin, Ira and the rest of the 2nd platoon ran toward the mountain's base.

Almost immediately, the defenders reacted. Suddenly the air was filled with deadly missiles and the men of Wells' platoon, in the lead, started falling. Wells, Henry Hansen and Don Ruhl were first to reach a blockhouse at the base of Suribachi. The trio encountered some enemy soldiers in a trench behind the blockhouse. As Ruhl and Hansen fired at these, a satchel charge landed on the ground nearby. Ruhl yelled, "Look out, Hank" as he dove on the charge just as it exploded. The next time anyone asked, "Did you hear about Ruhl," it would be about his having earned the Medal of Honor for sacrificing his life to save a comrade.[40]

As Pennell's platoon moved forward, Ira and Franklin ran in a zig-zag from one hole to the next. Japanese soldiers usually tapped a grenade on their helmet as was required to start the fuse of that weapon. On one occasion a Japanese soldier wearing no helmet ran toward them. Just as the man tapped a grenade on his head, Ira dropped him with a single shot from his M1. Before he fell, he threw the missile into the hole with the Marines. Ira and Franklin stared at the object as if hypnotized. When the grenade did not explode, Franklin said, "I guess his head wasn't hard enough."

"Guess not," Ira replied shoving a fresh clip into his rifle. "And a good thing, too. I'd hate to see you get killed by a dead Jap."

In the next hole over, Tex Stanton was not so lucky. A mortar round fell in his hole and blasted him high into the air. He fell to earth badly burned, but was able stay on the field.

Harlon Block gestured for the fire team to assemble. Ira, Franklin, Lewis and Bill all dove into the same hole. This near the base of the mountain, they could see, for the first time, the effects of the naval and artillery fire. Many of the defensive sites were blasted into bits, but many were still active, too. "There's a flame-thrower team over there," Block said. "Franklin, you and Ira move up this side; Lewis, you and Bill come with me. We'll take out this pillbox just like the others."

When the men were in position, Franklin peppered the pillbox's firing port while the others moved. When Ira had fired his clip, the other team fired while Ira and Franklin advanced. In a few minutes the flame-thrower team was close enough to unleash its stream of flaming napalm on the pillbox. "I love the smell of roasted Jap," Ira cracked as a demolitions team prepared to blow the pillbox to prevent further use.

Just as Lieutenant Pennell joined the action, a mortar whizzed nearby. All dove to the ground; the round landed between Pennell's legs, blowing off his left heel, part of his right buttock and peppering him with shrapnel. The same round killed Lewis Hesse. A few holes over, a machine gun bullet wounded Dick Mathewson, so Strank's squad had suffered two casualties in as many minutes. Ed Pennell would survive, and earn a Navy Cross, but his war was over. Platoon Sergeant Joe McGarvey took over command of 2nd platoon.[41]

Lieutenant Keith Wells of the 3rd platoon was wounded in the legs in the same attack that killed Don Ruhl. After Doc Bradley treated him and administered morphine, Wells refused to leave the field. His platoon had lost one-third of its men since the attack began, so Wells felt that every man counted. Hence, he stayed, continuing to direct his men toward the mountain. Later, though, his activity re-opened his wounds and he collapsed on the ground. Bradley gave him another shot of morphine. Then the Pharmacist's mate, Second Class ordered the Lieutenant to the rear. When Wells reluctantly complied and turned his command over to Platoon Sergeant "Boots" Thomas, all three of Easy's platoon leaders were out, Lieutenant Stoddard of the 1st having been hit and evacuated earlier in the day. Wells would also be awarded a Navy Cross for his heroics.[42]

Mike Strank gathered his squad. "Hold up, men," he said. "Smoke 'em if you got 'em," he advised as the weary men fell to the ground. "Navy observation planes have spotted some Japs massing in front of us and the carrier planes are on the way." The boys watched in fascination as the planes strafed and bombed the would-be bonsai chargers. When the planes flew away, Strank jumped to his feet. "Come on! Let's show these sonsabitches what a real bonsai charge looks like," he shouted, running forward.[43] With a Pima war whoop Ira stood and ran. Franklin let out a scream that would have made his Cherokee ancestors proud as he followed. Harlon and what was left of the squad charged into the fray.

Aided by the finally-arrived tanks and Easy's mortar and artillery sections, the company was at the base of Suribachi as dusk set in. The gains had been costly: the Americans had sustained nearly 5400 casualties in three days fighting. On balance, Easy Company had knocked out more than fifty defensive sites. How many Japanese had been killed is unknown as many were roasted or buried in their underground emplacements. "We gotta move around to the left," Sgt. McGarvey ordered. "There's some caves around there we're to take out. We'll move up on 'em, toss in a few grenades and then barbeque 'em before the demolition boys blow the entrance with a charge."

"That ought to kill 'em pretty dead," Franklin joked.

"They can't get too dead for me," Ira muttered, moving to the attack.

The cave entrances stretched around the eastern face of the mountain's base. When darkness finally bought D + 2's activities to a halt, Easy Company was in a bad spot, isolated along a ledge about 50 feet above the surf crashing into the rocky shore. Cries of "Corpsman" came from wounded who could not be reached and the entire company was low on food and ammunition. The continuing cold rain did not improve anyone's spirits.

"Can't dig into this rock," Ira said, striking the volcanic surface with his entrenching tool.

"Diggin' in won't matter none when they start rollin' grenades down on us," Franklin commented, turning to look up the face of Suribachi.

"You got anything to eat?" Ira inquired, dropping to a sitting position.

"Half a D ration chocolate bar," Franklin replied, handing it to his pal. Ira broke off a small chunk and handed the remainder back as the evening's first star shell burst above them.

Suddenly every ship in the fleet snapped on its searchlights, the shafts of light pointing skyward. "Look," Franklin cried as one of the lights speared a plane bearing the "meatball" insignia of the Rising Sun. "They're Japs!"

"Oh, hell," Ira shouted. "They're gonna strafe us."

But no. The planes were interested in the American ships. The Marines ashore observed in horrified fascination as the Japanese planes nosed over, each headed for a ship. The air was filled with criss-crossing red tracers as the fleet's anti-aircraft batteries sought the enemy planes. Many were blasted from the sky, but some got through to plunge into a ship. When the bomb-laden plane impacted the ship, a massive explosion resulted. The Japanese called these suicide pilots *kamikaze*.

The night was long, wet and cold, but many Marines got the first sleep they'd had on Iwo Jima, sleeping, despite the cacophony and light, from sheer exhaustion. The dawn of February 22, D + 3, brought heavier rain and colder temperatures. These elements were enhanced by an increased wind howling from the northwest; that prevailing wind being the reason the eastern beaches had been selected for the landings. Perched on a rocky ledge high above the rocky shore at the base of the mountain, the men of Easy Company's 2nd platoon were in a position to observe the conditions on Green Beach where they'd landed what seemed like months ago.

"They're gonna have a time landin' any supplies today," Franklin opined. "Look at that surf!"

"I hope they bring us somethin' to eat," Ira commented.

"And some ammo and grenades."

"And water!" This last came from both in unison.

A roar from the sky caused both men to look up. A Navy Corsair making a bombing run on Suribachi caught their attention. As they sat helplessly, the plane turned toward them.

"Oh, hell," Ira said, "he thinks we're Japs."

Franklin waved his arms above his head and screamed, "We're Americans." The shouts and gestures were to no avail. As the sea-blue plane roared over them, they could see the bomb descending in a graceful arc. Fortunately, the missile fell short of their position.

"That's what they call 'friendly fire,' ain't it?" Franklin asked.

"An American bomb will kill you just as dead as a Jap one will," Mike Strank informed sliding to where his men huddled. "Captain's already yelling to HQ about it." He plunked himself down and gathered what was left of his squad. "All right. Today, we're gonna go on around the base of this mountain. Before the day is over, we'll have the whole damn thing surrounded. Intelligence says there's some more caves around this side and we'll take 'em out the same way: shoot at 'em, roast 'em and blast 'em shut. They also say to watch out for any Japs you see laying out in the open."

"They playin' 'possum?" Franklin asked.

"If that means actin' like they're dead, yes," Strank said, managing a smile. "Most times, they've got a grenade or a pistol close at hand. If you get close, they'll let you have it, so watch out. There's an amtrac comin' up now with supplies, so as soon as we get refitted, we'll move out."

With a fresh supply of rations, water, ammunition and grenades, they set out around the south side of Mt. Suribachi. Through the morning, they successfully took out all the caves they encountered. A little after noon, Strank called a halt on a wide flat plain. "Take a break," he said.

Franklin, Ira and Joe flopped to the sandy ground. "I'm hungry," Franklin announced, opening a K ration carton.

"I can remember when you didn't have no appetite," Ira said.

"A man can get used to anything," Joe said in Franklin's behalf.

"Listen," Franklin commanded with a shooing gesture. Leaning his ear to the ground, he said, "I hear Japs japperin' down there."

The others placed their ears to the ground. "I hear it too."

With his entrenching tool, Ira quietly scooped up some soil. At a depth of about two feet, he uncovered a wooden beam. Digging to the side of that, he soon broke through into an open space. "Gimme a grenade," he ordered.

Taking the "pineapple" Franklin handed him, he ordered, "You guys get over there." When everyone was at a safe distance, he pulled the pin, dropped the deadly missile in the hole he'd fashioned and ran. The resulting muffled explosion lifted a hunk of earth, sand and rock a foot in the air. When they returned to the spot, no sounds were to be heard below.

In mid-afternoon, they were ordered to retrace their steps back around to the north. By dusk, they'd returned to the morning's starting point. In the lull, Ira Hayes was playing around with his harmonica while he fashioned little mounds in the earth. "Looks like miniature graves," Franklin said.

"That's right," Hayes replied. "This one's for you, Sousley." He made a show of playing "Taps." "Just in case I ain't around when you get it."[44]

Buddy or not, Franklin was not pleased and frayed nerves came into play. He stepped over and kicked the mounds away. Ira stood, quickly drew his Ka Bar knife and lunged at Sousley.

"Knock it off," Strank commanded. "If you boys ain't had enough fightin', you'll get your fill tomorrow." Everyone turned to look at the Sergeant. "We're goin' up this hill in the morning."

Chapter 14

Friday, February 23, 1945
D-Day + 4 on
Iwo Jima, Volcano Islands

P oised at the base of Mt. Suribachi, Easy Company awoke to clearing skies. The sun made an appearance and although it soon ducked
behind the thinned overcast, the departure of the rain lifted everyone's
spirits. Early in the morning, a small patrol had discovered – amazingly –
no resistance as they climbed the mountain. When that news reached the
Company command post (CP), the order had come down from Lieutenant Colonel Johnson to "occupy and secure the summit" of the 550-foot
high mountain. In the military, as in most walks of life, the reward for a job
well done is often to be given more of the same kind of work. Accordingly,
the chore fell to Easy Company. Captain Severance ordered Easy's executive officer, Lieutenant Hal Schrier to take the 3rd platoon, now under the
command of Sergeant "Boots" Thomas to find a path up the steep slope
and feel out enemy resistance.[45]

The cost of Iwo Jima so far to the three battalions of the 28th Marines was about 1000 casualties, nearly one-third of its initial strength.
Those losses, which included Platoon leader Lieutenant Keith Wells, had
shrunk Easy Company's 3rd platoon's ranks, so Schrier had to supplement
his patrol with a machine gun section bringing his effective total to about
40 men. As the men prepared to move out, they were joined by Marine
Corps photographer Louis Lowery, two teams of stretcher bearers along
with Doc Bradley and a radio man, Pfc. Ray Jacobs. Just before they left,
Col. Johnson handing Schrier a small (28 x 54 inches) folded American
flag, said, "If you get to the top, put this up. If you can't get all the way up,
just come on back down, don't try to go overboard."[46]

The smaller patrols had already determined that the only feasible
path to the top was up the north (near) face of Suribachi, so about 08:00
Schrier ordered, "Move out." As the starting point was close to the base

166

of the mountain, reaching the steep slope took only a few minutes. Soon, the incline was so sharp that it could only be climbed on hands and knees and the heavily laden men had to stop often to rest. Schrier sent flankers out to guard against enemy attack. It could be, after all, that the enemy had allowed the smaller patrols to pass in hopes of luring a larger target up the slope. Many cave entrances were seen, but, just as earlier, no enemy resistance was encountered as they climbed.

About 10:00 the first of the men, with Lt. Schrier in the lead, reached the summit. A narrow circular rim framed the concave core of the extinct volcano. Many cave openings were evident, but no Japanese were sighted as more men arrived at the rim. "Find me something to use for a flag pole," Schrier ordered. In response, several men moved down into the crater.

One of the men in the crater spotted a Japanese soldier climbing out of a hole. The man fired and the Japanese soldier dropped back into the hole. This action seemed to alert other enemy soldiers in the area as grenades began flying out of several of the cave entrances. The Marines responded in kind and the action soon died down

"I gotta pee," somebody said, as he stepped up to the rim of the crater.

"That's Imperial Japanese territory you're pissin' on there, son," Schrier informed, laughing.

"Gee," the Marine feigned shock. "I hope it don't insult the Japs none."

The idea instantly spread to everyone within hearing. Several men stepped to the rim of the crater and proceeded to wet the concave slope below them.[47]

As there is no fresh water on Iwo Jima, the Japanese had been obligated to construct cistern systems to capture rain water for drinking. Schrier's men found a water pipe; a remnant of such a facility destroyed by the bombardment. Ernest Thomas, who had earned the nickname "Boots" back at Camp Pendleton because he would not shower barefooted, fired a shot through the pipe to create a hole and tied the flag to it. About 10:20, as they hoisted the pole, the American flag began snapping in the wind. As, in an effort to inspire the defenders, the Japanese government had made Iwo Jima an integral part of the Empire, this was the first time any foreign flag had ever flown over Japanese territory. Photographer Lowery preserved the image of the flag raisers: Schrier, Thomas, Pfc. Louis Charlo, Sgt. Henry Hansen, Pfc. James Michels and Cpl. Chuck Lindberg with the flag for *Leatherneck* magazine.

On the island below, many men had watched the progress of the patrol as it made its way up the side of the mountain. The sight of the Stars and Stripes fluttering in the breeze brought a cheer from every throat. "Would you look at that," was heard everywhere. The ships off shore took up the applause, sounding all available klaxons, foghorns and whistles. Those unloading supplies on the beach and even men involved in active combat took a moment to shout approval. It was a great moment in American history; for many Americans, this represented the exact moment the sneak attack on Pearl Harbor was avenged. If the issue of taking this island had been in doubt, that fluttering flag made American victory a sure thing in every man's mind. Now, how much time and how many lives would be required were the only variables. And, as of now, that evil monster which had rained shells on the men below was the property of Easy Company of the 28th Marines.[48]

Landing on the beach about the time the flag went up was a landing craft carrying Marine General H.M. (Howlin' Mad) Smith and the Secretary of the Navy, James M. Forrestal. The flag atop the mountain had the same spirit-raising impact on these two men as it did for everyone else. Turning to Smith, Forrestal said, "Holland, that flag raising means a Marine Corps for the next five-hundred years."

At the battalion CP, Lt. Col. Johnson had to strain his neck to see the flag. Thinking aloud, he said, "Some son of a bitch is gonna try to get that flag as a souvenir, but it belongs to us!" Turing to his adjutant, he ordered, "Find another flag to replace that one and bring the first one to me." Then, as an afterthought, he added, "Make it a big one."[49]

At the same time, Lieutenant Schrier radioed from the summit that his radio batteries were running low. Col. Johnson called Easy Company's Captain Severance and ordered him to send a detail to string a telephone wire up the mountain. Looking around to see who was available, Severance spotted Mike Strank's squad resting from their morning's patrol around the base of the mountain. Severance hung up the phone and ordered, "Strank, the Colonel's got a little chore for you."

"Saddle up, boys" Strank said, wearily getting to his feet.

"Didn't we just get back from a patrol?" Ira groused.

"What was all the hollerin' about?" Franklin asked.

"They put a flag up on the mountain a little while ago," Severance informed. "Get ready. You're goin' up the hill yourselves."

On Johnson's order, a large (48 x 96 inch) flag, which happened to be a Pearl Harbor survivor, had been located on one of the LST's. Back at the Battalion CP, Johnson gave the flag and some radio batteries to company runner Rene Gagnon and told him to report to Captain Severance at Easy Company's CP.

"Well, well. Look what the cat dragged in." Strank said when Gagnon arrived carrying the batteries and the folded flag under his arm.

None of the men were particularly happy to see Gagnon, who had been discontent all through training. Nonetheless, the affable Franklin had a smile and a nod for his former tent mate.

"Sergeant," the Captain said to Strank, "take your squad, a spool of telephone wire and Gagnon up the hill. As you know, Schrier is already up there with a patrol from the 3rd platoon. When you get up there, put up the flag Gagnon has and you damn well make good and sure the other one gets back to the Colonel."

As the men turned away, Severance added, "Sousley, leave your BAR here. That mountain's pretty steep and that spool of telephone wire is gonna be encumbrance enough without that extra weight. You will probably not encounter any resistance anyway."

"But, sir." Franklin had managed not to address Lt. Pennell as "sir," but could not bring himself to call Captain Severance by name. "I'll feel naked without a weapon."

"Well, take an M1 if you want."[50] With that, Strank, Block, Hayes, Sousley and Gagnon began a trek up the face of Suribachi.

The slope was as advertised. Soon the men were crawling on hands and knees. With a borrowed M1 strapped over his shoulder, Sousley was feeling the effects of the effort. "Harlon, take this spool for a while," he pleaded.

"Let's take a break," Strank ordered. The men gladly dropped the heavy spool and flopped to the ground. "Keep a sharp eye out," the Sergeant advised. "I heard they had a little fight up top just after they raised the flag. There's a hell of a lot of caves around here and there figures to be Japs in some of 'em."

"You seen any Japs?" Franklin asked his buddy.

"A few dead ones puttin' out an awful smell back there," Ira said, wrinkling his nose.

While Strank's squad was climbing, so were three photographers; Joe Rosenthal of the Associated Press and two Marine photographers, Private Bob Campbell and Sergeant Bill Genaust. The two Marines had gotten wind of a replacement flag going up so were going up to photograph that event. The Marines carried weapons, but as a civilian, Rosenthal was armed only with his Speed Graphic camera. In addition to their weapons Campbell had a still camera and Genaust had a movie camera loaded with color from Hilltop to Mountaintop

film. Given the competition between the military and civilian photographers, in another situation, the Marines might not have shared what they knew, but Campbell and Rosenthal were friends, having worked for the same newspaper in San Francisco. The three decided to make the climb together. On the way, they met Lou Lowery, who had photographed the first flag raising, descending. "You're too late," Lowery gloated, emphasizing the antagonism between the civilians and the military. "The flag's already up." Then, softening a bit, he added, "Hell of a view from up there, though. It's worth the climb." The photographers, knowing what Lowery didn't about the replacement flag, pressed on.[51]

Thirty minutes climbing brought Strank's patrol to the summit. Following the tradition established by the men already there, the newcomers dutifully urinated into the volcano's crater. "Would you look at that," Franklin said in wonder. Below them the entire island stretched away to the northeast. They had a perfect view of the landing beaches, the three airfields in the center of the island and even the rocky terrain in the north. They could even see the men fighting on the central plains.

"No wonder the Japs could rain shells on us," Harlon observed, awed by the view.

"Quit yer gawkin', we got work to do," Strank said. Turning to Sousley and Hayes, he ordered "Find me a flag pole." The Sergeant took the larger flag from Gagnon and handed it to Lt. Schrier. "The Colonel wants this flag to replace the first one. He said to put it up high enough so that every son of a bitch on this whole cruddy island can see it."[52] Pointing at the flag whipping in the wind, he added, "And, he wants that one delivered to him personally."

"All right," Schrier said, handing the flag back to Strank. "It's cost a lot of lives to get that flag up and we will not give up control of this mountain, even for one second. Let me know when you're ready and we'll take it down at the same time the new one goes up."

Sousley and Hayes walked a few hundred yards down the west side of the mountain where they located a 20-foot length of iron pipe that had been part of the Japanese water collection system. "That'll do," Ira said.

"Damn, this thing is heavy," Franklin commented as they strained to drag the pole back up to the summit.

The pair of Marines had nearly reached the summit when they encountered the photographers. "What's doin', guys?" Rosenthal asked.

"We've been ordered to put up a larger flag," Franklin explained. "We're gonna put it on this pole."

170

"Where?"

Franklin pointed to the north rim where Harlon had scraped out a level spot and was stacking rocks to steady the base of the pole. Strank walked up with the replacement flag. "We're gonna put this one up at the same time the other one comes down," he informed, pulling a length of cord from his pocket.

Given that information, the photographers scattered to find vantage points from which to shoot. Campbell positioned himself where he could get a shot of both flags; one going up while the other came down. The diminutive Rosenthal, who stood only 5'4", stacked some rocks to stand on. Genaust, with only a few feet of movie film in his camera, took a post just to Rosenthal's left. Lt. Schrier stood between the two flag positions, ready to direct the activity.

With the flag tied on the pipe, Strank gathered the cloth in his hands and placed the pipe over his right shoulder. Ira took a position behind the Sergeant and to his right as Harlon, crouching near the ground, grasped the end of the pipe. Franklin, standing in front of Hayes on Strank's right, placed his hands on the pole. Gagnon joined in, positioned in front of Strank. Seeing the men struggling with the heavy pipe, Doc Bradley jumped in between Sousley and Block to lend a hand. From Rosenthal's perspective, Strank and Gagnon were hardly visible; Hayes, Sousley, Bradley and Block, being between those two and the camera.

"I'm not in your way am I, Joe?" Genaust asked.

"No, you're fine," Rosenthal said, turning to address Genaust. Then, catching movement from the corner of his eye, he shouted, "There it goes!"

The movement Rosenthal had sensed was the men pushing forward. The action happened in less time than it takes to describe it. Block shoved the end of the pipe into the ground between the stacks of rocks he had built while Bradley, Sousley, Gagnon, Hayes and Strank walked forward, shoving the pole before them and up. Mike, sensing that Franklin's grasp was slipping, wrapped his fingers around Sousley's wrist to steady his hand. Just as the pole escaped Ira Hayes' grasp, Rosenthal swung his camera up. With no time to even look through the viewfinder, he clicked the shutter an instant after the following breeze billowed the banner away from the men.[53] Campbell got his shot of both flags and Genaust recorded the scene on color movie film. The time was about noon; the Stars and Stripes now flew over Iwo Jima to stay.

As soon as the staff was upright, two observers standing near photographer Campbell's position snapped to attention and saluted.

"Did you get it, Joe?" Genaust asked.

"I don't know. I hope so," Rosenthal answered.

As the flag raisers held the standard in place and attempted to shove the pole farther into the ground, others gathered to attach guy ropes to the pole. With additional rocks buttressing the base, the flagstaff was soon secured. "You guys can take a break," Strank said.

"How come nobody ain't cheerin' for us like they did the first flag," Franklin wondered, lighting a cigarette.

"Nobody noticed," Ira said.

"How could they not notice? That flag's twice as big as the first one."

"Maybe they're busy," Rene suggested.

"We're as far above that beach as if we were on the top of a 60-story building, you know." Harlon said.

"Yeah? So?" Franklin was puzzled.

"Let me put it to you this way," Block said, taking Franklin's cigarette to light his own. "Let's say you're walking down Ninth Avenue in, what is it, Hilltop, Kentucky?"

"That's right," Franklin agreed, recognizing Harlon's teasing attitude. Both men knew that Hilltop consisted only of a general store and a few houses. There was certainly no Ninth Avenue. Block returned his cigarette.

"OK, then, you look up on the top of one of them 60-story buildings lining Hilltop's street and you say, 'Why! That ain't the same flag they had up there a few minutes ago.'"

"I see what you mean," Franklin confessed. "We are a long way up here, ain't we." After a moment's thought, he added, "It's interesting you should put it that way, 'cause, you know, I was in your hometown, Weslaco, Texas last year and spent the night on the 58th floor of that 60-story hotel. It was a long way up." The country boy had learned to give as good as he got.

"Yeah?" Block responded. "The one downtown or the new one out by Weslaco International Airport?"

The photographer approached. "Hey, guys," he yelled. "How 'bout gathering under the flag to let me get a shot?"

"OK," Mike said, rising. "Come on, boys. Let's get our picture took for the folks back home."

Lieutenant Schrier, Ira Hayes, Mike Strank, Franklin Sousley, Doc Bradley, Hank Hansen and several other men posed under the newly erected banner to allow Joe Rosenthal to get what he called a "gung ho" shot. "It's my job to get photographs worth showing in the newspapers," he explained to Schrier. "This may be the only one I get up here that's worthwhile." The joyful men raised their weapons and helmets in the air and shouted as Rosenthal climbed back on his perch and clicked the shutter. "Thanks, guys," he said. "that should be a good one for your mommas to see."

When the telephone wire Strank's team had brought up was connected, Lt. Schrier reported to Capt. Severance that his assignment was accomplished. Severance ordered that everybody atop the mountain was to stay put, clean out and seal whatever caves they encountered. The order soon came up, however, that General Smith wanted the 3rd platoon's Boots Thomas to report to him on his flagship.

When the day's work was done, Franklin and Ira settled down on the north rim of the crater near the flag. From that vantage point, they had an excellent view of the activity on the island. "Look over there, "Franklin said pointing just inland from Green Beach where a bulldozer was at work scraping a smooth road toward Suribachi.

"I'll hope they bring us some hot food up here," Ira expressed for every Marine on the island.

"I bet they will," Franklin said. "They've got to resupply us with ammo and water."

"Yeah," Ira agreed. Thinking of Easy's decimated ranks, he added, "They'll be sending up some replacement troops, too."

The two studied the scene below in silence. On the southern part of the island, they saw men planting poles to raise the telephone lines off the ground. Although the day's combat activity was dying down, they could see that the Marines attacking the airfields on Iwo's central plain were in the open while the Japanese fired at them from caves, pillboxes and "spider traps." Neither voiced the thought that the entire island would have to be taken in that fashion. Nor did either man comment on the cemeteries they could see under construction. Those were the only orderly spots on the island, their white crosses and Stars of David's standing in perfect military alignment, starkly outlined against the black sand.

"Hey," somebody yelled, "did you guys hear the news?"

"What's that?" Franklin asked.

"Tokyo Rose predicts that the Rising Sun flag will be flying here in the morning!"

As darkness fell, Franklin found a little security – his first since landing – in the flapping of the flag above him. That feeling was soon overcome, however, by the shells being fired from the north of the island as the enemy tried to knock the flag down. "You think one of us ought to stay awake?" he asked.

When Ira did not answer, Franklin moved a little closer to observe that his buddy was sawing logs. Despite his resolution to remain awake and the booming artillery, sheer exhaustion soon took over and in the relative security of the mountaintop, Sousley slept, too.

His slumber did not last long. A different, muffled boom jolted him awake. "What the hell was that?"

"Japs blowing themselves up in tunnels below us," Ira informed drawing from his experience on Bougainville. "They would rather die than surrender and they know they're cut off, so they just hold an exploding grenade to their chest and get it over with."

During the night, a fully equipped field kitchen had been brought up, so along with daylight came the hot breakfast for which they'd hoped. "If it comes in a can, we've got it," the kitchen's sign proclaimed. Another unexpected treat was a morale-raising mail call. Mail had been flown in from Guam and the distribution indicated that a post office was in operation on Iwo Jima. Franklin was delighted to receive a letter from his Aunt Mildred and a month-old issue of the *Fleming Gazette*. "What's the water level in the reservoir?" Ira inquired with a grin. Even back at Camp Pendleton, when the Pima – a native of arid Arizona – read Franklin's newspaper, the report of the reservoir's weekly water level was all he could find of interest.

With no specific duties, D + 6 provided a much appreciated day to rest, refit the equipment and write letters. A highlight was provided when a couple of men blew open a previously sealed cave to hunt for souvenirs. Although they came out with a goodly haul, the booty was not worth the massive chewing out they earned. The officers made sure that no one else would be so stupid as to re-open a cave. Late in the day, Boots Thomas returned to account for his foray into the land of the brass and media. He'd made a radio broadcast to the States, he said, and assured everybody that he'd credited all of Easy Company for the conquest of Suribachi.[54]

The major highlight, however, was that Thomas reported that he'd encountered his wounded platoon leader, Lt. Keith Wells, on the flagship. Wells' wounds, while not life-threatening, were serious enough to keep many a man out of action. But not Keith Wells; the sight of his platoon sergeant was more than the Lieutenant could stand so he slipped on the boat which was returning Thomas to the island and reported to Easy Company's CP.

"What the hell am I to do with you?" Capt. Severance demanded. "Your platoon's up on the hill top and you are in no condition to climb up there."

Wells pondered only a moment. Picking up the telephone connecting the CP to the hilltop, he ordered two of 3rd platoon's strongest men to come and get him. When they arrived, huffing and puffing, at the summit, Wells was deposited amid the cheers of his men. The outcome of the war against the Japanese had long been in doubt, but every man knew that with that kind of *espirt de corps* prevailing among the Marines, the issue was settled.[55]

"Well, it's over for us." Franklin enthused. "We did the job they sent us here to do."

"I hope so," Ira agreed. "I'll happily sit out the rest of the war in peaceful obscurity right here on this mountaintop."

Both men were wrong on both counts.

Chapter 15

Wednesday, February 28, 1945
D-Day + 8 at
Iwo Jima, Volcano Islands

G iven the state of photographic and communication technology, photographic images did not move around the world at great speed. Photographer Rosenthal's film was flown to Guam where it was developed and a lab technician was the first to see his iconic photograph of the replacement flag raising. As soon as the on-site Associated Press (AP) editor viewed the image, he forwarded it, via radio telephone, to AP headquarters in New York from where it went out over AP's network to newspapers all over the United States.

Readers of those newspapers were well aware of what was going on at Iwo Jima, the progress of the battle having been front page news for the last week. Americans were aware of the clever and formidable Japanese defenses, the horrific casualties, the action around the airfields and the fierce fighting at the base of Suribachi. On February 24, the papers had trumpeted the fact that the 28th Marines had reached the summit of the mountain. The following day, the Sunday editions of most major newspapers printed Rosenthal's image on the front page.

No one on Iwo Jima had seen the picture, but they soon heard about its affect on Americans at home. While the end of the war against Germany was in sight, the Pacific struggle was another matter. Previous battles against the Japanese had convinced all Americans that the fight would be long and bloody until the bitter end. The terrific casualty toll on Iwo Jima did little to change that attitude. The anticipated invasion of Japan was projected to cost one million American casualties. Suddenly, here at long last, in one breath-taking image was visual evidence that Japan was being defeated. A study in American courage, discipline, muscle and teamwork, Rosenthal's photograph galvanized the American public and word of that had come to the Marines on Iwo by radio.[56]

Joe Rosenthal thought this photo best portrayed the Marine spirit on Iwo Jima. Associated Press/ Joe Rosenthal.

Japanese pillboxes carved into the rock presented tough objectives. Price family collection.

A fire team at work. The riflemen provide cover for the brave flame-thrower operator. USMC photo.

A Marine guarding the patrol's flank has no time to appreciate the view from atop Mt. Suribachi. USMC photo.

Donald J. Ruhl received the Medal of Honor for sacrificing his life to save his comrades. USMC photo.

Louis Lowery's photo of the first flag raising. USMC photo.

Bob Campbell got this shot of the first flag coming down as the replacement went up. Lieutenant Hal Schrier, at left, directs the action. USMC photo.

Perhaps the most famous photograph of all time. Associated Press/Joe Rosenthal.

Rosenthal's "gung ho" shot, the only one he was sure he had. Ira Hayes is seated on the ground at left, Mike Strank with his thumbs in jacket pockets, Franklin Sousley raising his rifle behind Strank, John Bradley with a shadow across his face to Franklin's left. Associated Press/Joe Rosenthal.

Bob Campbell caught Joe Rosenthal posing his "Gung ho" picture. USMC photo.

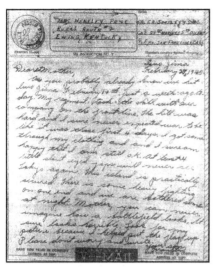

Franklin's last letter home. "Look for my picture because I helped put the flag up. Please don't worry and write." Price family collection.

Barren terrain of Northern Iwo Jima. USMC photo.

There was nowhere to hide. Even the wounded awaiting evacuation were exposed to enemy fire. USMC photo.

Marines cautiously climb over a rocky ridge. USMC photo.

The Fifth Division's part of the cost of Iwo Jima. Associated Press/Joe Rosenthal.

Joe Rosenthal pays his respects at Franklin Sousley's grave. Associated Press/Joe Rosenthal.

Saying goodbye to a buddy. USMC photo.

April 7, 1945

STATEMENT BY MARINE PRIVATE FIRST CLASS RENE A. GAGNON
CONCERNING THE DEATH OF PRIVATE FIRST CLASS FRANKLIN R.
SOUSLEY ON IWO JIMA ON OR ABOUT MARCH 12:

I knew PFC. Franklin R. Sousley since March,
1944 when I joined the Fifth Division.

I moved into a tent with him at that time and have
been a tentmate of his since that time.

Sousley was one of our group of six which raised
the large flag on Mount Suribachi.

A Browning automatic rifleman, he was one of two men
left in his squad at the time he was killed. A rifle shot
hit him in the back and came out through his chest while
he was engaged with a small group of Marines in cleaning out
a pocket of Japanese at the north tip of the island.

He was killed instantly. The time was about 1430. His
body remained where he was killed until the following morning.
I saw the stretcher bearers bringing back his body. The body
was covered by a poncho. I asked them who was on the
stretcher. They said it was Sousley. I lifted the poncho
and recognized that it was Sousley.

When the funeral services were held at the Fifth Division
Cemetery March 30 I saw Sousley's grave at the cemetery.
His name was on the cross and his dogtags were hanging over
the cross. I looked at the dogtags. They were Sousley's.

Rene A. Gagnon,
Private First Class, USMC.

Gagnon's affidavit identified Sousley as one of the flag raisers and gave the details of his death. National Archives.

TELEGRAM
(KTA)

IDENTIFICATION NUMBER   942297

DGU -296 - J8

FROM: COMMANDANT OF THE MARINE CORPS

TO: MRS GOLDIE PRICE (MOTHER)

R R #2

EWING KENTUCKY

DEEPLY REGRET TO INFORM YOU THAT YOUR

RELATIONSHIP
RANK-NAME
CLASSIFICATION   SON PRIVATE FIRST CLASS FRANKLIN R SOUSLEY USMCR

WAS KILLED IN ACTION

DATE-LOCATION   12 MARCH 1945 AT IWO JIMA VOLCANO ISLANDS
IN THE PERFORMANCE OF HIS DUTY AND SERVICE OF HIS COUNTRY. WHEN
INFORMATION IS RECEIVED REGARDING BURIAL YOU WILL BE NOTIFIED   TO
PREVENT POSSIBLE AID TO OUR ENEMIES DO NOT DIVULGE THE NAME OF HIS
SHIP OR STATION. PLEASE ACCEPT MY HEARTFELT SYMPATHY. LETTER
FOLLOWS.

RELEASED BY   M G CRAIG   A A VANDEGRIFT
                                        GENERAL USMC
DATE   9 APRIL 1945   COMMANDANT OF THE MARINE CORPS
                                        038214

Goldie received this telegram the same day the flag raisers' names were released. National Archives.

Above: Goldie could never escape the image. Price family collection.

Left: In this picture which appeared in newspapers on April 9, 1945, Rene Gagnon had misidentified Harlon Block as Henry Hansen and transposed the positions of Hayes and Sousley. Associated Press.

The first US postage stamp to depict a living person sold more than 137,000,000 copies.

The Mighty Seventh Bond Tour Poster. National Archives.

Emil Schram, president of the New York Stock Exchange presenting a $1,000 bond to (from left) Madeline Evelley (Hank Hansen's mother), Goldie Price, Martha Strank, Rene Gagnon, John Bradley and Ira Hayes. Price family collection.

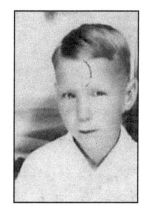

Julian Sousley. Price family collection.

An inventory of Franklin's personal belongings provided another reminder. National Archives.

Fresh off his furlough, Franklin accepted Christ by signing his Bible. Price family collection.

Staff Sergeant Eddie Sumrall stands guard over Franklin's flag-draped coffin at an Elizaville funeral home. Price family collection.

A final salute. Price family collection.

Goldie Price stands next to Kentucky's Governor Julian Carroll after placing a wreath on her son's grave. Price family collection.

Grave marker erected by the Commonwealth of Kentucky. In fact, one of the flag raisers was a Navy corpsman, but they did get the date right. Author photo.

Even thought the survivors (Rene Gagnon shown here) posed for sculptor Felix de Weldon their facial features were not used on the statue. Marine Corps War Memorial Foundation.

Trucks carried the figures from the Brooklyn, NY foundry to Virginia. Marine Corps War Memorial Foundation.

The figures being lifted into place atop the Memorial dwarf the workmen. Marine Corps War Memorial Foundation.

The Marine Corps Memorial is awe inspiring. Courtesy of John Snell.

Mike Strank's hand grasping Franklin Sousley's wrist. Courtesy of John Snell.

Goldie and Hensley Price meet Senators Earl Clements (KY) and Lyndon Johnson (TX). Price family collection.

Above: Goldie saved her dedication ceremony program. Price family collection.

A Marine bugler appears tiny atop the Memorial. Marine Corps War Memorial Foundation.

The crowd begins to gather for the dedication ceremony. Marine Corps War Memorial Foundation.

This booklet was circulated to raise funds for Franklin's monument. Price family collection.

Thanks to Tom White, this monument marks Franklin's Elizaville grave. The glass vial (in front of the flag) at the base contains Iwo Jima sand. Courtesy of John Snell.

Present at the Elizaville dedication were (from left) Congressman Larry Hopkins, Goldie Price, Congressman Carl D. Perkins, Tom White, Franklin's buddy Joe Rodriguez and General Trotter. Price family collection.

After nearly 30 years, Tom White is justifiably proud of his accomplishment. Author photo.

Joe Rosenthal autographed this picture for Dwayne Price. Price family collection.

Dwayne Price and daughter Brittani at the wayside panel identifying the flag raisers. Price family collection.

"Something just ain't right about this," Marine photographer Louis Lowery complained to Robert Sherrod who was covering the battle for *Time Life* magazines. Lowery was upset that Rosenthal, who had simply photographed a replacement flag, was getting national attention while he, who had covered what was *the* flag raising to those on Iwo, wasn't even mentioned in the newspapers. The fact that news moved more slowly through military channels and the jealousy between the military and civilian photographers were also factors in his ire. "Rosenthal must have faked something or posed his shot." Having seen neither his own flag raising image nor Rosenthal's, Lowery had no understanding of the marked difference between the two images or the psychological impact of Rosenthal's picture.

Sherrod sent Lowery's story to Time-Life headquarters at Rockefeller Center in New York with a stipulation that Lowery's suspicions should be verified before publication. Unfortunately, that did not happen and the story that Rosenthal's picture was a phony went out on a national radio broadcast.

Ironically, Joe Rosenthal himself added to the confusion. When he arrived at AP's installation on Guam, he was immediately congratulated on his wonderful flag raising photograph, which he had not yet seen. Asked, as a result of the Lowery/Sherrod radio story, if he'd posed his picture, he replied, "Yes, of course." He was speaking of the only picture he knew he'd taken; the "gung ho" shot which was clearly posed. Despite Lowery's later retraction of his accusations and the Campbell and Genaust films proving that Rosenthal's image captured a spontaneous event, Joe Rosenthal would spend the rest of his life defending his photograph's legitimacy.[57]

While all that action was going on around the world, it was "business as usual" for the Marines on Iwo Jima. After the flag raising, Schrier's patrol had remained atop the mountain while Strank's party had rejoined the majority of Easy Company at the base of Suribachi. Their relatively peaceful stint in reserve there was disturbed only by the Japanese shelling from the far north and the millions of green flies buzzing around the many corpses. Their depleted ranks were replenished by new men who had been serving in other capacities, unloading supplies or whatever. Many of these were untrained and all of them were strangers whom the veterans did not know or trust. During the lull Franklin found time to write. Knowing that he'd posed for Joe Rosenthal's "gung ho" shot, he alerted his mother to "watch for my picture, I helped put the flag up."

The respite there ended late on this Wednesday afternoon when they were ordered to prepare to move out. "We're goin' north this evening," Capt. Severance informed. "The fellows up there have made some progress while we rested," he said. "About half of this island's in our hands, but the attack has stalled on the west coast at a place they call Hill 362A. We'll be replacing a worn down company."

When the 3rd platoon came down to join up, Capt Severance spotted a badly limping Keith Wells. "Lieutenant!" he shouted to get Wells attention.

"Yes," Wells replied, approaching.

"You get your ass to the hospital. You're in no shape to go where we're goin'."

"But, sir...."

Severance's booming "Go!" ended the discussion as well as Wells' active service on Iwo Jima.[58]

Dusk was thickening as Easy Company moved through the men they were replacing on the front lines just south of the hill. "Those guys look like hell," Franklin observed.

The retiring men were grimy with dirt and sweat, black circles rimmed their eyes and their clothing was stiffened by dried blood. The two groups eyed each other as Easy occupied their foxholes but nobody could find any words to say, so they passed in silence.

"Don't look in the mirror," Bill said, "that's what we'll look like in a few days."

"If we're still alive," Ira commented, settling into a hole with Franklin.

About 02:00, Franklin was jolted awake by the loudest boom he'd ever heard. "What the hell was that?"

"Japs hit an ammo dump," Ira, who was on watch, laconically noted.

Neither man slept any more as March roared in; the rest of the night was filled with shooting flames, sparks and explosions as the ammunition was consumed.

The first day of March began, as did most others on this island, with a naval bombardment of the ground over which the men were to advance. When the gunfire ended, the 28th Marines attacked, moving north, with all three battalions in line, the 2nd being in the middle. The ground was rock-strewn, devoid of vegetation and criss-crossed with ravines between sheer cliffs. Although most were not obvious, the area was also honeycombed with interconnecting caves and tunnels which sheltered the Japanese. "This is the ugliest country I ever saw," Franklin observed, moving forward in a crouch.

"It's as barren as west Texas," Tex agreed, "but there's a hell of a lot more rock here."

"And more tunnels with Japs in 'em." Ira said. The men had observed that when a tunnel entrance was blown, smoke would puff out of other entrances to the same cavity, sometimes an amazing distance away.

As they approached the hill, under constant fire, Henry Hansen was observed on the left, peeking around a boulder. "Watch out, Hank," Tex Stanton yelled as Hansen moved around the rock.

The same warning Don Ruhl had yelled did not save Hansen this time. "You worry too much," he replied, stepping into the open. In the next instant, he was dead, shot by a Japanese rifleman. Doc Bradley's best efforts failed to save him.[59]

Late in the morning, the men were pinned down by a machine gun. Franklin, Mike, Ira, L.B. and Joe gathered in a cluster of large rocks. Strank motioned for the rest of the squad. While they waited, Mike, eyeing a dead Marine, said, "You know, Holly, that's got to be a hell of an experience." Before L.B. could ask what he meant, the others arrived. As Mike was explaining a possible way to attack the machine gun nest, a shell – maybe a Japanese mortar, maybe an American Naval shell – landed nearby. Sousley and Holly were blasted into the air and landed dazed but unhurt. Joe Rodriguez was wounded, unable to move his legs. As Sousley and Hayes dusted themselves off, Strank, lying on his back, did not move. When they rolled him over, they saw that the shell had blasted his chest open, literally ripping out his heart. The event had the same effect on those who knew, loved and respected Strank. "You're the best damn Marine I ever saw," L.B. Holly said to a corpse. The taciturn Hayes, whose admiration for Mike knew no bounds, simply walked away.[60]

Realizing what Mike had meant, L.B. said, to no one in particular, "He told me he was gonna die."

"When?" Tex asked.

"Just now, two seconds before he got hit."

When the remaining men looked around, they were horrified to realize that the same blast had killed Harlon Block.[61] Two of the six men in Rosenthal's photograph died at the same moment.

"Let's go," acting platoon leader Sgt. Joe McGarvey, ordered. The men implemented Strank's plan and gained the top of the hill. On the north (far) side was a sheer cliff about 40 feet high. A rise called Nishi Ridge lay 300 yards beyond. The cliff left no option but to attack around the base of the hill, so the squad took the left side, nearest the west beaches and spent the remainder of the day trying to advance toward the ridge.

That evening a Marine, who's tidy appearance was in stark contrast to the grubby veterans, approached where the men were huddled. "Is this 2nd Platoon?" he asked, hesitantly.

"What's left of it," answered Sgt. McGarvey.

"They sent me up as a replacement," the young man said, clearly ill at ease as he looked from face to face.

"Get down before you get shot," McGarvey advised. "What's your background," he inquired as the new man slid in beside them.

"I'm just six weeks out of boot camp," he replied. "I've been unloading supplies on the beach since I've been here."

McGarvey shook his head and heaved a sigh. "Well, keep your head down and don't lose touch with the man next to you. When you are ordered to move, run like hell, zig-zaging as you go. When you hit the deck, roll away from where you landed and find a hole to get in quick as you can. You can dig in with Ranous." With that combat instruction, the new man settled in.

The next morning, the cold wind and rain returned causing Easy Company to battle the elements as well as the Japanese for the next two days. Another of the first flag raisers, "Boots" Thomas joined the ranks of the dead on the third day of March and Joe McGarvey, acting 2nd platoon leader, was wounded. Franklin and Ira shared a hole while Bill Ranous and the replacement were dug in next to them. Despite his 'training,' when the new man stood upright, he was immediately shot through the head. "What was his name, Bill?" Franklin absent-mindedly asked.

After a moment of silence, Ranous said, "I don't know. He never said." "Didn't you ask?"

"No. I didn't want to know."

Later in the day, L.B. Holly peeking around a boulder, spotted a bunker. "Gimme a bazooka!" he yelled. When the weapon was passed forward, he stepped around the rock, blasted away the steel door of the bunker and peered inside. Running back around, he shouted, "I need a flame thrower." Supplied with one, Holly dashed back to the bunker entrance and sprayed the inside, roasting the Japanese occupants. In the sudden quiet, Franklin and Ira wondered what had become of their friend. At that moment, they heard a tinkling sound as L.B. rounded the boulder riding a Japanese bicycle ringing its bell for all he was worth.[62] Franklin and Ira shared a laugh, a rare event on Iwo Jima.

March 4th was filled with the same kind of action as they advanced through what was aptly termed Death Valley. The highlight of the day came when the Marines saw what they were fighting for: a B-29, returning from a raid on Japan appeared over Suribachi with its landing gear down. The silver aircraft, landing south to north, was shelled by the Japanese as it reached the far end of the runway. Superfortress *Dinah Might* immediately turned to taxi back to the safer environs to the south. On secure ground the crew jumped out and kissed the runway that had saved them from having to ditch at sea. The Marines, who considered this island as "hell with the fire out," watching that action questioned the airmen's sanity, but knew they'd earned the "fly-fly boys" eternal gratitude.[63]

"Good news, men," Capt. Severance announced. "We get tomorrow off!" That announcement met with cheers all around. We'll move back south a little," he went on. "And, I've got an idea. How'd you guys like to go swimming?"

"You wanna go swimmin'?" Franklin asked.

"Well," Bill said, eyeing his buddy, "we could use a bath."

"I'd sure like to wash the smell of dead Japs off me," Ira commented.

As the men arrived at the beach, some stripped, but most waded right in, boots and all. Despite the sulphurous quality of the water, a few bars of soap emerged and men scrubbed their bodies and their clothes. Soon the Pacific waters were teeming with naked young men. These Marines, who had amply proven themselves to be men, were treated to a rare chance to be boys once again.

Had they been on the other side of the island, they might have seen the 3rd Marines, the last of the floating reserve, sail away headed for Guam. Although these fresh men had been called for several times and their commitment would have shortened the fight, they would not be used here. The overall plan called for the invasion of Okinawa soon and somebody was going to have to hit the beach there.[64]

Back in the line, the days wore on with what came to be regarded as monotony. Some days they accomplished an advance of as much as 25 yards. On other days, they did not even manage to move to the next shell hole. The one constant was casualties: Death Valley cost the 28th Marines an average of 236 killed and wounded a day, nearly as much as that first disastrous day on the beach and more than the battle for Suribachi.

On March 14, the highest ranking Navy and Marine officers on Iwo Jima gathered at Marine headquarters a few hundred yards north of Mt. Suribachi. A proclamation from Admiral Chester Nimitz, Commander in

Chief of the Pacific Fleet, declared that "forces under my command have occupied this and other of the Volcano Islands. All powers of government of the Japanese Empire are hereby suspended." Easy Company's flag atop the mountain came down as a flag was run up at headquarters.[65]

March 16 was a significant day for everyone on Iwo Jima and for a few of Easy Company's men in particular. On this date, the highest level of the American military declared the island secure, in essence officially ending the battle. The actual reason was that the invasion of the next island, Okinawa, was scheduled for April 1, so the Navy's ships and especially the landing craft had to be released.

"Are they crazy?" Bill Ranous wondered.

"We're still getting shot at, ain't we?" Franklin added.

As if to emphasize Sousley's point, Joe Senoracke was struck by a burst of machine gun fire as he ran carrying a light machine gun up the ravine. "I'm hit!" he screamed as he fell.

"Corpsman!" Franklin cried, rushing to his friend's side. "How you doin', Joe?" he asked pulling the wounded man behind a boulder.

A corpsman arrived almost instantly and started dressing Joe's wounds. He simply shook his head in answer to Franklin's unspoken question. Blood pouring from Joe's abdominal wound saturated Franklin's trousers.

"We'll get you fixed up and evacuated," Franklin said, cradling Joe's head to his chest while stroking the wounded man's hair.[66] Noticing that the corpsman had stopped working, Franklin saw in the medic's eyes that Joe was dead. The corpsman moved on to where he could be of help. L.B. Holly scrambled in the space the corpsman had just vacated and started to say something, but as he looked at Franklin and saw the white streaks created by the tears streaming down the Kentuckian's grimy face, no words were necessary.

That evening, Franklin lay alone in a shell hole about as despondent as any one person could be. He was alone only physically though; every one of the finely tuned fighting men who'd landed on this island 26 days ago was now a dull android, physically bone-weary, dirty and swollen, mechanically going through the motions without feeling. "Hey, Sousley!" somebody shouted "where are you?"

"Over here," Franklin yelled, unenthusiastically.

"Look at this," Rene Gagnon said, sliding in beside him. In his hand was a copy of *Life Magazine*. "Look," Gagnon repeated, "My Mom sent it! That's us! She says this picture is all over the place back home!"[67]

Franklin took the glossy page and beheld Joe Rosenthal's flag raising photograph. "Wow! That is us." he exclaimed, perking up a bit. "That's a hell of a picture. I didn't know he took that."

"Nobody did," Gagnon agreed, "but that's us. We're famous! I gotta show it to Chief." With that, he dashed to the next hole where Ira was nestled with Bill Ranous.

Ira Hayes viewed the photograph and somehow immediately grasped the impact it would have on the men in the image. "I'll kill if you tell anybody that's me," he said, thrusting the magazine back.[68] A giggle died in Gagnon's throat as he saw the Indian was serious. "That goes for you too, Sousley," Hayes shouted. "I'll cut your gizzard out."

"What about Doc Bradley?" Franklin's voice was humorless. "You gonna kill him too?"

"No need to worry," Gagnon informed, eager to get away from Hayes. "He was wounded and evacuated the other day. He's gone."

The next day, Dave Severance got what he considered an annoying request from 2nd Battalion Headquarters – they wanted the names of the men in Rosenthal's photo. "I've got other things to worry about," Severance shouted into the phone. Informed that the order was straight from the President, Severance considered who would know the names of the men involved. The Captain didn't know who they were, but he did know that he had sent the flag up with his runner. "Gagnon!" he shouted. "Get over here with that magazine."

Gagnon approached, the magazine in his hand and fear in his heart, suspecting what the Captain wanted. "Who are these men," Severance demanded, "you can't see any of the faces."

Gagnon studied the grainy picture. "Me, Sousley, Bradley, Strank and, uh…." With great concentration, he tapped his finger on the back of the man on the right at the base of the pole, and said, "That's Hank Hansen." Sousley and Gagnon were the only ones named who were still alive and unwounded. For reasons best known to himself, Gagnon did not mention Block or Hayes. No one noticed that he'd only supplied five names while six figures appear in the picture. The five names went back up the chain of command.

Easy Company was pinned in place by Japanese fire for the next several days. Franklin and Ira lay in a shell hole where the Japanese fired at them anytime they moved. Close by were Tex Stanton and Rolla Perry. Hayes and Sousley burrowed deeper when they heard the distinctive whine of an incoming mortar round. The shell landed in the hole sheltering Tex and lifted him into the air, one foot gone and the other attached only by a tendon. "His war's over," Franklin observed, somewhat enviously, as stretcher bearers carried his friend away.[69]

On the morning of March 21, Capt. Severance briefed what was left of Easy Company. "Men," he began, "we're damn near to the Northern tip of this island and that means the battle is about over. In fact, as you may have heard, the 4th Division has already pulled out and Army troops are landing on the beaches right now to take over garrison duty. Intelligence thinks there are no more than a couple of hundred Japs left, but they are hard-core and will give us all the trouble they can. The sooner we kill 'em all, the sooner we'll be out of here."

"We will be attacking our final objective today. As you've seen the last few days, the resistance has been getting stiffer as we've moved north, but I think we've seen the worst of it. Let's clean out this last pocket and then we'll all go home."

There was no cheering, not even much conversation, as the men prepared to move forward. They were too tired, too blood-stained, too overwhelmed to show any such emotion. Acting on nothing more than instinct and training, they moved to the attack as they'd done so many times before.

About 14:30 that afternoon, Ira and Franklin, who were all that remained of the 1st squad, were moving toward Kitano Point at the Northern tip of Iwo Jima. "There's a spider trap over there," Ira yelled, pointing to his left. "Keep his head down."

"I see it," Franklin noted. "Wait 'til I get in position." He jumped to his feet making for a better angle for his covering fire. As he stood, a single rifle shot entered his back and blew out the front of his chest. He stood a moment, absently swatting at his back as if stung by a wasp. He was dead before he fell.[70]

"Franklin!" Ira screamed, as he saw Sousley fall. Running to his fallen friend oblivious of the bullets whizzing around him, he dragged the body to a safer location. "Franklin, talk to me." Franklin Runyon Sousley, aged nineteen years, six months and two days would never again answer the call.

At the same time Franklin died, a Navy Chaplin was speaking at the dedication of the 5th Division Cemetery at the foot of Mt. Suribachi. The site where Harlon Block and Mike Strank and nearly 2000 other 5th Division men were buried was only a couple of miles to the south of where Franklin lay beneath his poncho. "Somewhere in this plot of ground there may lie the man who could have discovered the cure for cancer," the Chaplin began. "Under one of these Christian crosses or Jewish Star of David there may now rest a man who was destined to be a great prophet – to find the way, perhaps for all to live in plenty, with poverty and hardship for none. Now they lay here silently in this sacred soil, and we gather to consecrate this earth in their memory.

"This is a difficult thing to do. Here before us lie the bodies of comrades and friends. Men who until yesterday or last week laughed with us, joked with us and trained with us.... Some of us have buried our closest friends here. We saw these men killed before our very eyes. Any one of us might have died in their places. Indeed, some of us are alive and breathing at this moment only because these men who lie here beneath us had the courage and strength to give their lives for ours...."[71]

Five days later, the remnant of Easy Company was pulled out, the battle was over. The battle that was predicted to take "3 or 4 days," had actually taken 36 and cost the Americans nearly 28,000 casualties. Captain Severance's figures showed that his company had landed with 7 officers and 235 enlisted men. During the course of the battle they had received some 70 replacements and suffered a total of 240 casualties – more than 100% of the original strength. Severance was the only officer still standing.

On March 26, these men, Easy's 60 survivors (only 35 of which were members of the original company and some of them walking wounded) marched to the cemetery to say good bye to their buddies who would be staying on Iwo Jima.[72] They were amazed and gratified to see that Iwo Jima had become an American military base complete with roads, Quonset huts and tents everywhere. No flag flew atop Mt. Suribachi, the summit being occupied by radar, weather and navigation equipment. After a brief memorial service, the men broke up to wander silently through the orderly rows of graves. Ira Hayes and Rene Gagnon found their way to grave # 2189 in Plot 8, Row 7. Ira knelt at the cross marked "Sousley, F. R., P.F.C., 942297 while Gagnon inspected the dog tag tacked to the wooden banner. "Franklin's?" Hayes sobbed. Tears streamed from his eyes as Gagnon simply nodded. Yes, it was Sousley's dog tag.[73]

The weary and grimy survivors loaded on transport ships for the trip back to camp in Hawaii where they would train for the invasion of the Japanese mainland. Few looked back as Iwo Jima slipped into the distance. The Fifth Marine Division – The Spearhead – which left so many of its men there, had fought its first and only battle.

Chapter 16

Monday, April 9, 1945
Ewing, Kentucky

Springtime came early to the Bluegrass State this year. The sweet fragrance of the flowering crabapple trees wafted on the gentle breeze flowing over the hillsides that were colored by lime green buds and pink redbud blossoms. As Goldie Price sat in a rocker on her porch, she was enjoying the weather, but only in an absent-minded way; other thoughts occupied her mind.

"What have you heard from Franklin," her brother Ray asked, coming through the gate. He had a rolled up newspaper in his hand. He noted the concern in her face as he took the chair next to her.

"Nothin'." She practically spat the word. "Not a word since the end of February."

"Well, that don't mean anything. You know that lots of times they're too busy to write."

She rocked in silence for a few moments. "Yeah, I do know that." She took a couple of swings before saying what was on her mind. "I also know that the fightin's been over at that place he wrote from – Iwo Jima, it was – for two weeks now. I ain't heard nothin' from him."

"Well, you got some letters he wrote from a ship before, ain't you? How long did they take to get here?"

Setting her jaw, she rocked. "A long time, sometimes. I wish we had one of them telephones."

"That wouldn't do no good," Ray said, laughing. "The Navy don't have no telephone on those ships and if they did, they sure as hell wouldn't let the Marines use 'em." He picked up the copy of *Life Magazine* resting on the windowsill behind him. It was open to Joe Rosenthal's flag raising photograph. The caption below the picture read, "OLD GLORY ON MT. SURIBACHI." "You've studied this?"[74]

"'Course, I have," she said, rocking furiously while staring straight out over the valley. "You can't recognize none of those people, though."

"No, you can't see their faces. The thing is, though, we don't know for a fact that this is the picture Franklin was talkin' about."

Goldie stopped rocking to stare into his eyes. "He wrote the letter from Iwo Jima and said 'Look for my picture, I helped put up the flag.' Now how many flag raisin's on Iwo Jima pictures have you seen?"

"This is the only one," Ray had to admit.

"Well, then. It's got to be the one he was talkin' about, ain't it?"

In fact, Rosenthal's flag raising photograph could not have been the one Franklin referred to in his letter written February 27 as neither he nor anyone else on Iwo Jima knew that the picture existed at that time. No doubt, Franklin meant Rosenthal's "gung ho" photograph which he did know about as he'd purposely posed for that one. But, Goldie and Ray didn't know that!

"It could be," Ray sighed. "It probably is. If so, Franklin's gonna be famous."

"How's that?" She resumed her rocking.

"Why, this photograph is causing all kinds of stuff to happen. Haven't you been readin' the paper?"

"I got two boys to raise, a husband to feed and cows to milk," she said. There was no bitterness in her voice, but Ray thought he heard a trace of weariness. She did not mention that worrying about her son in the Marine Corps consumed as much of her energy as anything else. "I ain't got time to read newspapers." After a couple of rocker swings, she asked, "What kind of stuff?"

"Oh, all kinds of stuff," he replied, enthusiastically. "For one thing, some congressman suggested that the Government build a memorial based on this picture."[75] He tapped the printed image for emphasis. "He said that it would be a tribute to the courage and achievement of the entire Marine Corps."

She stopped rocking, but not abruptly this time. "Are you serious?"

"You think I'm makin' this up? He said that there was nothing any artist could dream up that would rival this picture."

"Reckon they'll do that?" A push of her foot restarted the rocker.

"Probably," he opined. "I think so because Congress has already approved using this image as the symbol for the war bond tour comin' up."

Her rocking again stopped abruptly. "Why, if they do that, whoever those boys are will be famous! In the newsreels at the movies, I've seen Clark Gable and Carole Lombard and Gary Cooper and Mickey

Rooney and Judy Garland and all manner of movie stars mixed in with military heroes." She began rocking again as she contemplated the possibilities.

"Oh that ain't all." Ray was happy to see that he'd taken her mind off her worries. "Yep, those war bond tours are organized by the Treasury Department, you know. They appear at stadiums and theaters all over the country and draw huge crowds." His voice trailed off as he knew what his sister was thinking. But he knew something she didn't and was not yet ready to tell her. "And, that ain't all. The United States Senate has proposed that the Post Office issue a stamp with this image on it."

"Wow!" Her gaze remained out over the valley, her mind racing.

"Here's the best part." Now he stopped rocking, leaned toward her and placed his hand on her shoulder. "Some newspaper man suggested to President Roosevelt that these men," again he tapped the magazine, "whoever they are be brought home to be a part of the war bond tour.[76] The war'll be over for them."

She took the magazine from him and stared at it. "Well, then that brings us right back around, don't it? We don't know if this is the picture Franklin meant and we don't know who these people are."

Ray Mitchell had been thinking hard all morning. Rosenthal's photograph had impacted the nation, he thought, in the same way the idea of dedicating a tomb to an unknown Great War soldier had twenty years before. That Monument in Arlington Cemetery allows every American woman to think that perhaps the man honored there might be – just could be – her husband or brother or father or son. In this case, there were some 80,000 American women who knew that her serviceman had been on Iwo Jima. Because of Franklin's letter, Goldie Price had much more reason than most to think her son was in that picture. The moment Ray had been dreading all day had arrived.

"Well," he said with a deep sigh, "we do." He slowly unrolled the newspaper he'd been holding and handed it to her.

Rosenthal's image was reproduced one more time, but this one had captions pointing to each of the men. The one at the base of the pole was identified "Sgt. Henry O. Hansen (Dead)." Moving to the left, the others read, "Pfc Rene A. Gagnon, PhM2C John H. Bradley (wounded), Sgt Michael Strank (Dead) and Pfc Ira H. Hayes." The last figure, the one with his poncho stuffed in his belt, was labeled, "Unidentified Marine (Dead)."

"Now, Goldie," he said before she could react, "like we said, we don't know nothin'."

She stared at the grainy image for a long moment. At length, she cleared her throat and asked, "How is it that they know the names of all these others, but don't know this one?"

Ray had not considered that question. "Well," he said, thinking fast, "things get pretty confusin' in a battle." Trying to sound confident, he added, "Why sometimes it takes years to sort out who was where, who did what and such." If either suspected the truth – that the "unidentified dead marine's" next of kin had not yet been notified, neither voiced that suspicion.

Her chin fell to her chest. "Well," she drew the word out, "that's Franklin.' She was unconsciously caressing the printed image of the last figure in the photograph.

"You don't know that," Ray insisted. "There's no way to identify any of them."

"Franklin hates to wear a coat, you know that. This man here has his coat stuffed in the back of his belt. That's Franklin."

Unknown to Ray and Goldie, as well as most of the rest of the world, a Presidential directive had snatched Rene Gagnon off the transport *Winged Arrow* and assigned him a priority seat on a plane to Washington D.C. When word got around the ship that Gagnon was to leave the transport at Eniwetok, Ira Hayes knew that what he'd suspected about the glare of publicity was coming true. He sought out Rene Gagnon and reiterated the murder threat should his identity be revealed.[77] At Marine Headquarters, careful inspection had revealed six men in the photograph and Gagnon had only named five. In one of his last acts as President, an ailing Franklin Roosevelt had ordered that the survivors of the flag raising be brought home to appear in the Seventh National War Bond Tour, so they had to be identified. "Who's the sixth man?" the highest brass in the Corps demanded when Gagnon arrived on April 7. However reluctant he may have been, a Pfc does not ignore a Major General; Gagnon released Ira Hayes' name. So now, the Marine Corps, and soon the press, had the six names. Evidently in honest error, Gagnon had misidentified Hank Hansen and transposed Sousley and Hayes' positions in the photograph.[78]

That same day, Gagnon dictated a statement for the record. He certified that Franklin Sousley was one of the pictured flag raisers and documented what he knew about Sousley's death. He stated that Franklin had died instantly, that he (Gagnon) identified the body as stretcher bearers carried it away and that he verified that Sousley's dog tags were hanging on the cross bearing his name in the division cemetery.

In the south Texas town of Weslaco, near the tip where the Lone Star State adjoins Mexico and the Gulf, another American mother was scrutinizing the same newspaper photograph. "That's your brother," Belle Block told her younger son. "I said so the instant I first saw that picture." Indeed, Belle had insisted that the figure pushing the pipe into the ground was her son Harlon despite the fact that no names were initially supplied and despite the fact that only the man's posterior was visible. Gagnon's misidentification did not cause her to waiver. "I reckon I know my boy," she persisted.[79]

Everett Neal was standing on the porch of the Hilltop General Store enjoying the spring weather and swapping stories with the loafers gathered there when a noise down the road caught his attention. Conversation stopped as everyone looked toward the sound. Slowly, a leather-helmeted head appeared over the crest of the hill, then shoulders came into sight, then the full figure of a man mounted on a roaring motorcycle. The machine slowed and slid to a stop just off the porch. A Western Union logo graced the side of the gas tank in front of the rider's knee. "Can I help you?" the proprietor asked.

The man stepped off his mount, removed his goggles, dusted himself off and retrieved an envelope from the saddlebag. "Got a telegram here for," his eyes fell to the envelope, "a Mrs. J. Hensley Price." Ignoring the rider's expectant look, Mr. Neal said nothing. At length, the messenger asked, "Can you get it to her?"

"I reckon so," he replied, reluctantly. The messenger held the envelope at arm's length, but Mr. Neal did not want to touch it.

The Western Union man stepped up on the porch to hand the message over. "Thanks for your help," he said as he hopped on his cycle. In a roar and a cloud of dust, he was gone back the way he came.

"Is it sealed?" somebody asked.

Neal inspected the small brown envelope. "Nope."

"Well, are you gonna read it?"

"No need to," he sighed. "You'll know as well as I do that these telegrams only bring one piece of news and it ain't good news, either." Eyeing the men gathered there, he asked, "Any of you want to take it to her?" Amid mumbled excuses, the men hurriedly cleared out.

Everett Neal stood for a moment reviewing his long friendship with Goldie and Franklin. With a deep sigh, he turned to go in and tell his wife to mind the store while he delivered the telegram. He'd only reached the door when somebody shouted, "Hey, Mr. Neal. How ya doin'?"

He turned to see young Tom Alexander approaching at a lope. "Come to get me a bottle of pop. Beautiful day, ain't it?"

"Weather wise, yes it is," Mr. Neal agreed as the young man extracted a bottle from the cooler and yanked off the top with the opener dangling on a string.

"I got a nickel here," Tom said, fishing around in his pocket.

"Tell you what," Neal offered, "the pop's on the house if you'll do a little chore for me."

"You bet! Just name it."

"Well, Western Union just dropped off this telegram here for your cousin Goldie. How 'bout you take it to her?"

Although he was only 19, Tom Alexander knew as well as everyone else what the telegram said. Sensing the young man's reluctance, Neal said, "It'd be better coming from family. Easier for her."

His exuberance instantly evaporated. Tom accepted the envelope and wordlessly walked away.

Goldie was sitting like a statue in her rocker when he entered the gate. She was not rocking and her unseeing eyes stared over the far hilltops. "Hello, Cousin," he said.

She did not move or change her gaze. "Hello, Tommy." Her voice was barely audible.

He waited, but she said no more and still did not even twitch. "I've got… uh, Mr. Neal gave me…." Not finding the words, with a sigh, he offered the brown envelope he pulled from his hip pocket. Still she did not move. He laid the telegram on her lap and stepped back.

Since she'd identified the picture to Ray earlier, she'd hoped against hope that she was wrong that somehow "unidentified marine (dead)" was not her son. That faint hope had allowed her to keep her emotions in check. The envelope in her lap evaporated the last shred of hope. Tears gushed from her eyes and a loud shriek escaped her lips. Tom tried to say something but could think of nothing and she was screaming so hysterically that the words would have been lost anyway, so he simply walked away, trying not to run.

A quarter of a mile down the road, he could still hear her screaming. "What's goin' on?" Charles Cowan asked as Tom passed in front of his house.

"She just found out Franklin's been killed." Charles would hear those screams all through the night. Tom Alexander would hear them for the rest of his life.[80]

Chapter 17
Sunday, May 13, 1945
Cincinnati, Ohio

A springtime shower drizzled down on the bustling street outside the Queen City's Union Terminal as the Navy Packard sedan rolled to a stop before the main entrance. The young sailor driving jumped out, ran around the car and opened the door for Goldie and Hensley Price. Retrieving their luggage from the trunk, he sat it by the curb and addressed his passengers. "Well, this is it, folks. That Marine there will take it from here." Before Goldie could even express her thanks, the young man was gone.

A Marine, resplendent in his dress blues, respectfully approached. Goldie nearly burst into tears at the sight of him, but managed to rein in her emotions. She'd shed so many tears in the last five weeks that she wasn't sure there were anymore in her. She'd received condolences from the Commandant of the Marine Corps, General Motors, Kentucky's Senator A.B. "Happy" Chandler, the district Congressman, Joe Bates and many other mothers who had also lost sons in the war. Each of those communications had mixed results: no words could lessen her grief or staunch her tears, but those commiserations were, nonetheless, some small consolation. Among her most cherished items was an especially touching personal letter from Captain Dave Severance, who informed her that Franklin did not suffer and said that her son "was a fine, courageous young man and a good Marine." Those words from his commanding officer were treasured beyond value. Also, she'd received a letter from Ira Hayes' mother. In it, Nancy Hayes struggled – and failed – to find some explanation for the fact that while their two boys had faced death shoulder to shoulder, Ira came home and Franklin died. Nancy said, and Goldie believed, that she understood Goldie's sacrifice.[81]

The young man waiting for her to acknowledge him reminded her so much of Franklin when she'd last seen him in the back yard wearing his dress uniform. Steeling herself, she turned to face him. Seeing that she'd noticed him, he inquired, "Mrs. Price?"

"Yes." A deep sigh escaped her lips.

"The train is about ready to go. May I help you with your luggage?" He picked up her suitcase without waiting for her to answer. Turning to Hense, he started to grasp the other bag. "Sir?"

"No, thank you." Hense seemed insulted by the offer.

"Follow me, please." The Marine turned to enter the terminal building.

Goldie was taken aback by what she saw. A 10-foot high bond poster featuring a reproduction of Joe Rosenthal's photograph hung above the main entrance. Below the men's figures was the caption, "Now... All Together." At the lower corner it said "7ᵗʰ War Loan." Her heart swelled with pride every time she saw the representation of her son, but each instance also renewed her grief. And that war bond poster was everywhere – shop windows, movie theaters, banks, everywhere. They'd even seen it on a couple of billboards along the highway. Her pride/grief would perhaps have been even deeper had she known how pervasive the image actually was: more than a million shop windows, 200,000 factories, 30,000 railroad and bus stations, 16,000 movie theaters and 15,000 banks displayed the bond tour's poster.

Through the lobby, the couple waited on the concrete ramp in total awe of the gleaming, polished chrome Pullman car before them. Just up the track, a locomotive throbbed its eagerness to be off. "I ain't too sure about this," Goldie shouted into her husband's ear. "I'm as far away from home right now as I've ever been."

"Well, they've set this deal all up for us. It's surely good enough to get us to New York." Seeing her look of dismay as she eyed the car, he added, "We don't have to go, you know."

"Of course we have to go," she snapped. "President Roosevelt himself – rest his soul – decided that the Iwo Jima flag raisin' was to be the symbol for this War Bond drive. 'The Mighty 7ᵗʰ,' he called it. So, it's an honor to my son and I aim to be there for the kick off." She hesitated as her attitude softened. "It's to raise money to feed and clothe and equip the men still fighting...." She paused as her voice cracked. "Besides, I want to see Times Square and Central Park and the Waldorf-Astoria. I want to meet Franklin's friends, too." Hense had his reservations about the whole thing, but seeing now that his wife was more excited than she had cared to let on, he did not share his concerns with her.

"They're ready for you to board, Ma'am," the Marine escort said. With a nod to Hense, he added, "Ready, sir?"

Hense took his wife's arm as they followed the young man up the step into the car. She was pleasantly surprised by the luxury of the car's interior. "I expected a metal bench seat," she said.

"The Government's evidently doing this up in style," Hense commented, glancing at the Marine accompanying them.

The young man, taking no notice of Hense's comment, indicated a leather seat. "This is yours, Mrs. Price." His other hand gestured to an identical seat across the narrow aisle, "Sir." Stepping back, he said, "All set?"

These three were the only occupants of the car. "Wow," Hense exclaimed, "they sent this monster just to get us!"

The Marine nearly lost his footing as the train suddenly lurched forward. Both Goldie and Hense were glued to their windows as the car moved out of the shed into the weak light beneath the gray sky. She watched with fascination as first the city streets and then the southern Ohio countryside flew by the window. Realizing that someone was speaking to her, she tore her attention away from the scenery. "Can I get you anything?" the young Marine repeated. "Coffee?"

"No, thank you," she replied, managing her first smile of the day.

"Well, just settle back and relax. We'll have dinner in a little while. Then the porter will fix up your bed for you later. We'll be in New York when you wake in the morning."

The evening flew by as the day faded to twilight. A full seven-course meal – with wine even – was laid out for just the two of them. She giggled a little to herself hoping that the folks back in Hilltop didn't find out about the wine. She was ready enough when the porter came to prepare the bed. He was just stepping away when the Marine reappeared. "Sleep tight," he said with a smile. "You have a big week ahead of you!"

Safely ensconced in her berth, Goldie's thoughts drifted. Now that the Germans were whipped, the country could concentrate its efforts on the Pacific War. That's why the poster said "Now," she decided. The poster! Well, she'd read that the war was costing $175,000 a minute. That figure was incomprehensible, but still, the money for bullets and uniforms and tanks and planes had to come from somewhere. Yes, but did they have to torture her with her dead son's image plastered everywhere she looked? Wasn't dealing with his loss enough for her to bear? An all-expense paid trip to New York! Times Square! Broadway shows! The clickety-clack of the rails lulled her to sleep as she realized that every revolution of the wheels carried her further from her roots, Fleming

County where she belonged, where her family was, where Franklin... Goldie fell asleep, as she did every night, with tears in her eyes and a name on her lips – Franklin.

The sun was shining brightly as the train rolled into New York's Grand Central Station. Once again Goldie was confronted with what she'd come to think of as *The Photograph* as it was prominently displayed in the Station. She and Hense were whisked to the Waldorf-Astoria where the government had reserved a room for them. Over the hotel's front entrance hung *The Photograph*, 20 feet high.

Their room was more elegant than anything she'd ever dreamed existed, but they had little time to enjoy it before being summoned. That evening, they had a fabulous dinner at the Hampshire House overlooking Central Park. "I thought dinner was at noon." Hense said. Goldie was not sure if he was joking.

Informed that Central Park was New York's impressive green space, Goldie said, "What's the big deal? We've got as many trees on our little ole farm."

Later that evening they were taken to Radio City Music Hall where they saw a production of *Valley of Decision* featuring the world famous Rockettes. The show was a predictable romance story set in 1873 Pittsburg. The parlor maid falls in love with the mill owner's son and after many troubles, all comes right in the end.

"How'd you like the show?" Hense asked in the cab.

"I thought it was pretty silly," she said. "I knew he was gonna throw out that tramp he'd married in favor of the maid. She was his true love."

"I noticed that you cried anyway there at the end."

"How'd you like it?" she inquired, playfully slapping his knee.

"I thought the Rockettes looked pretty damned good."

The next day, May 15, was the big day. John Bradley, Ira Hayes and Rene Gagnon rolled in from a tour stop in Boston for a return visit to New York City. Hayes and Gagnon had escaped Iwo Jima unhurt but Bradley was on crutches, having been released from the hospital just for the bond tour. The day began with a rally at the Sub-Treasury Building on Wall Street. Goldie stood on the speakers' platform where she was placed next to Martha Strank and Hank Hansen's mother, Madeline Evelley. The ladies tried to carry on a polite conversation, but found it awkward and Mike Strank's mother did not speak English very well, anyway.

At one point, Madeline whispered to Goldie, "Big crowd, don't you think?" They faced a sea of perhaps 10,000 faces.

"More people than I ever saw at one time," Goldie said with a forced smile.

"This is a historic spot," Madeline said. "it was right here that George Washington took the first oath as President."

The program's beginning interrupted the talk. On their left, a Coast Guard band struck up *The National Anthem*. After some opening remarks, the band played *Anchors Away* followed by a speech by an Admiral. Then a speech by an Air Corps General followed *Off We Go Into the Wild Blue Yonder*. Then, the big moment: with a drum roll, the three "Gold Star" mothers, whose sons had died on Iwo Jima, and the three surviving flag raisers were introduced to thunderous applause. In the crowd, Hensley Price said, "I wouldn't have come if I'd known what a dog and pony show this was gonna be," to whoever might be listening.

After Bradley, Hayes and Gagnon ran up a flag while a bugler sounded *Call to the Colors*, each of the survivors and mothers was presented a $1,000 Series E War Bond. At 12:35, the band's rendition of the *Marines Hymn* brought the ceremonies to a close.[82]

Grateful when that was over, they were whisked off for lunch at the New York Stock Exchange. At the lunch table, Goldie was seated between her husband and Mike Strank's brother, John. Again, conversation was awkward. Directly across from her sat Ira Hayes flanked by Bradley and Gagnon. She longed to talk to the men who had served with her son, especially Ira as she knew that he and Franklin were close. The width of the oval table – at its maximum between her and Ira – prevented them from speaking, however.

When the meal was finished, each of the six honorees was introduced to Greta Garbo and then given a few free minutes before they were to go the gallery above the floor of the Stock Exchange. One of the swarming newspaper reporters approached Goldie and asked if she was enjoying the visit. "It kinda weights a woman down, sort of. You can't remember all the sights, they come at you so fast and I did want to tell the folks back home all about it."

"How do you feel about what your son did?"

"Well, he was just a farm boy. When he was home on furlough, he told me that he was going to do something to make me real proud." She paused to gather her thoughts then added, "I don't think he could have done anything greater than to raise that flag on Iwo Jima."

Laying his pencil aside, the reporter agreed, "No ma'am. No one could."[83]

Rene Gagnon was interested in hob-knobbing with the various big wigs while John Bradley and Hank Hansen's mother were occupied in quiet conversation. Goldie approached Ira. "Mr. Hayes?"

"Yes," Ira turned. The instant their eyes met, tears began to flow down the Marine's cheeks. Wordlessly he stepped up and put his arms around Goldie. "I tried to save him," he sobbed into her shoulder. She thought she smelled whiskey on his breath.

Holding her emotions in check was a constant struggle. At this moment, she lost the struggle and the tears she'd been holding back began. "I know," she managed to say. The crowd respectfully gave them space.

After a few moments, each managed to recover some composure. "Can you tell me about it?" Goldie asked, wiping her eyes with a handkerchief.

"You're sure you want me to?"

"Yes. I want to know how my son died."

"Like a Marine," Ira said. "We were cleaning out a small pocket of resistance. Franklin was moving from one hole to the next when a single shot hit him in the back." His voice cracked, but he cleared his throat and went on, "He did not suffer. I ran over. I was with him within ten seconds, but it was too late." Again he wrapped his arms around her. "I'm so sorry. Franklin was a good boy, a good Marine and a good buddy. I miss him terribly."[84]

They stood in silence for a moment. Then Goldie said, "So do I. I just wish Franklin was here to share in all this. He deserves it."

"Yeah, he does," Ira agreed. "As much as me or Gagnon or Bradley." After a pause, he added, "And so do Mike and Harlon." A look of dismay instantly covered his face.[85]

"Harlon?" Goldie asked, puzzled. "Who's that?"

"I have to go," Ira mumbled as he hurried away.

The rest of the day was a whirlwind tour. Another flag raising at the Bank of Manhattan was followed by a visit to the Barr Brothers Brokerage firm on the 55th floor of the Manhattan Company building. "Hell of a view, ain't it," Hense asked, looking out over the sprawling island.

"I don't know whether we came here to see or been seen," Goldie commented. She'd picked up on what Hense had been thinking all along.

"Huh!" he snorted. "Like I been sayin', a dog and pony show."

After a visit to the Statue of Liberty, they returned to the Waldorf-Astoria via East River Drive. Dinner was served on the Starlight Roof overlooking Park Avenue. Then it was off to Broadway for a live stage production of *Oklahoma!*, which had been playing at the St James Theater for more than two years.

A tired couple was delivered back to the hotel. "Wanna move to New York?" Goldie asked.

"I never dreamed I'd miss the smell of cow manure," Hense said with a smile. "I'm ready to go home. How 'bout you?" They stepped into the elevator.

"I'm doin' this for Franklin," she said. Thinking, she added, "And for the ones still fightin'." They walked to their room in silence before she sighed, "I'm tired of fancy food and fancier people. Give me just plain Kentucky folk any day. Well, it's only one more day."

May 16 was filled with the same kind of activity for the Prices. Lunch at the famous Stork Club, a complete tour of Rockefeller City where a model of the latest design in aircraft carriers was on display, a visit to former Presidential candidate and New York Governor, Al Smith's home, a tour of St. Patrick's Cathedral on Fifth Avenue and a shopping opportunity at Saks was topped off by dinner on the St. Regis' Roof and another Broadway show, *Bloomer Girls*.

A tired but relieved couple ignored the bond tour posters as they walked through Grand Central Station, happy to bid farewell to old New York. Physically exhausted and emotionally drained, Goldie slept most of the way but was awake after they ate dinner.

"Goldie," her husband said, hesitantly broaching a topic which had occupied his mind for weeks, "what are you gonna do with the money?" He had carefully chosen to ask "you" rather than "we."

"The $1,000 bond?"

"No," he looked into her eyes. "The $10,000 life insurance money Franklin left you."[86]

"Oh. I've tried not to think about it." After a long pause, she said, "do you have any ideas?"

"Well, it's your money," he said, "but I do think you ought to keep the fact that you got it private." Again he chose "you."

"It really isn't anybody's business," she agreed. "You know, there's a couple of pieces of property around that we could pick up. Maybe we could run a real dairy operation. That's what Franklin always wanted. It's his money and that'd honor him."

Her father, Charlie Mitchell, sisters Florine and Mildred and Julian were waiting when they stepped off the train at the Flemingsburg station.

"Well, daughter, how was the trip?" he asked, wrapping his arms around her.

"I cannot possibly tell you how happy I am to be home," she confessed, smiling.

"How'd you like New York?" Mildred asked.

"It's a right smart place they got up there," she replied with a grin, "but I don't believe it's ever gonna amount to nothin'."

"Why not, Mom?" Julian inquired.

"Well," she said slowly, "'cause it's just too far away."

Chapter 18
Saturday, May 8, 1948
Ewing, Kentucky

G oldie was awake early on this spring morning. More accurately, she was out of bed early, as a matter of fact, she had hardly slept at all. Today would be the day for an event she'd been anticipating and dreading for more than six months.

Back in August, nearly a year before, she and Julian had suffered a terrible day when the Marine Corps had returned Franklin's personal effects. In a tidy little green canvas bag came all that was left of him: the cigarette lighter he'd purchased in Honolulu, his watch, high school class ring and a silver ring, the small New Testament and two pennies. Handling these items was a traumatic chore for the two of them.

Julian opened the small blue Testament and saw Franklin's signature with the date inside the front cover. "January 19, 1944. That's the day he left here, isn't it, Mom," he asked.

"Yes," she said, eyeing the page.

"Look at this," Julian exclaimed when he saw his brother's signature inside the back cover of the Bible and the date. "August 29. That's just after he was home on furlough." Before he went overseas, Franklin had accepted Jesus Christ as his personal Savior. Gaining knowledge of that fact was a small comfort to Goldie, but she battled back her tears as she held the small Book in her hand.

Then, in September her heart was broken again when she received a Government check for $133.05, the military pay the Marine Corps owed Franklin for his service right up to the day he died. A few days later, Julian received the "gratuity" Franklin had told him about, a check for $388.80. Because Julian was only 12 and his father was dead, Goldie had appointed the People's Bank of Fleming County as his financial guardian, so the legal hassle involved did nothing to ease the process.

In October a Government notification had arrived informing her that all the servicemen's bodies were to be removed from Iwo Jima. She was offered the option to have her son's remains buried in an overseas National Cemetery – probably Hawaii's Punchbowl – or a National Cemetery in the continental United States or returned for burial in a private cemetery. Although she briefly considered having him buried in Arlington National Cemetery, the decision was not hard: Franklin belonged in Kentucky. Accordingly, she chose to have his remains shipped to Elizaville's Price Brothers Funeral Home for burial in that town's cemetery.

Near the end of March, notification had arrived that Franklin's body, along with 65 other Kentucky servicemen and 162 Ohioans killed in action in the Pacific, was enroute to the United States aboard the Army transport *Walter W. Schwenk*. At the time, the Government was not sure of an arrival date but promised further notification.

On May 6, the proverbial pine box, escorted by Marine honor guard Staff Sergeant Eddie Sumrall, arrived at the funeral home. The personnel there – who were only distantly related – took charge of transferring the remains to a proper casket. Despite Goldie's offers to feed and house him, Sergeant Sumrall stayed with the coffin all the while it was at the funeral home. Goldie had obtained a burial flag through the postmaster, and the rigid Marine beside the flag-draped casket was a memorable sight. With a heavy heart, she wrote a check for the $75 funeral expenses. The fact that the Government would reimburse that money made no difference. Uncle Sam would also supply a standard military headstone – the small flat marble marker – but she had not yet filed the application.

Mixed emotions again filled Goldie as she scanned the front page of the *Fleming Gazette* that afternoon. In the center of the page was a picture of the new $4,500 Franklin R. Sousley science lab at Fleming County High School. Beside that article, on the right, was Franklin's picture accompanied by the announcement of his remains arrival.

"Are you ready?" Ray Mitchell was at the door.

"As soon as I gather up these youngun's."

Hense came in from the bedroom with baby Janice in his arms. "Jake," he commanded, "you help keep J.H. quiet when we get there." Franklin's half-siblings were aged two and five.

"Florine and Mildred will look after him," Goldie informed.

Outside, the Sousley side of the family waited. Franklin's uncles Leslie and Hoover and the grandparents were standing in the shade smoking cigarettes and talking quietly.

There was no conversation during the short ride to the Elizaville cem-

217

etery. All were amazed at the size of the crowd gathered there. "There must be 2000 people here," Hense guessed.

"Biggest funeral I ever saw," Mildred agreed.

Near the crest of the hill, a Price Brothers tent had been erected over the gravesite. In the rows of folding wooden chairs beneath the tent sat some of Franklin's closest friends. The tent also shaded the burial plots of Duke and Malcolm Sousley, and an open grave. Sgt. Sumrall stood at his post by the flag-draped coffin. Two front rows of vacant chairs awaited the family.

Beside the tent, standing at attention in bright sunshine, was an honorary firing squad provided by Flemingsburg's Will Nelson Fant American Legion Post. Behind the guard, who held their rifles at order arms, was a contingent of perhaps 50 uniformed men representing all branches of the service.

The family held back to allow Goldie to enter the tent first. The hum of conversation ceased as she ducked inside and took her seat in front of the casket. Hense with Janice, Julian, J.H., Mildred, Florine, Ray, Leslie and Hoover filed in to fill out the front row.

After an old family friend, the Reverend Gilbert Fern, offered an opening prayer, a Marine Corps chaplain conducted the standard military service. Then Rev. Fern took over. "Franklin was simply one of the millions of boys we sent out to fight for our way of life," he began. "They fought for our American democracy and our Christian hopes. They preserved the freedom our forefathers earned nearly 200 years ago.

"Perhaps, in time, the name of this particular boy may be forgotten, but as long as there is democracy in this land, the picture of which he is a part will be symbolic of a heroic act in a great cause....

"When Franklin left here, he had a date with destiny.... He gave not one whit more than the other sixty-six Fleming County men or the thousands of other American men and women who died in this war. They all had courage; they all gave their lives; all were heroes. Franklin gave no more than any one of these – no one could – but it was his fate to become an enduring symbol of every man who fought and died for his country."[87]

As Rev. Fern sat, a sharp order caused the honor guard to raise their rifles. The other servicemen rendered a hand salute. "Ready... Aim... Fire!" The loud report from eleven rifles caused Goldie to flinch. Despite her being prepared, each of two more repetitions also startled her. The sound from the third volley had barely faded away when a bugler standing under the flag behind the casket sounded *Taps*.

The final poignant note lingered still in the soft spring air as an echoing bugled *Taps* began from somewhere over the crest of the hill. Two Marines stepped forward, lifted the flag from the casket and folded it into three corners. One of the men handed the thick triangle to Sgt. Sumrall who stepped in front of the softly weeping Goldie Price. Bending so his face was near hers, he quietly said, "On behalf of a grateful nation," as he placed the flag on her lap. Those who were not weeping openly certainly had tears in their eyes.

Hense handed Janice to Mildred so that he could take his wife's arm as they stood to exit. She ran her hand over the smooth casket surface whispering, "my son, oh, my son." Everyone gave her a respectful space. At length, she said to Hense, "Well...." He led her from the tent into the sunshine.

A round, bespectacled man stepped forward. "Mrs. Price," he said, taking her hand, "I'm Earl Clements."

"Governor!" Goldie exclaimed. "It's an honor to see you here."

"I just thought the State Government should be represented here today," he said. "We're all mighty proud of your boy."[88]

Franklin Runyon Sousley, the boy who'd predicted he'd come back a hero, had kept his word.

"We'd better get a sweater or go in," Goldie said from the semi-darkness of the porch. "There's a little nip in the air tonight."

"Well, it is October," her husband observed, rising from his rocker. "It's nice out, though. I'll get you a sweater."

He had only taken a step when a police car slid to a stop in the drive. A short fat man emerged from the car, his flat-brimmed hat in his hand. "Evenin', Sheriff," Hense greeted him.

"Evenin'" he replied, clearly ill at ease.

After a few moments of awkward silence, Hense asked, "What can I do for you?"

"Well," the policeman began hesitantly, "I came to talk to Goldie."

"I'm right here," she said, standing.

With a deep sigh, the Sheriff said, "There's been an accident and...."

"Jake?" There was dread in her voice.

"Yes, ma'am, I'm afraid so."

"How bad?"

"I really don't know. He's in the Hayswood Hospital up at Maysville. I'll take you up there, if you want."

In the car, Goldie could see the driver's face only when it was lit in the glare of on-coming headlights. "What happened?" she demanded as they rode north toward the river.

"Well, he was out with four other men. They'd been over to Aberdeen on the Ohio side." The man's face faded from view as the car passed.

"Drinkin'?"

"Yes, ma'am, I think so." An on-coming car again briefly lit his features.

"Who was he with?"

"Well, it was J.L. Hawkins who was driving. He just failed to make a curve on Highway 52 near the pay lake out there. The State Police said the car rolled four or five times. Hawkins was killed at the scene and Bill McKee is hurt pretty bad, so they tell me. R.D. Hunt – it was his parents' car – and Bill Galliher, in addition to your son are in the hospital. Hunt and Galliher were thrown clear."

"They're all older than Julian," she said, "he didn't have no business out runnin' with that bunch. What about…."

"I've done told you all I know," the Sheriff interrupted. He was relieved when he delivered her at the front entrance of the hospital. Without bothering to express her thanks, she ran up the steps to the information desk. Given the directions, she dashed along the tiled corridor to the intensive care unit's nurses' station. "That's his doctor there," the nurse said, inclining her head toward a white-coated figure standing behind her.

"I'm Dr. Denham," the tall, white-haired man said, taking her hand. She found no clues to her unspoken fears in his face.

"How bad is he hurt?" she implored.

"His injuries are rather serious," he answered. "Your son has some deep lacerations and several serious body contusions, but," here he paused to polish his glasses with a handkerchief, "the fractured skull is the worst of it."

"Oh, Lord," Goldie said as Dr. Denham helped her sink into a plush chair. "Will he recover?" Before the doctor could answer, she blurted, "Will his mind be OK if he does?"

"Well," the Doctor said, noncommittally, "there's the finest staff and facilities here and I'm doing everything I can."

Three agonizing days later, on October 4, 1951, Julian Martin Sousley, youngest son of Duke and Goldie Sousley was dead.[89] None of the three boys had lived to see age twenty.

A little more than three years after Franklin's funeral, Goldie Price stood on the same spot in the Elizaville cemetery. Beneath the same Price Brothers Funeral Home tent sat the same family and friends and the same Reverend Gilbert Fern. This time, the tent covered the graves of Duke, Malcolm, Franklin and an open grave. Kneeling beside Julian's casket, Goldie gathered her two remaining children, Janice and J.H., now five and nine in her arms. Her face betrayed no hint of what was going through her mind.

Chapter 19

Tuesday, November 9, 1954
Blue Grass Field
Lexington, Kentucky

G oldie and Hensley Price stepped through the gate onto the concrete ramp where the blue, green and silver Eastern Airlines Lockheed Constellation waited. At the top of the rollaway stairwell, its side door stood agape revealing a dark interior. Admiring the plane's gleaming finish, sexy curves and triple-tail configuration, Hense remarked, "What a beautiful aircraft!"

"I ain't so sure about this," Goldie worried aloud. "If the Lord had intended me to fly, He'd have given me wings."

"Instead of wheels?" Ignoring the nasty look she gave him, Hense took her arm as he guided her toward the stairs. "This is the same plane President Eisenhower flies on and he goes all over the world. Surely it'll get us to Washington, D.C."

"Oh, I reckon it will," she said with a sigh as she hesitantly started up the steps. At the top, a uniformed pretty girl looked at the ticket and ushered them to their seats. Hense took the window seat. Soon the four mighty engines were roaring and the plane started to roll. With only a brief pause at the end of the runway, the machine accelerated, pushing the passengers back in their plush seats. With her eyes closed, Goldie asked, "Are we off the ground yet?"

Before Hense could answer, they both felt the thrill everyone experiences when he or she feels the wheels leave the ground for the first time. "Let me see," she squealed, leaning across him to look out the window. She watched in fascination as the bluegrass fields and white fences whizzed by below. Her view was improved when the wing dipped as the plane turned to the east. "How long is this gonna take?"

"The ticket says we'll be there about 4 PM," he replied. "So that's about three hours." In a moment, he added, "You're the one who dealt with 'em in setting this up, is somebody gonna meet us?"

"No. Something called The Marine Corps War Memorial Foundation is in charge. They raised the funds to build the Marine Corps Memorial, selected the site, designed the Monument and oversaw everything. They also made reservations for us at the Washington Hotel and, as you know, paid for the plane ticket and sent some expense money. We're on our own as to how to get around and how long we stay."[90]

"All this is just to honor Franklin and those other guys that raised that flag?"

"Lord, no," she snapped. "It's the Marine Corps Memorial – not Iwo Jima – it honors all Marines who've served their country. I'm proud, and you should be too, that my boy will forever be the symbol of so many."

"Seems to me they didn't have much design work to do. The statue is just Joe Rosenthal's photograph, ain't it?"

"I don't know how much work they've had to do," she said, settling back in her seat. "I guess there's some difference between a picture and a statue."

Indeed, Goldie had no idea of the work, money and time that were behind the Marine Corps Memorial that was to be officially dedicated the next day. During the war, Felix de Weldon, a trained sculptor, was serving in the Navy when he became one of the many who were captivated by Joe Rosenthal's image of the second flag raising. Within days, he took it upon himself to fashion a small three-dimensional model in clay and then he made a life-sized model. The Marine Corps liked his work so well that they had him produce a 36-foot tall plaster model, which was unveiled in front of Washington's Navy Building in 1946.

On July 1, 1947 Congress proposed, and ultimately approved, an act allowing for "the erection of a memorial to the Marine Corps dead of all wars to be placed in the District or immediate vicinity." The memorial was to be privately funded by the Marine Corps League, but located on public property. The League, in turn, established the Marine Corps War Memorial Foundation to raise the money and oversee the project. While the Congressional bill mentioned neither Rosenthal nor de Weldon, no other design was ever considered, although the original concept was much larger than the final product turned out to be. The first location considered, near Haines Point, proved unsatisfactory, so the Nevius tract in Arlington, Virginia adjacent to the national cemetery was selected. Ultimately $850,000, donated almost entirely by Marines, was needed to complete the memorial on that site.

The surviving flag raisers, Gagnon, Hayes and Bradley, posed for de

Weldon and the sculptor also used pictures and available physical statistics to create figures representing Sousley, Block and Strank. In the end, the facial features were not used as the Memorial was to honor all Marines killed in all wars, so resemblance to any particular individual was not desirable. In an effort to make the body images as realistic as possible, the sculptor first created them as nudes and then added the clothes. Also, converting a two dimensional image to a three dimensional statue required some rearrangement of the figures.

Ninety–six tons of plaster was required for de Weldon to craft a model with the 32-feet tall men's figures, a 60-foot flag pole, 16-foot rifles and a 32-quart canteen. This model was cut into more than 100 pieces before being moved to New York to be used as a mold for casting. The resulting bronze figures were carried by truck down the seaboard to Arlington in September 1954.

Site preparation had begun with a groundbreaking ceremony on February 19 – the ninth anniversary of the Iwo Jima invasion. Excavation began in May, and that same month a Marine Corps time capsule was placed in the concrete being poured.

When the bronze figures arrived at the site, cranes lifted them into place atop a ten-foot concrete base. As access to the interior was required to bolt and weld the various parts in place, a door was cut in the cartridge pocket of one of the figures. The men were oriented facing south so that the prevailing north wind would cause the flag to billow away from them, just as in *The Photograph*, most of the time. The statue was also purposely aligned so as not to be on an axis with the Washington Monument and Lincoln Memorial on the National Mall across the river. By late September, the figures were fixed in place.

Black Swedish granite facing completed the base. Carved in a band running around the top of the base are the names of every battle in which the Marine Corps fought from the Revolutionary War (1775 -1783) to Korea (1950). On the east side stands the Marine Corps globe, anchor and eagle emblem and the words:

"IN HONOR AND MEMORY
OF THE MEN OF THE
UNITED STATES MARINE CORPS
WHO HAVE GIVEN
THEIR LIVES TO THEIR COUNTRY
SINCE 10 NOVEMBER 1775."

On the west side, surrounded by a wreath, are the stirring words Admiral Chester Nimitz used to describe the Americans who served on Iwo Jima:

"UNCOMMON
VALOR
WAS A COMMON
VIRTUE"

In the tails of a ribbon beneath the wreath is the Marine Corps motto:

"SEMPER FIDELIS."

By the next month, work was complete and the American flag first flew over the Memorial on October 8, 1954. Official dedication was set for November 10, the 179th anniversary of the creation of the Marine Corps. The surviving Iwo Jima flag raisers, including those from the first flag raising, and the parents of those killed were invited to take part in the ceremony.[91]

Goldie would soon be surprised to learn that the parents would not include Madeline Evelley, Hank Hansen's mother, whom she had met at the bond tour rally nine years before. In the fall of 1946, Mrs. Ada Belle Block had gotten wind of the fact that Ira Hayes had informed the Marine Corps that the figure at the base of the pole in Rosenthal's picture was – just as she had insisted all along – her son, Harlon. In answer to a letter from Mrs. Block, Ira had written, "God knows how happy I was to get your letter. I have prayed and waited for such a happening as this. When I did arrive in Washington [April 19, 1945] I tried to set things right, but some Col. told me not to say another word, as the two were dead, meaning Harlon and Hansen. And besides, the public knew who was in the picture and [the Marine Corps] didn't want any last minute commotion."[92] At Mrs. Block's instigation, the Marine Corps had obtained an affidavit from Ira and interviewed Gagnon and Bradley as to the identity of the man with his back to Rosenthal's camera. Ira Hayes pointed out, among other facts, that in Lowery's pictures, Hank Hansen was wearing a cloth cap while all the figures in Rosenthal's photograph were helmeted. In answer to Marine Corps investigations, Gagnon and Bradley admitted that, "it could be Block." Ira was absolutely certain that the man was Harlon and, as the facts indicated that he was correct, the Marine Corps officially declared that the man at the base of the flagstaff was Harlon Block.[93]

Goldie was relieved and disappointed when the plane's wheels squeaked against the pavement at Washington's National Airport. She was happy to be on the ground, disappointed that the flight was over and apprehensive about the ceremonies to take place in the morning. "Want to do some sight-seeing?" Hense asked. "I hear the Lincoln Memorial is worth the trip."

"Maybe tomorrow," she replied as they waited for their bags. "Senator Clements has invited us to visit him at the Capitol, so we'll be over there anyway."

"Pennsylvania and 15th," Hense instructed the cab driver.

"A little wider than the Licking, ain't it?" Goldie observed as they crossed the Potomac. They did manage to view a few sights, as they passed near the Jefferson Memorial, were awed by several government buildings and spotted the Lincoln Memorial in the distance, before they arrived at the Washington Hotel.

November 10 – a day which Kentucky's Governor Wetherby, to honor Franklin, had proclaimed Iwo Jima Day back home – dawned gray and cold in the District of Columbia. Despite the chilly weather, a crowd of some 7,000 people were gathered at the site of the Memorial just outside Arlington Cemetery. After Goldie and Hense met Belle Block, Joe Rosenthal, sculptor Felix de Weldon and Deputy Secretary of Defense Robert Anderson, they were seated in the front row of the crowd with Ira Hayes, Rene Gagnon, John Bradley and first flag raisers Chuck Lindberg and Jim Michels. Goldie grimly noted that, of the eleven men who had participated in the two flag raisings, only five were alive and present to witness this tribute. On the speakers stand before them sat Vice President Richard Nixon, Secretary Anderson, the Commandant of the Marine Corps, General Lemuel Shepherd, de Weldon and assorted other dignitaries. Behind the platform, the Monument, covered by a giant tarp, loomed against the gray sky. Evidently as a surprise, President Eisenhower showed up to add his dignity to the proceedings.

The ceremony began with a concert by the Marine Corps band. Following a prayer by Navy Chaplin Admiral E.B. Harp and a few brief remarks by Colonel Moreau, President of the Marine Corps War Memorial Foundation and Orme Lewis, Assistant Secretary of the Interior, General Shepherd stepped to the microphone.

Stunning in his dress blues with a chest full of ribbons, the Commandant began slowly but soon warmed to his topic, saying that the statue represented a great moment in American history. "This is not simply a monument to the departed past, it is a graphic message for the future....

"May it stand for ages yet to come as a symbol of American courage and determination, of indestructible faith and of unity of purpose. For with that spirit, however severe may be the trials which lie ahead, our nation will endure and the cause of human freedom will triumph...."

Tears streamed from Goldie's eyes as she heard him say, "In this sense the five Marines and the sailor depicted here are, in themselves, only a symbol. These men do not represent just the Marine Corps – nor is this a monument to war.

"To all who shall ever view this Memorial, it will speak of the courage, the spirit and the greatness of the American people – the people from who these men and their comrades came."[94]

A tug on a cord caused the tarp to fall away revealing de Weldon's work. "Franklin will live forever," Goldie said through her tears. While a collective gasp went through the crowd, Ira Hayes, sobbing away, leaned toward Goldie and placed his head on her shoulder.

The remainder of the program was anticlimactic. Sculptor de Weldon explained some differences between his work and Joe Rosenthal's photograph, detailing the changes he had made to enhance the perspective of a viewer on the ground. Leaning close to his wife so Mrs. Block would not hear, Hense whispered, "He moved Harlon's ass to a less exposed position, too." Goldie slapped his hand.

Vice President Nixon then took the opportunity to make a foreign policy address. "This statue symbolizes the hopes and dreams of American and the real purpose of our foreign and military policy.... We realize to retain freedom for ourselves, we must be concerned when people in other parts of the world may lose theirs. There is no greater challenge to statesmanship...." At that point, Goldie stopped listening and studied the figure that represented her son. From her vantage point, she could not see the face, but did credit the sculptor for duplicating Franklin's body frame.

When the festivities ended, Goldie and Hense met the dignitaries and pictures were taken all around. She took an immediate dislike to Richard Nixon, as he was looking at someone else in the crowd when he shook her hand. Although she considered that an insult, it really didn't matter, as she wouldn't have liked him anyway – he was a damned Republican. After the crowd melted away, Goldie and Hense walked around the statue with Joe Rosenthal and his family. Joe expected to find his name carved into the base and Goldie expected to see her son's name. Both were disappointed – the only name carved in the granite was that of the sculptor.[95]

"Look at that," she exclaimed, pointing.

"What?"

"That man next to Franklin has his hand wrapped around Franklin's wrist! Who is that?"

"That's the Sergeant. Strank. Why is he holding Franklin's wrist?" Hense wondered aloud.

"Maybe he couldn't reach the pipe," she speculated. "Maybe he was helping Franklin hold on."

They stood in silence for quite some time. Sensing that Goldie was reluctant to leave, Hense walked away, giving her distance and time to reconcile her thoughts. She walked to his side when she was ready to go.

"Well, it's an impressive Monument," Hense said, in the car returning to the hotel. "You had it right – with that statue of him up there, Franklin will live forever."

"Yes," Goldie said, sobbing softly.

Hense gathered her in his arms. "Something for us to always be proud of," he said. "Not many of us ever gain that kind of immortality."

"You're right," she replied softly, "but he surely paid a mighty high price."

Chapter 20

Sunday, June 3, 1984
Elizaville, Kentucky

If you want to visit Franklin Sousley's grave, you'll need to get to the Elizaville Cemetery. From Cincinnati or Lexington, travel on US 68 and turn toward Flemingsburg on KY 165. If you're to the east, you can take state roads from either Morehead or Mt. Sterling to Flemingsburg. In any case, you'll end up traveling on KY 32 over the same beautiful hills and valleys that Franklin saw from the school bus. After you turn south on Route 170 at the caution light in downtown Elizaville, a drive of about a half mile will bring you to the cemetery on the left. As soon as you enter the cemetery, you'll see his tall rectangular grave marker standing black against the sky.

The man we have to thank for that is Thomas White. Tom White grew up in neighboring Nicholas County and like any other Kentucky boy, took pride in knowing that a country boy from just up the road was immortalized in Joe Rosenthal's photograph. White's pride swelled even more when he joined the Marine Corps in the mid-1960's and learned that the spirit exemplified by the Iwo Jima flag raising is an integral part of Marine philosophy.[96]

One day, in the summer of 1982, White had business in Flemingsburg. As he passed through Elizaville on the way home, he decided to visit the cemetery to pay his respects to Franklin Sousley. "I couldn't find his grave," White says. "I was a little pressed for time, so I decided to come back another day." On his second visit, he still could not locate Sousley's grave, so "I decided I'd look at every stone in the cemetery until I found it."

On the third try, when he finally did locate the grave, he was stunned to see that it was marked only with the standard Veteran's Administration stone, a flat marker about 18 by 24 inches. "I was mad, probably madder than I had ever been in all my life," White said. "After all, Franklin was a part of the most famous photograph ever taken. To me, he is a hero and he deserves more than that."

White did not know it at the time, but Franklin's mother thought her son deserved something more, too. In July 1958, Goldie had petitioned the Marine Corps to provide some recognition on his grave identifying him as one of the Iwo Jima flag raisers. For her effort, she received nothing more than a letter informing her that such matters were under the jurisdiction of the Quartermaster General, Department of the Army.[97] Several years later, the Commonwealth of Kentucky did erect a small metal sign proclaiming that Franklin was "one of six Marines who raised the flag on Iwo Jima, 23 February 1945." Evidently, somebody didn't know that one of the men was a Navy Corpsman.

Leaving the cemetery, White wondered if any of Franklin's family might still be around. A stop at the local post office gained him the knowledge that Goldie Price was, indeed, alive and living just down the road. "I just had to talk to her," White said with a grin. He learned, as everybody in Fleming County knew, that "Miss Goldie" had a wonderful sense of humor and even though nearly 80 years old, was a very active woman. "I really enjoyed Goldie's company," he said. "In fact I fell in love with her – she was a piece of work." The two of them shared a common passion to get additional recognition for Franklin. White came away not only determined to do what he could, but to get it done while Goldie was still alive.

Tom White was in the Marine reserves at that point, part of the First Military Police unit in Lexington. Back at the office, he mentioned to the First Sergeant, Larry Napier, that he had located Sousley's grave and was disappointed to find nothing more than the standard flat stone. "He inspired me when he said, 'Let's do something about it.'" White says. White and Napier and the other non-commissioned officers formed a committee with the intent of "doing something about it." The committee rolled up their sleeves, and on November 4, 1982, the Franklin Runyon Sousley Foundation, Inc., a non-profit agency created for the specific purpose of raising money to build a fitting monument on his grave came into existence.

White, Napier and the other committee members created and distributed a brochure featuring a picture and description of the memorial they intended to build as well as some information about Franklin, Goldie and the battle for Iwo Jima. They proposed a three-tiered monument made from black marble. The lower level would present a brief biography of Franklin, the middle section would have his name and birth and death dates with the Marine Corps emblem on each side, while the upper section would feature a carving of Rosenthal's famous photograph with the Sousley figure highlighted. The upper section would also include the appropriate inscription:

Semper Fidelis
Always Faithful
I am defender of my country. My actions are governed by those of my forefathers whose courage and valor beyond the call of duty enabled this country to remain independent. I will never forget that I am dedicated to those principles which let our flag fly free throughout the world. I have always placed my trust in God and in these United States of America. I have given my life in their defense.

On the back, the upper section would present the names of the six flag raisers. The proposed memorial would be six feet wide and about ten feet high, weigh about ten tons and cost some $16,000. If it were possible, the committee intended to obtain some of Iwo Jima's black sand to complete the project. White hoped to complete the monument within a year or so and dedicate it on February 19, 1984, the 39th anniversary of the Iwo Jima invasion.

The committee members spoke at every Veterans of Foreign Wars (VFW) post, American Legion hall, Rotary Club and civic club they could schedule, asking for donations. Kentucky's major newspapers lent their support, publishing articles detailing the project and asking for public contributions. A similar article ran in the Marine Corps magazine, *Leatherneck*.

White worked closely with the American Legion post in Flemingsburg and sought Goldie's approval on every move. "I visited her at her home one day," he said, "and there was another lady there. As Goldie and I discussed the plans for Franklin's memorial, the other lady burst into tears." White choked up a bit as he said, "the lady sobbed, 'I lost my son, too.' That's when I knew that this monument – like the one at Arlington – isn't simply for Franklin, he's a symbol for all those who saved democracy for us."

Despite tireless efforts, the results were somewhat disappointing. By July 1983, only about $6,000 had been raised and so the committee began to think in smaller terms. Perhaps a less ambitious project could be accomplished. "No!" Tom White declared in redoubling his efforts. "Franklin Sousley deserves a proper memorial," White said, "and I wasn't going to make him settle for less." After he persuaded the newspapers to run the appeal again, money began to flow in. In mid-January 1984, the required money was in hand. Ultimately more than $22,000 was donated.

However, considering the time required in obtaining the necessary permits and for construction, it was too late to make the February date. In consideration of Goldie's age, the decision was made not to wait another year but to have the monument constructed and dedicated as soon as possible. With much time and materials being donated by various companies and individuals, work forged ahead at full speed.

Kentucky's Congressman Larry Hopkins, a former Marine himself, became involved and managed to cut through the governmental red tape involved in obtaining sand from Iwo Jima's beach. "I have no idea how he did it or what was involved," says White, "all I know is that the most beautifully crafted Japanese box I ever saw arrived packed with black sand. Opening that box was a dramatic moment." It is possible that Franklin walked on the same sand, and, considering the small size of the island and the ferocity of the battle, that sand is almost surely blood stained.

By summer, the monument, just as originally envisioned, was in place including a glass vial in the ground at the base containing the black Iwo Jima sand. On a clear June Sunday afternoon, a crowd of about 800 people gathered at the Elizaville cemetery for the unveiling ceremony. Among those present were the Maysville community band, a Marine honor guard, Congressmen Larry Hopkins and Carl D. Perkins and one of Franklin's Marine buddies, Joe Rodriguez.

Following some opening remarks by Marine Major Stephen Shivers and an invocation by a Navy Chaplin, Tom White stepped to the microphone to explain the how and why of the creation of the monument. After Brigadier General Richard P. Trotter addressed Franklin's importance to the Marine Corps, Joe Rodriguez shared a few memories of the flag raisers, noting that he "thought Franklin was making up the names of those Kentucky towns until I came down here and drove through some of them." Congressman Hopkins made the keynote address, praising Franklin for his heroic service. "It's not corny for us to love our country, it's not corny to respect the flag and it's not corny to be proud to be an American," Hopkins said.[98] With a tug on the cord, the monument was exposed as the honor guard fired a 21-gun salute and four Marine Corps jets roared across the blue sky overhead.

All donated funds not expended on the monument were turned over to Flemingsburg's Franklin R. Sousley VFW post #1834 to establish a scholarship fund in Franklin's name. About $4,600 was invested at the Peoples Bank of Flemingsburg in hopes that the interest it earns would be sufficient to provide a small financial aid to deserving Fleming County students. An officer of the bank, a member of the VFW and the Fleming County High School principal formed a committee to award the $500 scholarship.

Twenty-five years after that June day, Tom White stood beside Franklin's monument, his face covered with obvious and justifiable pride. "I have two regrets," he said. "I'm sorry that the carving of Rosenthal's photograph isn't better, but it's all we could afford." And secondly, "This should have been done much sooner."

The practical interpretation of the Marine Corps motto, *Semper Fidelis*, means that a Marine is always faithful to the mission at hand, to his fellow Marines and to the Corps. In his work on behalf of Franklin, Tom White exemplifies that spirit above and beyond the call of duty.

Chapter 21

Saturday, November 9, 2002
Arlington, Virginia

In the 27 years that have elapsed since the flag raising ceremony, when my primary interest in my Uncle Franklin was praying he'd provide some way for me to get a ride in that helicopter, I have come to a better understanding of the significance of the Iwo Jima flag raising and his part in it. When my Mamaw – everybody else called her Miss Goldie – died in 1988, her sister Mildred became the keeper of the Franklin legend. Mildred and Florine couldn't keep up with all the requests for interviews and so on, so my dad – who was Franklin's half-brother – being gone, the torch was passed on to me.

I'm not sure how the word got around, but evidently it did, that Dwayne Price was the person to talk to if you wanted information on Franklin Sousley. I knew that the Marine Corps League held a ceremony at the Elizaville cemetery every year sometime around February 23 to commemorate the anniversary of the flag raising, but I was a bit surprised at the number of requests for interviews from newspaper reporters, magazine editors and history students. Mamaw saved everything: all Franklin's letters, his certificates, his grade school and high school records, letters of condolence to her – everything, so we have plenty of documentation. In answering so many questions, I've had occasion to study all that data and have been required to learn a lot about World War II in general and Franklin's part in it in particular. The on-going interest is a source of family pride.

Given that, it was not too much of a shock when a letter from Edward Block, Harlon's cousin, rolled in asking if we were interested in joining him in an effort to have the flag raisers' names added to the Marine Corps Memorial. As soon as we got that word, I, too, felt that the names should be included and so did the other families. It seems that Mr. Block was visiting the Memorial when he pointed out to a friend that one of the figures represented his cousin. "How do you know?" she asked. "There are no names."

At that point, he decided the names should be there. "If those guys had been Generals, the names would be there," he declared. Mr. Block enlisted the families' aid and the Commandant of the Marine Corps, General James Jones. With General Jones and all the flag raisers' families behind him, Mr. Block took on the National Park Service (NPS).[99]

Two generations of Americans, and Japanese, born since that memorable day in 1945 understand neither the significance of the battle for Iwo Jima, nor the impact that the flag raising had on the two countries. That's a part of the reason the Memorial is there, of course, but it is a monument to all Marines who died in all wars, not just Iwo Jima and not just WWII. Therein lies the reason the names were not made an integral part of the Memorial which is under the auspices of the NPS.

However, the NPS has learned over the years that many of the thousands of people who visit the Memorial every year want to know who the men are and the significance of Iwo Jima on world history. So, at Edward Block's instigation, a compromise measure was reached. The NPS decided to install four "wayside panels" which would answer the most frequently asked questions. The Marine Corps History Division provided the text for the wayside panels and the Marine Corps Heritage Foundation graciously provided funding for the project. The panels are designed to: (1) provide an overview of Marine Corps history; (2) explain the battle for Iwo Jima; (3) describe the two flag raisings and (4) provide some data on the Memorial itself. The third panel identifies Joe Rosenthal as the man responsible for the picture and includes pictures, ranks and hometowns of the six men involved in the second flag raising. Of necessity, each of the descriptions is brief.

In August, we received a letter from Mr. Block inviting us to participate in the dedication of the wayside panels at the Marine Corps Memorial in Arlington. The ceremony was to be held November 9 in conjunction with the annual celebration of the founding of the Marine Corps.

"What?" my wife, Tina exploded. "You wouldn't seriously consider going to Washington right now, would you?"

"Of course, I'm going. Why not?"

"Because that D.C. sniper is running wild up there. Do you want to get shot?"

"Oh, they've arrested him. That's over."

"Well," she admitted, "just because they've made an arrest doesn't mean they got the right one. And besides, there may be a copy cat."

I was adamant. "Mamaw would go," I declared. "She'd go if the sniper called up and personally told her that he was specifically after her. And anyway, that Memorial is an impressive thing and so special to us I'd like to see it again."

"I'm sure you're right about Goldie," she sighed. "If you're going, I'll go too. What's the deal?"

"The Marine Corps has a ceremony at the Memorial every year on November 10 to celebrate its birthday and remember all those who've died to keep us free. This year, they're going to dedicate the wayside panels on the day before. We'll get to meet some of the other flag raisers' families."

"Franklin's aunts ought to go, too," Tina suggested.

Mildred and Florine would have loved to attend, but aged 96 and 86 respectively, they were just not up to the trip. So, my mom, my sister Penny, Tina and I and our daughter Brittani had the honor of representing the Sousley family. We ended up at the Marine Corps Community Services Center at Henderson Hall in Arlington on the morning of November 9 where we did meet each of the other flag raisers families. Edward Block was there, of course, as was Ira Hayes' brother Kenny and his daughter, Sara Bernal. Rene Gagnon's wife Pauline and their son Rene, Jr. were in attendance as well as Mike Strank's brother John and sister Mary Pero. A gaggle of Bradley's were on hand including James, son of corpsman John Bradley and who, with Ron Powers, produced the book *Flags of our Fathers*. We arrived first and just after we were seated on the van for the ride over to the Memorial for the dedication and ceremony, Kenny Hayes and Sara joined us. We had an interesting conversation and discussed the relationship between our relatives. Let me tell you that anybody who thinks history is boring or that these things didn't really happen has never had such an experience!

The ceremony began with a concert by the Marine Corps Band. At the finale, everyone came to rigid attention while the band played a stirring rendition of the National Anthem. A couple of speeches by assembled Marine dignitaries were pretty routine. For me, the highlight was hearing Edward Block get in a lick for our enlisted men relatives. He used an analogy quoting the Queen of the Netherlands when she was putting up a bell cotillion. "There are big bells and sometimes they drown out the smaller bells when ringing, but we also need to hear the smaller bells to appreciate the song." He said that this represented the enlisted men embedded in stone silence without their names. He later told me that he felt it was a great day for America to hear the smaller bells tolling for a change.

My getting to view the Memorial up close and personal was a thrill. A solemn moment occurred at the close of the ceremony when a Marine bugler standing at the men's feet atop the base of the Memorial sounded *Taps*. Seeing a live person standing beside the figures gave a lasting impression of the grandeur of the statue. The blue-coated Marine looked so tiny in comparison!

In walking around the base, I noticed that Joe Rosenthal's name had been added to the base of the Memorial. I later learned that President Reagan had approved that addition in October 1982. I also learned that the Memorial is one of just a few places where it is authorized for the American flag to fly 24 hours per day. That measure was approved by President Kennedy in 1961.

We had an opportunity to inspect the new additions and talk to the other flag raisers' families. It's impossible to explain, but I felt a kinship with each of them in knowing that our pasts were linked by the famous event in which our relatives participated. Being related to Franklin Sousley has always made me proud to be an American, but I was never prouder of my heritage, and never more humble, than when I stood with the other families at the flag raisers' feet. Seeing the same emotions in their faces made it an extra special event as in no other company could anyone experience what we shared.

Looking up at the figures, I tried – and failed – to imagine what Mamaw must have felt 48 years earlier when she viewed the image of Franklin 30 feet tall. Given the pride that swelled within me, I cannot envision how her heart must have fluttered. I also tried – and also failed – to put myself in Franklin's place back in 1944 when he joined the Marine Corps. Franklin was, just like me, a good ole Fleming County boy and while I know the Memorial is for all Marines, I could not help wondering what would he think about seeing himself up there?

Saturday, May 1, 2010
Bardstown, Kentucky

There are a number of items which I feel are important for complete-ness of the story but which did not fit in anywhere in the narrative. So, I'll chunk them in here. First are the Iwo Jima statistics. The battle, which was projected to last 4 or 5 days, actually took 36, a tribute to the military genius of the Japanese commander, Tadamichi Kuribayashi. Nearly all of the estimated 22,000 Japanese troops were killed; less than 1,000 were captured. For the Americans, 6,821 were killed (this is the number buried there and eventually repatriated), 17,372 were wounded and there were 2,648 cases of combat fatigue. It's the only battle in Marine Corps history in which the Corps suffered more casualties than the enemy. A total of 27 Medals of Honor – the nation' highest award – were bestowed on the participants. This represents one-third of the total 82 Medals of Honor awarded in World War II.

On balance, 2,251 B-29's landed on Iwo Jima's airstrips during the remainder of the war. Each of these planes carried a crew of 11 and while it would not be accurate to say that the availability of Iwo Jima's landing strips saved 42,751 (2251 x 11) lives, undoubtedly many were saved by not having to ditch at sea or fly on to Tinian or Saipan.

There are reports (which I could not verify) that Army Chief of Staff George Marshall wanted to use poison gas to kill all the occupants of Iwo Jima. That action would have preventing having to invade the island and saved all those American lives. President Roosevelt, however, had pledged that gas would not be used and in overruling General Marshall, stuck to that promise.

Ira Hayes is the best known of the flag raisers partly because Univer-sal Pictures released a movie detailing his life in 1961. *The Outsider* stars Tony Curtis who wears heavy make-up in an attempt to look like a Native American. The writers took some liberties with the truth, but the movie is a fairly accurate depiction of Ira's post-war troubles. It is interesting to note that while Franklin Sousley and Mike Strank were two of his best friends, neither character appears in the movie, but actor Forrest Compton portrays John Bradley.

The next year, folk singer Peter La Farge wrote a song about him. While *The Ballad of Ira Hayes* was recorded by several artists, Johnny Cash's version is the most famous. The lyrics tell a bit of Ira's story between repetitions of the chorus:

> Call him drunken Ira Hayes.
> He won't answer any more.
> Not the whiskey drinkin' Indian.
> Nor the Marine who went to war.

It is true that Ira Hayes identified the man at the base of the pole as Harlon Block, not Hank Hansen when he arrived at Marine Headquarters in April 1945. He was ordered to keep his mouth shut as the plans for the bond tour, including Hansen's mother were already in place. In the fall of 1946, out of the Marine Corps by then, Ira hitchhiked all the way across Arizona, New Mexico and Texas to notify Harlon's family of the correct identity. Harlon's parents were separated, so Ira only managed to tell Harlon's father. When Belle Block found out about it, declaring that she'd known it all along, she wrote to Ira for written confirmation. The data he provided launched the investigation that corrected the misidentification. Although the hitchhiking story does not appear in Ira's biography, *Pima Marine*, Harlon's cousin, Edward Block, assures me it is true.

On that score, *The United States Marines on Iwo Jima*, published by the History and Museums Division of the Marine Corps says (page 11): "Because of the haste with which their bond-selling tour was organized, none of the surviving flag raisers seem to have had time to examine closely the Rosenthal picture. At any rate, Hayes did not mention his doubts concerning the identity of any of the deceased flag raisers until the winter of 1946. He then claimed that the person at the base of the flagpole was Corporal Harlon Block. An investigation proved him correct, and the list of flag raisers was altered."

As for the transposition of the Sousley and Hayes figures, I could not determine when that was definitely straightened out. Newspaper and magazine articles published as late as 1975 incorrectly identify the figure on the left with the poncho on his belt as Sousley. Bill Genaust's color movie film, which is available on the Internet, clearly shows the rear figure

239

to be Ira Hayes. When I showed that footage to Franklin's Aunt Florine, through her tears, she identified the second man from the left to be her nephew. Today, all accounts correctly identify Ira Hayes as the figure on the left and Franklin Sousley as the one with the M1 over his shoulder.

The monument that Tom White was instrumental in placing on Franklin's grave took some room in the cemetery. Goldie Sousley Price had saved a plot for herself where she intended to be buried alongside her first husband and three sons. Franklin's monument, however, took that spot. In the last of her many sacrifices for her sons, she gave up her plot so that Franklin could have the recognition he deserves. Goldie is buried beside Hensley Price in another section of the Elizaville cemetery.

Franklin didn't simply "buy the farm" for Goldie and Hense, he bought four farms. Within a year of Franklin's death, they used the $10,000 insurance money to purchase four tracts amounting to about 100 acres of Fleming County land. Hensley Price passed on in 1958; Goldie outlived him by 30 years. Her estate left a net total of $20,493.82 to her heirs.

Colonel Chandler Johnson, who was killed on Iwo Jima, was determined that the flag that flew over Suribachi belonged to the Marines. That determination paid off, today the flags from both raisings are at the Marine Corps Museum at Quantico, Virginia. The second flag flew from February 23 until March 14, 1945. On that date, a bugler competed with battle noise as a flag was run up at headquarters as the one on the mountain came down. The flag from Rosenthal's photo shows the effects of the stiff wind in which it waved for 20 days.

That flag appears in the movie *The Sands of Iwo Jima*. The film was released by Republic Pictures in 1950 staring John Wayne, John Agar and Forrest Tucker. The movie also features, in basically a publicity stunt, Ira Hayes, John Bradley and Rene Gagnon. The surviving flag raisers appear in one brief scene in which the Duke hands the actual flag to Gagnon while Hayes and Bradley look on. Their screen time is less than five seconds. In a larger role is Hal Schrier, the man who led the patrol up Mt. Suribachi. Schrier, a captain by the time of the film, ordered Wayne up the mountain and handed him the flag. Incidentally, the movie also features the baby-faced Richard Jaeckel who seems to have appeared in every WWII movie ever made. This movie also earned an Academy Award nomination for Wayne and was dear enough to him that he had the concrete for his marker on Hollywood's Walk of Fame mixed with Iwo Jima's black sand.

The Sands of Iwo Jima is also partly responsible for the persistent myth that the Marines fought a bloody battle to get to the top of Mt. Suribachi.

Wayne's patrol, aided by Naval gunfire and tanks, killed many Japanese and lost several men, including the picture's star, before the flag raising was recreated. In an attempt to get at least one fact right, the fine print at the beginning of the movie contains a "historical note" to the extent that the first flag to fly over Mt. Suribachi was put there by Sergeant Ernest I. Thomas.

The print media have a hand in that myth as well. The battle on Iwo Jima occupied the headlines for five days following the landing on February 19, 1945. On Friday, the 23rd, the papers duly reported that the top of the mountain had been gained. As there was little to report on Saturday, evidently some creative journalism took over. On February 24, the *New York Times* banner headline screamed:

SURIBACHI REACHED IN A FIERY BATTLE

Other papers printed paragraphs such as "The fierce resistance in the northern sector was paralleled on the steep fortified slopes of Suribachi. Some marines of the 28th Regiment, Fifth Division fought their way to the summit Friday forenoon and planted the American flag amid volcanic ash and lava rock."[100] Joe Rosenthal's picture appeared in the same papers the next day.

That picture gained the photographer the 1945 Pulitzer Prize for photography as well as everlasting fame. In awarding the prize, the Pulitzer Committee described the photo as "depicting one of the war's great moments," a "frozen flash of history."

When Franklin left home at the end of his furlough in August 1944, he left his dress uniform in his mother's closet. He did not know that he was going to Iwo Jima, but he surely knew that he'd soon be going overseas where he'd have no need for it. The uniform hung in Goldie's closet for nearly 40 years until a family emergency created an urgent need for money. I imagine that it broke her heart to part with it, but she placed Franklin's uniform, on consignment, in an antique shop near her Ewing home. A private buyer purchased it on the condition that he'd never try to profit from it. The uniform is on display at the Bluegrass Heritage Museum in Winchester, Kentucky.

Marian Harding married Earl Fant Hamm on April 5, 1949. The marriage would last until Mr. Hamm's death and produced three children. A life-long Fleming County resident, Marian was active in community and church affairs. She died as a highly respected citizen on December 15,

2009. Earl Hamm, ironically, was the President of the People's Bank who helped establish the scholarship in Franklin's name with the money left over from the monument fund.

The fate of flag raisers is a frequently asked question. Franklin Sousley, Mike Strank and Harlon Block were killed on Iwo Jima. Mike Strank's body was reinterred in January 1949 in Arlington National Cemetery. Harlon Block's remains were reburied in private cemetery in Weslaco, Texas. Ira Hayes died on the reservation in Arizona on January 24, 1955 and is buried in Arlington National Cemetery. Rene Gagnon died in New Hampshire in October 1979 and was buried there. Later, at his widow's request, he was reinterred in Arlington National Cemetery. The last survivor, John Bradley, died in January 1994 and is buried in Antigo, Wisconsin.

Various accounts assign different men to the BAR in Easy Company's 1st platoon. That military designation, by the way, has to be one of the worst misnomers in history – the life of that company was surely never easy! Company Commander Dave Severance says that every man in the company was qualified with that weapon. Franklin mentions that he carries the BAR in several of his letters and indicates that he will continue to do so in combat. In answer to my inquiry as to why Rosenthal's photograph shows Franklin with an M1 strapped over his shoulder, Severance, who retired as a Colonel, informed me that he ordered Franklin to leave the heavier weapon behind as the spool of telephone wire was burden enough and no resistance was expected.

Visitation to Iwo Jima today is restricted as control of the island was returned to the Japanese government by an act signed by President Lyndon Johnson in 1968, much to the chagrin of the Marines who fought so hard to wrest that control away. In all my reading and interviewing, one of the best quotes I found was from one such man who said, "I hope to hell they know what they're doing, 'cause I ain't goin' back."

After the battle for Guadalcanal, Marine Pfc James Donahue penned a little poem which is appropriate for all the men who served in the Pacific theater in WWII and for Iwo Jima Marines in particular:

When he gets to heaven
To St. Peter he will tell
"Just one more Marine reporting, sir
I've served my time in hell."

Are the Iwo Jima flag raisers heroes? I asked that question of many Marines. The Iwo Jima veterans say that if there were any heroes, they died there. Others say that anyone who set foot on that island is a hero. By either definition, Franklin Runyon Sousley, the boy from Hilltop became a true American hero on a mountaintop on Iwo Jima.

Endnotes

[1] Franklin's Aunt Florine doubts the truth of this story, but his friends say it actually happened.

[2] Sousley, Franklin letter to his mother December 29, 1943 gives these details.

[3] Sousley's first letter from boot camp, undated describes his trip.

[4] Sousley described this incident in a February 15, 1944 letter.

[5] National Archives Records Administration (NARA). The score is as recorded in Franklin's service record.

[6] Conner, Howard B., *The Spearhead, The World War History of the 5th Marine Division*, Infantry Journal Press, Washington, D.C.:1950 15

[7] Wheeler, Richard, *Iwo*, Castle Books, Edison, NJ: 1980. 47. Mr. Wheeler was a member of Easy Company and so provides a wealth of information on the Company's personnel, whereabouts and movements.

[8] Conner, *The Spearhead*, 24.

[9] Wheeler, *Iwo*. 56

[10] Gagnon's affidavit from Sousley's personnel file. See page 183.

[11] Dave Severance provided the second platoon's roster.

[12] Sousley letter to his mother March 25, 1944.

[13] Severence

[14] Sousley letter April 27, 1944

[15] Sousley letter March 25, 1944

[16] Sousley letter April 27, 1944

[17] Bradley, James with Ron Powers, *Flags of Our Fathers*, Bantam Books, New York: 2006. 113

[18] Conner, *The Spearhead*, 42.

[19] *Ibid.* 43

[20] NARA. The date of Franklin's furlough supplied by his service record.

[21] Franklin's Aunt Florine supplied the details of his furlough.

[22] NARA. The date and ship from Sousley's service record.

[23] Conner, *The Spearhead.* 55

[24] Wheeler, *Iwo.* 47

[25] Bradley, *Flags.* 119

[26] Sousley, letter October 14, 1944

[27] NARA. Service record.

[28] Franklin's lighter and other belongings are on display at the Fleming County Public Library.

[29] Wheeler, *Iwo.* 61

[30] *Ibid.* 62

[31] *Ibid.* 65

[32] *Ibid.* 65

[33] Bradley, *Flags.* 159

[34] Wheeler, *Iwo.* 94

[35] *Ibid.* 105

[36] *Ibid.* 110

[37] *Ibid.* 105

[38] *Ibid.* 122

[39] Bradley, *Flags.* 176

[40] Wheeler, *Iwo.* 136.

[41] *Ibid.* 137

[42] *Ibid.* 141

[43] *Ibid.* 142

[44] Bradley, *Flags.* 197

[45] Wheeler, *Iwo.* 155

[46] Buell, Hal, *Uncommon Valor, Common Virtue,* Berkley Publishing Group, New York: 2006. 99. Hal Buell worked with the Associated Press for 40 years, knew Joe Rosenthal well and collected the photographer's war stories.

[47] Bradley, *Flags.* 204

[48] Buell, *Valor.* 101

[49] Wheeler, *Iwo.* 161

[50] Severance, Dave letter. In answer to my question as to why the platoon's BAR man is shown in Rosenthal's photograph with an M1 over his shoulder.

[51] Buell, *Valor.* 106

[52] Wheeler, *Iwo.* 161

[53] Buell, *Valor.* 107

[54] Wheeler, *Iwo.* 177

[55] *Ibid.* 178

[56] Buell, *Valor.* 182

[57] *Ibid.* 181

[58] Wheeler, *Iwo.* 186

[59] *Ibid.* 188

[60] Bradley, *Flags*. 231

[61] Hemingway, Albert, *Ira Hayes: Pima Marine*, Lanham, MD, University Press of America, Inc: 1988. 112

[62] *Ibid.* 115

[63] Wheeler, *Iwo*. 201

[64] *Ibid.* 204

[65] Haynes, Fred, *The Lions of Iwo Jima*, Henry Holt and Co., New York: 2008. 205

[66] Bradley, *Flags*. 244

[67] Severance, Dave. Speech at American Veterans Center, November 8, 2008. Available at www.greatamericans.com. Colonel Severance says they saw the picture on Iwo Jima about March 15, 1945.

[68] Bradley, *Flags*. 268

[69] *Ibid.* 243

[70] NARA Gagnon's affidavit, see page 183. Joe Rodriguez imparted the same information to Tom White at Elizaville, KY June 3, 1984.

[71] Haynes, *Lions*. 227

[72] Wheeler, *Iwo*. 227

[73] NARA, Gagnon's affidavit.

[74] *Life Magazine*, March 5, 1945.

[75] National Park Service, *Historic American Landscapes Survey*, Washington D.C.: 2000. 3

[76] Bradley, *Flags*. 267

[77] *Ibid.* 268.

[78] NARA, Gagnon's affidavit.

[79] Harlon's cousin, Edward Block verified this story, interview March 10, 2010.

[80] Dwayne Price. This story is Price family lore.

[81] Price family collection. Goldie saved menus, programs, seating charts, letters, etc. to document her trip.

[82] *New York Times*, May 16, 1945

[83] *Ibid.*

[84] Florine Moran interview. Goldie related this conversation to her sisters.

[85] Hemingway, *Pima Marine*. 130. Ira Hayes identified the man at the base of the pole as Harlon Block, not Henry Hansen, but was ordered to keep quiet.

[86] NARA. Insurance papers in Sousley's service record.

[87] Louisville *Courier-Journal*, May 9, 1948.

[88] *Ibid.*

[89] *Fleming Gazette*, October 6, 1951

[90] Price family collection documents.

[91] National Park Service, *Historic American Landscapes Survey*, Washington D.C.: 2000. 4-12

[92] Hemingway, *Pima Marine*. 149

[93] Nalty, Bernard C. and Crawford, Danny J., *The United States Marines on Iwo Jima: The Battle and the Flag Raisings*, History and Museum Division, Headquarters, U.S. Marine Corps, Washington D.C.: 1995. 11

[94] *New York Times*, November 11, 1954

[95] In October 1982, President Reagan signed into law a Congressional act which allowed Rosenthal's name to be added.

[96] White, Tom, interview January 12, 2010

[97] NARA. Letter J.F. Hogsett to Goldie Price, 13 Aug 1958

[98] *Fleming Gazette* June 6, 1984

[99] Block, Edward, Interview March 4, 2010

[100] Louisville *Courier-Journal*, February 24, 1945.

Bibliography

Alexander, Joseph, *Closing in: The Seizure Of Iwo Jima*, History and Museum Division, Headquarters, U.S. Marine Corps, Washington, D.C., 1994

Bartley, Whitman S., *Iwo Jima: Amphibious* Epic, Historical Division, Headquarters, U.S. Marine Corps, Washington, D.C, 1954

Block, Edward, Interview March 4, 2010

Bradley, James with Ron Powers, *Flags of our Fathers*, Bantam Dell, New York, 2000

Buell, Hal, *Uncommon Valor, Common Virtue, Iwo Jima and the Photograph that Captured America*, Berkley Publishing Group. New York, 2006

Conner, Howard B., *The Spearhead, The World War History of the 5th Marine Division*, Infantry Journal Press, Washington, D.C., 1950

Courier-Journal, Louisville, KY, various issues 1945 - 2010

Fleming Gazette, Flemingsburg, KY, various issues 1940 - 2010

Haynes, Fred and Warren, James, *The Lions of Iwo Jima*, Henry Holt and Company, New York, 2008

Hemingway, Albert, *Ira Hayes: Pima Marine*, University Press of America, Lanham, MD, 1988

Lexington Herald-Leader, Lexington, KY, various issues 1940 - 2010

New York Times, New York, NY, various issues 1940 - 2010

Moran, Florine, interview, Sept. 26, 2009 and November 14, 2009

Nalty, Bernard C. and Crawford, Danny J., *The United States Marines on Iwo Jima: The Battle and the Flag Raisings*, History and Museum Division, Headquarters, U.S. Marine Corps, Washington, D.C., 1995

National Archives and Records Administration, U.S. Marine Corps records of Franklin R. Sousley, St. Louis

Severance, David E., Personal letters, September 2, 2009 and January 12, 2010

Smith, Larry, *Jima World War II Veterans Remember the Greatest Battle of the Pacific*, W.W. Norton and Company, New York, 2008

Sousley, Franklin R., Letters August 1943 – February 1945

Rosenthal, Joseph and Heintz, W.C., *The Picture That Will Live Forever*, Fifth Marine Reunion Journal, Gallant/Charger Publications, 1978

Wheeler, Richard, *Iwo*, Castle Books, New York, 1980

White, Thomas, interview, January 12, 2010

About the Author

R on Elliott, a native of Lin-coln County, Kentucky, is a graduate of Stanford High School, Eastern Kentucky University and the University of Kentucky.

Ron's background includes working on the historic Apollo missions, which placed Americans on the moon and teaching in Kentucky's Community College system. Having a relative involved in the assassination of Kentucky's would-be governor, William Goebel, piqued his interest in history.

A popular speaker, Ron is the author of *Assassination at the State House*, *The Silent Brigade*, *Inside the Beverly Hills Supper Club Fire*, *Through the Eyes of Lincoln* and numerous magazine articles.

Semi-retired, Ron and his wife, Carol, currently live in Nelson County, Kentucky.

Index

A

Agar, John · 240
Alexander, Joseph · 248
Alexander, Tom · 207
Anderson, Robert · 226
Antigo, Wisconsin · 242
Anzio · 99
Arlington National Cemetery · 7,
188, 190, 223, 226
Arlington, Virginia · 223, 234

B

Bardstown, Kentucky · 238
Bartley, Whitman S. · 248
Bates, Joe · 208
Bernal, Sara · 236
Block, Belle · 206, 225, 226, 227,
239
Block, Edward · 7, 234, 235, 236,
239, 246, 247, 248
Block, Harlon · 109, 112, 115, 117,
119, 131, 133, 134, 146, 147, 152,
158, 159, 160, 161, 162, 169, 170,
171, 172, 184, 195, 199, 200, 206,
213, 224, 225, 227, 234, 239, 242
Bolton, Howard "Tex" · 88, 89, 92, 94
Boone, Daniel · 17, 25
Bougainville · 103, 108, 115, 117, 148,
151, 154, 174
Bradley, James · 236, 244, 245, 246,
248
Bradley, John "Doc" · 111, 151, 162,
166, 171, 172, 180, 185, 195, 199,
204, 211, 212, 213, 223, 225, 226,
236, 239, 240, 242
Bryant, Ron · 7
Buell, Hal · 245, 248

Busse, Alvin · 51, 52

C

Campbell, Bob · 169, 170, 171, 179,
180, 193
Camp Elliott · 104
Camp Lajeune · 104
Camp Matthews · 87, 90, 106
Camp Pendleton · 54, 60, 72, 73, 74,
102, 104, 110, 119, 122, 131, 134,
136, 167, 174
Camp Tarawa · 76, 134, 135, 136,
138, 148, 151
Carroll, Julian · 14, 15, 187
Cash, Johnny · 239
Chandler, A.B. "Happy" · 208
Charlo, Louis · 167
Cincinnati, Ohio · 208
Clements, Earl · 189, 219, 226
Cobb, Ty · 32
Cologan, Tommy · 32, 33
Compton, Forrest · 239
Conner, Howard B. · 244, 248
Cooper, Gary · 203
Cowan, Charles · 207
Crawford, Danny J. · 247, 249
Crockett, Davy · 17
Curtis, Tony · 238

D

Dayton Russell · 108
de Weldon, Felix · 188, 223, 224, 226,
227
Donahue, James · 242
Donovan, James · 7
Doran, Casimer · 109

E

Easy Company (Company E) · 73, 105, 106, 107, 108, 109, 110, 111, 115, 128, 131, 137, 139, 144, 146, 147, 156, 157, 158, 162, 163, 166, 168, 169, 173, 174, 193, 194, 196, 198, 199, 200, 201, 242, 244

Eisenhower, Dwight · 222, 226

Elizaville, Kentucky · 13, 38, 186, 191, 217, 221, 229, 232, 240

Elliott, Carol · 7, 76

Eniwetok · 144, 205

Evelley, Madeline · 185, 211, 212, 213, 225

Ewing, Kentucky · 97, 202, 216

F

Fern, Gilbert · 6, 218, 221

Fifth Marine Division · 72, 102, 104, 105, 108, 110, 115, 139, 182, 201, 241

Fleming Gazette · 98, 139, 174, 217

Flemingsburg, Kentucky · 48, 53, 101, 120, 124, 125, 129, 229, 231

Forrestal, James M. · 168

G

Gable, Clark · 203

Gagnon, Pauline · 236

Gagnon, Rene · 107, 110, 111, 112, 131, 140, 143, 147, 169, 170, 171, 172, 183, 184, 185, 188, 198, 199, 201, 204, 205, 206, 211, 212, 213, 223, 225, 226, 236, 240, 242, 244, 246

Gagnon, Rene, Jr. · 236

Galliher, Bill · 220

Garbo, Greta · 212

Garland, Judy · 204

Gehrig, Lou · 32

Genaust, Bill · 169, 171, 172, 193, 239

Graham, Jimmy · 86, 87, 89, 90, 93, 94

Guadalcanal · 100

H

Hamm, Earl Fant · 241, 242

Hansen, Henry "Hank" · 160, 161, 167, 172, 184, 185, 195, 199, 204, 205, 211, 213, 225, 239

Harding, Marian · 38, 41, 43, 48, 91, 120, 121, 125, 126, 127, 129, 130, 132, 138, 144, 241

Harp, E.B. · 226

Hawkins, J.L. · 220

Hayes, Ira "Chief" · 106, 108, 111, 112, 114, 116, 117, 118, 131, 133, 138, 139, 140, 143, 144, 145, 146, 147, 148, 149, 150, 151, 152, 153, 154, 155, 157, 158, 159, 160, 161, 163, 164, 165, 168, 169, 170, 171, 172, 173, 174, 175, 180, 184, 185, 194, 195, 196, 199, 200, 201, 204, 205, 208, 211, 212, 213, 223, 225, 226, 227, 236, 238, 239, 240, 242

Hayes, Kenny · 236

Hayes, Nancy · 208

Haynes, Fred · 246, 248

Heintz, W.C. · 249

Hemingway, Albert · 246, 247, 248

Henry, Heather French · 8

Hesse, Lewis · 108, 119, 152, 161

Hilltop, Kentucky · 18, 31, 55, 118, 135, 172, 210, 243

Hilo, Hawaii · 134, 135, 139

Hogsett, J.F. · 247

Holly, Lowell "L.B." · 105, 109, 111, 112, 117, 131, 133, 134, 135, 144, 195, 196, 198

Honolulu, Hawaii · 140, 141

Hopkins, Larry · 191, 232

Hunt, R.D. · 220

I

Iwo Jima · 6, 7, 8, 13, 14, 15, 17, 74, 78, 79, 141, 142, 143, 144, 145, 146, 153, 156, 157, 163, 166, 167, 174, 176, 181, 182, 191, 193, 194, 196, 197, 198, 200, 201, 203, 204, 209, 211, 212, 216, 223, 224, 225, 229,

230, 231, 234, 235, 238, 240, 241, 242, 243

J

Jacobs, Ray · 166
Jaeckel, Richard · 240
Japanese Mandates · 100
Johnson, Chandler · 157, 166, 168, 240
Johnson, Lyndon · 189, 242
Jolly, Francis · 41, 48
Jones, James · 235

K

Kaiama, Tsugi "Sue" · 138
Kennedy, John F. · 237
Kitano Point, Iwo Jima · 200
Kuribayashi, Tadamichi · 238
Kwajalein Island · 99, 100

L

La Farge, Peter · 239
La Jolla, California · 86
League of Nations · 100
Leatherneck magazine · 167, 231
Lewis, Orme · 226
Lexington, Kentucky · 222
Lindberg, Chuck · 167, 226
Lombard, Carole · 203
Louisville *Courier-Journal* · 247
Lowery, Louis · 166, 167, 170, 178, 193, 225

M

Maccio, Frankie · 88, 89, 92, 94
Mahar, Whitney C. · 7
Marcy, Phil · 88
Marine Corps Museum · 240
Marine Corps War Memorial
  Foundation · 7, 188, 190, 223, 226
Marshall, George · 238
Mathewson, Dick · 161
Maui, Hawaii · 139
May, Mildred · 7, 18, 19, 20, 21, 22, 23, 41, 97, 98, 99, 100, 101, 103,

121, 122, 174, 214, 215, 217, 218, 219, 234, 236
McGarvey, Joe · 162, 195, 196
McIntire, Cecil · 38, 39, 40, 41, 42, 43, 44, 45, 46, 47, 48, 49, 50
McKee, Bill · 220
McQueen, Jim · 7
McRoberts, Ralph · 90, 91
Michels, Jim · 167, 226
Miller, Joe · 88
Milstead, Ken · 109
Mitchell, Charlie · 29, 50, 51, 52, 53, 121, 214
Mitchell, Ortha · 29, 121
Mitchell, Ray · 7, 22, 23, 24, 25, 26, 27, 28, 29, 33, 34, 41, 50, 51, 53, 66, 92, 99, 100, 101, 102, 103, 121, 122, 129, 202, 203, 204, 205, 207, 217, 218
Moran, Florine · 7, 23, 41, 48, 71, 121, 125, 127, 139, 214, 217, 218, 234, 236, 240, 244, 246, 248
Moreau, Colonel · 226
Mt. Suribachi · 6, 76, 141, 142, 149, 151, 155, 157, 158, 159, 161, 162, 163, 164, 166, 173, 176, 178, 193, 197, 200, 201, 202, 240, 241

N

Nalty, Bernard C. · 247, 249
Napier, Larry · 230
Nash, Jim · 34
Neal, Everett · 18, 20, 22, 23, 35, 36, 37, 206, 207
New York City, New York · 210, 211
Nimitz, Chester · 197, 225
Nishi Ridge · 195
Nixon, Richard · 227

O

Oceanside, California · 54, 104
Okinawa · 197

P

Parris Island · 52, 54, 58, 104

Pearl Harbor · 33, 51, 100, 101, 139, 168
Pendleton, Bill · 34
Pendleton Island · 74, 118
Pennell, Ed · 105, 106, 108, 114, 116, 119, 132, 134, 135, 136, 142, 143, 146, 147, 148, 150, 151, 153, 157, 158, 160, 161, 169
Perkins, Carl D. · 191, 232
Pero, Mary · 236
Perry, Rolla · 109, 199
Possum Trot, Kentucky · 109, 135
Powers, Ron · 236, 244, 248
Price, Brittani · 192, 236
Price, Dwayne · 7, 13, 15, 16, 192, 234, 236, 246
Price, Goldie Sousley · 7, 14, 18, 19, 20, 21, 22, 23, 25, 28, 29, 30, 31, 33, 34, 35, 38, 40, 41, 50, 53, 65, 75, 97, 98, 99, 100, 101, 102, 114, 120, 121, 122, 125, 129, 130, 183, 184, 185, 187, 189, 190, 191, 202, 203, 204, 205, 206, 207, 208, 209, 210, 211, 212, 214, 216, 217, 218, 219, 220, 222, 223, 225, 226, 227, 228, 230, 231, 232, 234, 236, 240, 241, 246, 247
Price, Hensley · 31, 33, 34, 35, 38, 41, 42, 51, 53, 75, 97, 102, 121, 122, 124, 125, 129, 130, 189, 208, 209, 210, 211, 212, 213, 214, 218, 219, 222, 226, 227, 228, 240
Price, James Hensley "J.H." · 42, 217, 218, 221
Price, Janice · 217, 218, 219, 221
Price, Penny · 236
Price, Tina · 235, 236

Q
Quantico, Virginia · 104, 240

R
Rabaul, New Guinea · 99
Raisor, Jerry · 7
Ranous, Bill · 105, 108, 109, 111, 119, 143, 144, 151, 152, 194, 196, 197, 198, 199
Reagan, Ronald · 237, 247
Rockey, Keller E. · 104, 119
Rodriguez, Joe · 105, 109, 111, 112, 113, 116, 117, 119, 131, 132, 133, 136, 137, 138, 140, 141, 144, 147, 148, 149, 150, 152, 157, 164, 191, 195, 232, 246
Rooney, Mickey · 203
Roosevelt, Eleanor · 134
Roosevelt, Franklin · 74, 119, 204, 205, 209, 238
Rosenthal, Joe · 6, 14, 15, 16, 17, 71, 169, 170, 171, 172, 173, 176, 177, 179, 180, 182, 192, 193, 195, 198, 202, 203, 204, 209, 223, 225, 226, 227, 229, 231, 233, 235, 237, 241, 242, 245, 247, 249
Ruhl, Don · 110, 111, 117, 149, 156, 157, 159, 160, 161, 162, 178, 195
Russell, Dayton · 119, 152
Ruth, Babe · 32

S
Saipan · 141, 142, 144, 145, 238
San Clemente Island · 116, 131, 133, 152
San Diego, California · 52, 53, 54, 60, 61, 86, 90, 91, 92, 94, 98, 104, 113, 119, 131, 133
San Diego Recruit Depot · 52, 87, 92, 94, 95, 114
Schram, Emil · 185
Schrier, Hal · 166, 167, 168, 169, 170, 171, 172, 173, 179, 193, 240
Senoracke, Joe · 74, 109, 153, 198
Severance, Dave · 7, 105, 110, 118, 133, 135, 137, 141, 157, 166, 168, 169, 173, 175, 194, 197, 199, 200, 201, 208, 242, 244, 245, 249
Shannon, J.B. · 24, 25, 26, 27, 28, 32, 33, 34, 35, 36, 37, 120, 121, 127, 128, 129, 130
Shepherd, Lemuel · 226

Sherman, General · 153, 154
Sherrod, Robert · 193
Shivers, Stephen · 232
Sikes, Doug · 7
Simmons, E.H. · 14, 15
Simms, Billy · 54, 55, 56, 57, 58, 59, 60
Smather, Billy · 88
Smith, Al · 214
Smith, H.M. (Howlin' Mad) · 168, 173
Smith, Larry · 249
Snell, John · 7, 75, 189, 191
Sousley, Duke · 18, 19, 20, 22, 23, 24, 29, 65, 218, 220, 221
Sousley, Hoover · 24, 26, 27, 28, 33, 217, 218
Sousley, Julian "Jake" · 13, 24, 29, 31, 32, 41, 42, 50, 51, 53, 67, 75, 97, 120, 122, 123, 124, 128, 129, 130, 185, 214, 215, 216, 218, 219, 220
Sousley, Malcolm · 13, 18, 21, 22, 23, 36, 65, 89, 218, 221
Stanton, Art "Tex" · 109, 111, 112, 116, 117, 131, 133, 134, 135, 136, 137, 140, 144, 145, 147, 148, 149, 150, 156, 157, 161, 195, 199
Stoddard, Lieutenant · 133, 162
Strank, John · 212, 236
Strank, Martha · 185, 211
Strank, Mike · 108, 109, 110, 111, 112, 113, 115, 118, 119, 131, 149, 150, 151, 152, 153, 156, 158, 161, 162, 164, 165, 168, 169, 170, 171, 172, 173, 180, 189, 193, 195, 199, 200, 204, 211, 212, 213, 224, 228, 236, 239, 242
Sumrall, Eddie · 186, 217, 218, 219

T

Tarawa · 100, 145
Tea Run, Kentucky · 24
Tent Camp #1 · 73, 106, 119, 136
Thjorn, Marv · 88
Thomas, Ernest "Boots" · 162, 166, 167, 173, 174, 196, 241
Tinian · 142, 145, 238
Training Platoon 81 · 62, 70, 84, 87, 95
Treaty of Versailles · 100
Trotter, Richard P. · 191, 232
Truk · 99
Tucker, Forrest · 240

U

USS *Missoula* · 139, 143
USS *Talladega* · 144

V

Vella Lavella · 103, 108

W

Waikiki Beach, Hawaii · 140, 141, 149
Waimea, Hawaii · 138
Warren, James · 248
Washington, George · 17, 212
Wayne, John · 240
Wells, Keith · 133, 156, 160, 162, 166, 174, 175, 194
Weslaco, Texas · 172, 206, 242
Wetherby, Lawrence · 226
Wheeler, Richard · 244, 245, 246, 249
White, Tom · 7, 191, 229, 230, 231, 232, 233, 240, 246, 247, 249
Winchester, Kentucky · 241